WALKING ALONE

WALKING ALONE

The Untold Journey of Football Pioneer Kenny Washington

DAN TAYLOR

ROWMAN & LITTLEFIELD
Lanham • Boulder • New York • London

Published by Rowman & Littlefield
An imprint of The Rowman & Littlefield Publishing Group, Inc.
4501 Forbes Boulevard, Suite 200, Lanham, Maryland 20706
www.rowman.com

86-90 Paul Street, London EC2A 4NE, United Kingdom

British Library Cataloguing in Publication Information Available

Library of Congress Cataloging-in-Publication Data
Names: Taylor, Dan, 1957– author.
Title: Walking alone : the untold journey of football pioneer Kenny
    Washington / Dan Taylor.
Description: Lanham, MD : Rowman & Littlefield, [2022] | Includes
    bibliographical references and index. | Summary: "The inspirational
    story of African American trailblazer Kenny Washington, the first player
    to reintegrate the NFL and the first black football coach in the United States,
    considered by many to be the greatest football player of his time"—
    Provided by publisher.
Identifiers: LCCN 2021046982 (print) | LCCN 2021046983 (ebook) | ISBN
    9781538154366 (cloth) | ISBN 9781538154373 (epub)
Subjects: LCSH: Washington, Kenny, 1918–1971. | Football—United
    States—History—20th century. | Discrimination in sports—United
    States—History—20th century. | National Football League—History—20th
    century. | African American football players—Biography. | African
    American football coaches—Biography.
Classification: LCC GV939.W36137 T38 2022 (print) | LCC GV939.W36137
    (ebook) | DDC 796.332092 [B]—dc23/eng/20211109
LC record available at https://lccn.loc.gov/2021046982
LC ebook record available at https://lccn.loc.gov/2021046983

CONTENTS

Disclaimer: The terms "negro," "colored," and "colored person" are used only in direct quotes or titles and are used strictly for purposes of historical accuracy.

"A great football story will be written one day. The story of an All-American. The story of a Negro, his thoughts, his hopes, and his fears."

Eddie West
Santa Ana Register
1939

FOREWORD

It was not a big deal for me when I first met Kenny Washington. I mean, well, I was only about six, and he was about seventeen and a football player on my dad's team at Lincoln High School, located on North Broadway in Lincoln Heights, Los Angeles. We met on Lincoln High School's football field at an after-school practice. At home, my dad was a quiet father and never talked much about his teaching or coaching.

Actually, in those days I was more interested and involved in my own football playing on the playground—sandlot style. There were no Little League or Pop Warner games in those days. We had to organize our own "touch" football games on the local grammar school playground located one-half block from our home in San Gabriel, California. We played on dirt or asphalt surfaces. I always got to play or organize the games since it was my football that Dad had provided. Moreover, Lincoln High School was about eight miles from our home (seemed a lot farther), and since our family had only one car, which Dad had at school, I was never able to attend one of his games. Thus, I never saw Kenny play under my dad's coaching.

Dad never talked—or bragged—about Kenny or his family. Kenny's dad was named Edgar "Blue" Washington, a nickname given to him by the famous film director Frank Capra when they were both kids living in Los Angeles. Blue was an actor who played in seventy-four films. He also played baseball in the Negro Leagues. If you ever had a chance to see Kenny in action, it would be easy to see where his athletic skills were born—from Blue, of course. Dad was a big fan of Kenny's but never in awe of his superior athletic talent. Perhaps Dad's appreciation of Kenny was based on his (my dad's) own athletic talents. Dad was a high school star at Loyola High School (Los Angeles) and captain of the football, basketball,

Figure 0.1 Lincoln High School football coach Jim Tunney with his star player, Kenny Washington. *Photo courtesy of Jim Tunney Jr.*

and baseball (yes, all three) teams at Loyola College. Upon graduation from college, Dad played one year of professional baseball for the Oakland Oaks. He therefore knew talent and how to develop it. Dad was the teacher; Kenny was the student. They worked together famously.

My dad had some good teams at Lincoln High but none more powerful and famous than his 1935 team with Kenny as tailback. That 1935 Lincoln High team won the Los Angeles City Football Championship, defeating Fremont High School, 13–9. It's the only city football champion-ship Lincoln High has ever won, although it has had some excellent football teams and coaches throughout its 107-year history. Yet, the 1935 Tigers' football team is its only city champion! At that time, the Lincoln High student population was composed mostly of Eastern Europeans, Russians, Italians, and so forth. In fact, actor Robert Preston, at that time named Robert Preston Meservey, better known now to all as "the Music Man," was on that team.

Dad was vitally interested in Kenny's future education and encouraged him to go to college. Dr. Norm Duncan, who at one time taught physical education with Dad at Lincoln High, had moved on, obtaining his doctor-ate and teaching at the University of California at Los Angeles (UCLA), a small school located in Westwood (west Los Angeles). With the connec-tions of Dad and Dr. Duncan, they helped Kenny enroll at UCLA in the fall of 1937, where he continued his education on through graduation.

When Kenny graduated, the National Football League was thirty-seven years old, having started in 1920. Few African American players were allowed to play in the 1940s. It's interesting to note that Frederick Douglas "Fritz" Pollard, a small (5-foot-7-inch, 150-pound) running back from Brown University, broke the color barrier in 1919 playing for the Akron Pros. However, there were only a few Blacks attending UCLA, and only a handful were playing football. The Bruins had five on their team in 1939.

Joining Kenny on that Bruins football team were Woody Strode, Jackie Robinson, Ray Bartlett, and Johnny Wynne. Yes, *that* Jackie Rob-inson, who broke that same barrier in 1947 with the Brooklyn Dodgers. Although Kenny was on the UCLA baseball team, he was more widely known for his football prowess. But let's not overlook his college baseball skills. Kenny hit .397 for the baseball Bruins.

In the 1940 NFL draft, no Black players were drafted, despite Kenny's incredible college football career. So, Kenny played in the smaller Pacific Coast Football League for a team called the Hollywood Bears. My first time seeing Kenny play was when he was with those Bears. Dad was a college football official and also officiated those Bears games, as well as the Los Angeles Dons. The Bears played their home games at Gilmore Stadium in Hollywood, California, which is no longer there. It's now where CBS Television City and Farmers Market are located.

If I may digress for a brief note on Jackie Robinson. As a seven-, eight-, nine-year-old kid, I would carry my dad's gear bag when he was officiating. He officiated in the Pasadena Rose Bowl many times. In fact, Pasadena Junior College, where Jackie went to college before UCLA, played its home games in that iconic Rose Bowl. During one game, because of little or no security (well, maybe one cop), I got to sit on the PJC's bench. Jackie was the star running back for PJC. As clearly as if it were yesterday, I remember my dad approaching me at halftime of one of those games and saying, "You watch this colored kid [as most were called with no disrespect intended in 1938]; he's really gonna be something." As I said earlier, Dad was a great judge of superior talent.

When the Cleveland Rams of the NFL relocated to Los Angeles in 1946, they wanted to play in the Los Angeles Coliseum and signed Kenny to play for them. Kenny was the *first Black player* from the West Coast to be signed by an NFL team. The Los Angeles Coliseum was *not* going to allow the Rams to play in there unless they would allow Black players. Kenny, indeed, was the player that broke that "color barrier" in Los Angeles. Joining Kenny on that Rams team was his UCLA teammate, Woody Strode, as end.

When Dad retired from officiating in 1947, I was attending Occidental College in Los Angeles and focusing on my education and my athletic and officiating career and sort of lost track of Kenny. I do recall that Young's Market, a growing wine, beer, and spirits distributor, was wanting to build strong, positive relationships with the booming Southern California community. They hired Kenny. With the reputation Kenny had established at UCLA and with the Rams, he was the perfect man for the job in those days.

In 1971 I was working as the educational director of the (Herb) Alpert Family Foundation when I heard that Kenny was ill. He had big medical bills. I contacted Mike Frankovich, a UCLA alum and former Bruin football player and member of their Hall of Fame. In 1971 he was a film producer and had made more than thirty movies. When I talked with Mike about helping Kenny, he said of course, since he knew all about Kenny's UCLA accomplishments.

We decided to put on a dinner and through Mike's connections contacted the famous Hollywood Palladium, located on Sunset Boulevard in Hollywood. Our advertisement was mostly through word of mouth as well as through UCLA sources. Our entertainment was simple, with Mike as our master of ceremonies. Our attendance was about 1,000, and everyone was enthusiastic to meet and hear from Kenny. It was a *special* evening for him.

Lincoln High School has remembered its wonderful athlete by naming its football field as well as an annual football game in his honor. It always seemed sad to me that the Lincoln student body never got to meet such a legend. But I will always remember!

Jim Tunney Jr.
Thirty-one-year NFL official and son of Kenny's coach, Jim Tunney Sr.

ACKNOWLEDGMENTS

Deepest gratitude to my valued friend Artie Harris. From myriad conversations came the seed from which this project sprouted. Thank you. My thanks to the family of Kenny Washington; his daughter, Karin Cohen; and his grandson, Kirk Washington. Both were gracious with their time, supportive with their words, and tremendously helpful with the information shared. To Eve, my undying gratitude for your support, dedication, and Herculean assistance.

Resources utilized in this project include Ancestry.com, *Baltimore Afro-American*, Baseball-Reference.com, Bruin Life, *Chicago Defender*, Chicago Public Library, *Chicago Tribune*, *Daily Bruin*, *Daily Trojan*, *Fresno Bee*, IMDb, *Long Beach Independent Press-Telegram*, Los Angeles Public Library, *Los Angeles Daily News*, Los Angeles Police Department Museum, *Los Angeles Sentinel*, *Los Angeles Times*, Margaret Herrick Library, National Football Foundation Hall of Fame, *New York Age*, *New York Daily News*, New York Public Library, *New York Times*, Newspapers.com, *Oakland Tribune*, *Pasadena Star-News*, *Pittsburgh Courier*, Pro Football Hall of Fame, Pro Football Reference, *San Francisco Examiner*, Society for American Baseball Research, Sports-Reference.com, *Sporting News*, *Stanford Daily*, UCLA Athletic Communications, *Variety*, and Charles E. Young Research Library.

A great many offered invaluable assistance and enthusiastic encouragement. For that I thank Barry Anderson, Greg Baker, Bob Bishop, Saleem Choudhry, Brendan Coates, Gary Cunningham, Elizabeth Cathcart, Ittie Cutting, Simon Elliott, Ann English, Rachel Gutting, Eric Hardgrave, Ellen Hardy, Ed Hoffman, Paul Loeffler, Lee Lowenfish, Phil Marwill, "Bee" Mathews, Genevieve Maxwell, Nedene Myer, Rick Myer, Ron Munvez, Joshua Neuman, Christina Rice, Virginia Rookus, Larry Rubin,

Jaime Rupert, Daryl Slade, Russ Sloan, Mark Taylor, Jeff Tedford, Gayle Pollard-Terry, Jim Tunney, and Andrew Wagner.

To the team at Rowman & Littlefield, you are a joy to work with. Special thanks to Christen Karniski, Erinn Slanina, Nicole Carty, April Austin, the design team, and the publicity staff. Your enthusiasm, direction, and support provided motivation and inspiration.

Deepest thanks to everyone involved and to you, the reader, for enabling this remarkable life story to be shared.

INTRODUCTION

Bright floodlights illuminated the cavernous Los Angeles Memorial Coliseum. To many of the 40,000 who pressed through the turnstiles, more than just a lush, green playing field was brought from the darkness on this Friday night. An aura of anticipation wafted about the stadium. Football was back from its annual spring and summer dormancy. Long-suppressed expectation flowed freely in the form of an energetic buzz.

Among fans of the home team, UCLA, optimism spawned from third- and second-place finishes in the Pacific Coast Conference the previous two seasons. Many were anxious to see if the next three months would produce even better. Those confident that their Bruins would be a title contender reached that belief because of a heralded new player.

UCLA's fans had been teased throughout the summer months by notes in local newspaper columns, articles that featured provocative head-lines, and boasts about this new player, a sensation, certain to help the team ascend to new heights. This game with the University of Oregon would offer Bruins fans their first glimpse of the player, a talent they had been assured was unlike any they had ever seen before.

The September night was warm, 73 degrees. It was the kind of heat that, through summer months, produced a flawless playing field. As forty-eight players on the UCLA and University of Oregon sidelines readied for kickoff, Bill Spaulding approached his new halfback. "How do you feel?" he asked the gangly nineteen-year-old. "I feel alright," Kenny Washington answered.[1] The young man's voice, however, betrayed his words.

When the player tugged on his brown leather football helmet then jogged from the sideline onto the field of play, he was not only shrouded by the glare of bright lights that beamed from dozens of towers encircling the stadium, but also by the anticipation and a bit of skepticism that percolated from the stands. Both gave the unproven new Bruin much to live up to.

As the opening kickoff sailed through the night air, it wrought an eagerness in the home crowd. It sprouted from words about Kenny Washington like those typed by Braven Dyer of the *Los Angeles Times,* who exclaimed that Washington "is capable of flinging the ball 70 yards," adding that he "can put the ball in your hand with the accuracy of William Tell."[2] Skeptics encompassed the trite, aghast that Washington would wear an unlucky number, 13. There were the thoughtless with their gibes about Washington's gait, knock-kneed and pigeon-toed, caused by both a childhood bout with rickets and an accident in which he was hit by a car. "Reminds you of the peculiar Harlem dance," one sportswriter observed.[3] Beyond skeptical, however, were those downright truculent, a small minority who carried an ignorance, loathing, and even outright disdain for the young player based on nothing other than the color of his skin.

The skeptics gained fodder when Washington fumbled the ball away on the first play of the game. Amid a cascade of jeers, Oregon's scrambling defenders recovered. Those who brimmed with eagerness did not have to wait long, though, to get their first chance to gauge fact from fable. An interception set the stage. It happened on Oregon's third offensive play of the night, and it gave the ball right back to UCLA on its own 37-yard line.

The game-opening fumble did not cause Spaulding's confidence in his young back to waver. He made sure the first UCLA play after the interception went to Washington, who punched through the line for a 5-yard gain. It was on the very next play that the much-predicted and anticipated sensation burst forth. On second down and with 5 yards to go for a first down, Washington took the football. First, he darted to his right. His eyes searched for an opening in the mass of blockers and pursuers. As Washington reached the end of the line, he suddenly caught sight of a gap in the morass. Jerking his hips to the left, the Bruins' halfback turned his body toward the end zone and began a furious sprint. He left the first line of pursuers behind, then soon was past a second layer. A juke of the hips fooled an Oregon defender and cleared running room at midfield. Shouts swelled on the realization that there was nothing but open field between Washington and the end zone. The sight of an Oregon defensive back sprinting diagonally across the field in frantic pursuit made many in the stands flex their vocal cords to try to spur their new star's dash into a higher gear. When that defensive back's dive at the 10-yard line proved futile, the shouts of encouragement transformed into one mighty roar of jubilation, a celebration of the season's first touchdown, a 58-yard scamper by their new hero, Kenny Washington.

Elation unleashed by Washington's remarkable touchdown run would wane throughout the second quarter. Big plays vanished. One reason, a nighttime dew that coated the field and affected the running game. Worse yet was a slick football. The schools had agreed to use a white football, one that would allow for better visibility during a night game. However, the white leather ball with its black stripes absorbed the dew and became much more slick than its normal brown counterpart. A damp field led to mishandles. Fumbles, faux pas, and botched pass plays hampered execution. The two offenses sputtered and left it up to cheerleaders and card stunts, the well-orchestrated colorful panels held up by student rooters to spell out a saying or assemble a picture, to create enthusiasm within the stadium.

As intermission sent fans for hot dogs and soft drinks, UCLA held a mere 13–6 margin. If the Bruin faithful were made nervous by the score, it was understandable. The second half, however, would prove a much different tale. In the locker room at halftime, Spaulding made a bold move. The veteran coach decided he would put the game in the hands of his sophomore halfback.

When UCLA took possession early in the second half, the coach's decision would quickly yield dividends. A series of runs by Washington—one for 8 yards, another of 6, 3 in succession that picked up 7, and finally a twisting, spinning run that earned 5—drove UCLA from its own 36-yard line to the Oregon 18. It was then that, rather than run, Washington showed the throwing arm that evoked breathless marvel during his varsity play at Lincoln High School. He rifled a pass. The white football streaked through the air like a comet, was caught by Bob Nash at the goal line, and became a touchdown when the Bruins' receiver twisted free from a defender to score.

Whatever anxiousness was bottled up in fans burst out in the form of elation, the sounds of which echoed about the large Olympic stadium. Washington's heroics hiked confidence up and down the UCLA sideline and among the team's supporters in the stands.

After UCLA held Oregon's offense, Washington resumed his magic act. He faked a pass and then, spying an opening in the defense, took off running. Washington gained 18 yards before he slipped on the wet turf and toppled out of bounds. A Washington pass to Johnny Baida put UCLA at the Oregon 12-yard line. With everyone in the stadium expecting the ball to go to number 13, and eleven Oregon defenders expecting the same, Washington still somehow managed to deliver. He sliced through the scrum of grappling linemen and reached the end zone once again. His touchdown gave UCLA a 26–6 lead.

Spaulding motioned for Washington to come off the field. When fans noticed, they rose in voice and stature. With each step the young player took, the higher the decibel level grew. The roar was the loudest of the entire night. It enveloped the new Bruin in a hero's serenade as he exited his first collegiate game.

High above the stadium in the press box, fingers feverishly pecked typewriter keys. Stories were barked into phone receivers. There was far more to herald than simply a 26–13 outcome. Game statistics bordered on astounding. The team's new sensation not only accounted for 3 of UCLA's 4 touchdowns, 2 on runs and 1 via the pass, but carried the football 17 times and amassed 131 yards rushing.

So stirring was Washington's collegiate debut that the Southern California sporting landscape was about to change with seismic effect. Over the previous five months in 1937, two performers dominated the sports page headlines in Los Angeles. One was a cinder-churning distance runner seemingly devoid of fatigue. The second, a thundering 1,200-pound Thoroughbred racehorse. Zeal for Louis Zamperini was nourished by stories of a troubled, if not rebellious adolescence, conquered by development of his running skills. The University of Southern California freshman became a favorite of sportswriters and headline editors alike when he set the fastest mile time in the western United States during a meet in April. In June, Zamperini achieved hero-level status both locally and on a national scale when he won the NCAA title in the two-mile and helped his team capture a national collegiate championship.

A change of seasons shifted captivation from cinder running tracks to the dirt equine ovals around Southern California. Just as Zamperini commanded the adoration of sports followers and newspaper writers alike, fans of four-legged speedsters became enthralled by the achievements of a previously underwhelming Thoroughbred that went by the moniker "Seabiscuit."

Tales of how a new owner, an unobtrusive trainer, a partially blind jockey, and their peculiar training methods coaxed invincibility from a previously failed, undersized, idiosyncratic racehorse spawned fervor. A pair of stirring performances at Santa Anita Racetrack were cheered by celebrities—Bing Crosby, Clark Gable, and Douglas Fairbanks among them—and would vault Seabiscuit to prominence. The success convinced the horse's owner to take his prized speedster east for match races against several of the most highly regarded horses in America. By the end of summer Seabiscuit had beaten seven of them. Such was the level of enthrallment that 40 million people would listen to these races on radio.

That was then, and now, the morning after Kenny Washington's scintillating premiere, the city's largest newspaper, the *Times*, heralded the player in a page-one headline that read "Washington Hero of Bruin Win." Accolades flowed. "His debut was nothing less than sensational," wrote *Times* columnist Braven Dyer.[4] "Far and away the outstanding performance of the game," trumpeted Larry Mann in the *Progress-Bulletin*.[5] Ronald Wagoner went one further. In his game story for United Press, Wagoner intoned that Washington "was virtually the whole show for UCLA."[6]

Fans, who had left the Coliseum abuzz, carried with them sky-high expectations. But more substantially, the heralded harrier and the hallowed horse were knocked from receiving any future large type on Los Angeles sports pages. Never again would Zamperini or Seabiscuit command the kind of column inches or headlines as before. Los Angeles had a new sports hero.

1

BLUE, THE BREAK, AND THE ACCENT

Lincoln Heights was an area of Los Angeles defined by its sounds. The whistle from nearby trains was a reminder to many in the neighborhood of the journey they had made from faraway lands to pursue a better life in America. Frequent banging and clatter as freight trains were uncoupled and assembled at Taylor Yard, Midway Yard, or the Bull Ring Yard across the Main Street bridge signified the backbreaking manual labor many of the neighborhood's men carried out. The shouts and laughter of children playing in Downey Park on Spring Street and South Seventeenth Avenue told of the many young families that called the area home. And then there was the whine of the truck.

The sound did not come from just any truck. It was from a long Signal delivery truck, one that hauled produce to markets. A small handful of adolescents, buddies, kept an ear trained for the unmistakable whine of a truck shifting through its gears as it made its trek toward the neighborhood. The boys had become familiar with the driver's weekly route. It made deliveries to Viotto's Market on Fifth and Hewitt Streets, Eastside Market over on Alpine, and Lanza Brothers Market on North Main. At each, the driver would enter the store, leaving the truck unoccupied. More importantly to the boys, it left a tantalizing booty—fresh produce unattended.

Once opportunity presented itself, the boys would break from a slow walk into a speedy sprint. On reaching the truck bed, hands grasped at the plunder—juicy red apples, sweet round oranges, and if lucky, a delectable bunch of grapes. In a flash the real footrace began. The tallest of the youths, the one with an odd gait and ever so slight limp, was also the fastest. The boys sprinted around corners, down streets, between buildings until they reached a haven, a back alley, a vacant lot, one's house. It was there that they collected themselves, caught their breath, and feasted. Malice had

1

nothing to do with their thievery. This was spurred by one thing and one thing only. Hunger. Devourment trumped savoring. Haste overwhelmed sustenance. The speed at which they ate was not about eliminating evidence; it was more important than that. It was a rush to stop the pangs.

Lincoln Heights was unlike any other neighborhood in Los Angeles. Its residents were either directly from or were the children of immigrants from another land. Williams Street was home to several families from Greece. On Redondo Avenue were newcomers from Sweden, Germany, and France. Families from England and Switzerland dotted Avenue Nineteen. Those who emigrated from Italy had an especially large presence in the neighborhood.

The Washingtons were not unlike their neighbors. They worked hard, engaged in manual labor, and managed to keep a roof over their heads, all with the hope that they or their offspring would get ahead in life. Like many in Lincoln Heights, the Washingtons had migrated from somewhere else. That the Washingtons were Black mattered little to most of their neighbors.

The family matriarch, Susie Washington, was born in Missouri, where she married a man twenty years her senior. As the couple made their way to California, their first child, Lawrence, was born in New Mexico. A year later, the family grew with a second son, Julius. Within nine years Susie Washington had borne five children. A son, Edgar, followed Julius; then three years later came a daughter, Rebecca. Two years after Rebecca's birth came a fourth son, Roscoe.

Not long after the turn of the century, Susie Washington, by then in her early thirties, was widowed. She moved her children from an apartment house into the small home in Lincoln Heights, at 138 South Avenue Nineteen. With indefatigable strength the woman worked all hours to provide. She ran a day-care facility, handled janitorial work for the school district, and did laundry for families.

Like a great many who arrived from the South (i.e., below the Mason–Dixon Line), Susie Washington found Los Angeles far less discriminatory than her native Missouri. In a city with a population of 1.2 million in 1920, only one-tenth of 1 percent was Black. In Lincoln Heights that disparity was even greater. Discrimination was present; while still heinous, the intolerance was exhibited on a much lesser scale than in the Deep South. In Southern California, access to prime beaches was denied. The beach set aside for Blacks was derisively called Inkwell. In the Broadway Theater District, Blacks were either barred altogether or limited to balcony seating at the Lincoln, Tivoli, Angelus, and Globe theaters. Housing covenants existed in a handful of neighborhoods. Any real estate agent who attempted to sell to a barred buyer risked losing their license. Vandalism and violence often greeted Blacks who bought homes in previously all-white neighborhoods. In some cases, sellers risked lawsuits. Those whom they sold to might receive a menacing visit from members of a small local faction of the Ku Klux Klan.

Yet opportunity abounded. Home ownership was possible. So too was ascension into the middle class. Most schools were integrated. Born from denial, a collection of Black-owned businesses, restaurants, hotels, clubs, and churches grew on Central Avenue between Eighth and Twelfth streets. In time this area flourished. Unlike below the Mason–Dixon Line, there was no segregated seating on public transportation. On Saturday night, for instance, the V-Line was frequently packed with Blacks who traveled from Watts and Boyle Heights to enjoy the entertainment in the Central Avenue clubs.

Susie Washington pushed her children to achieve, and they responded. Her oldest, Lawrence, joined the Los Angeles Fire Department—first as a hose man, then ultimately achieving the rank of captain. After graduation from high school, Roscoe, the youngest, became a cop. He was one of the first Black patrol officers in Los Angeles, rose to detective, then achieved the rank of lieutenant. Julius hired on with Metropolitan Warehouse. Rebecca became a waitress. It was Susie's middle child, Edgar, who proved to be a handful.

Edgar Washington could do anything he set his mind to. At almost 6 feet 2 inches tall and 190 pounds, he was teeming with athletic talent. At fourteen, his build helped propagate a claim to be old enough to box professionally. Under the moniker "Kid Blue," Washington became known as a knockout artist in gyms and arenas around the Los Angeles area. A *Los Angeles Times* reporter wrote that Washington paid "the least attention to guarding anything."[1] Yet Washington's fights were filled with action. His punching power produced knockouts. He became popular with fans and drew big crowds to several Los Angeles–area venues, particularly Doyle's Arena in Vernon.

By 1915, the now seventeen-year-old walked away from pugilism for another sport. Edgar Washington joined a semipro baseball team, the Los Angeles White Sox, where his hitting and pitching skills impressed. In the fall of 1915, legendary team owner Rube Foster entered his all-Black Chicago American Giants in the Southern California Winter League. When the league concluded just after Christmas, Foster left Los Angeles with a new player, Edgar Washington.

In spring training during March 1916, Washington pitched brilliantly against Pacific Coast League teams. Tales of their new pitcher's performance whetted the appetite of Giants fans. But Rube Foster's enthusiasm for Edgar Washington would be quashed in the early days of the 1916 season. Washington pitched poorly in his first two appearances. While it left his manager frustrated, Foster's ire was not solely conjured by poor pitching. Rube Foster had no tolerance for shenanigans. When Foster learned that his new pitcher had blown his money on alcohol and was seen cavorting with white women, Edgar Washington was finished with the Chicago American Giants.

Life back in Los Angeles took two unexpected turns for Washington. The first came in March 1918, when he married a beautiful sixteen-year-old of Jamaican ancestry, Marion Lenán. Edgar Washington's bride moved into the family home on South Avenue Nineteen. Five months later, on August 31, the couple welcomed a son. They named him Kenneth Stanley Washington. He would be the couple's only child.

Despite Washington's failing with the Chicago American Giants, his love of baseball continued. The Los Angeles White Sox were all too happy to take him back, and he soon resumed his role as one of the team's top players. In the spring of 1920, another crack at professional baseball beckoned.

In Kansas City, Missouri, Rube Foster brought the owners of seven other Midwest ballclubs together. In that meeting on February 13, a professional baseball league, the Negro National League, was formed. Among the eight-member teams was a new club, the Kansas City Monarchs. Their search for players led them to Los Angeles and, ultimately, Edgar Washington.

Leaving his wife and young son behind, Washington boarded a train for Kansas City. Days after he joined the team, he went 4-for-4 to highlight an 11–1 Monarchs win over a semipro club, Davis Cleaners. The twenty-two-year-old continued to hit well in exhibition games. A week before Opening Day, the Monarchs' manager, José Méndez, lavished praise on his first baseman, calling Washington "a find, a hard hitter, and a player with lots of pep."[2]

When the Monarchs took the field in St Louis for their first game, Edgar Washington was the team's starting first baseman. By the end of May, Washington's hitting prompted Méndez to move him from seventh into the coveted cleanup spot in the batting order. Two days later in Indianapolis, Washington came through with a single that tied the game in the ninth inning. In all, he finished the afternoon with 3 hits.

It was, however, to be Edgar Washington's final hurrah in professional baseball. In the ensuing days, his hitting took a nosedive. Anxious to be competitive, the Monarchs tried out new players almost daily. It wasn't long before Washington's name became absent from the lineup card. In a last-ditch shot to determine whether Washington had value to his ballclub, Méndez gave him a turn on the mound. It was tainted by walks and wild pitches. When three new players arrived in mid-June and almost immediately shone, their inclusion on the team was at the expense of Edgar Washington.

Through connections in the spring of 1918, Edgar Washington received a bit part in a motion picture, a silent film titled *High Stakes*. After his second failed foray with professional baseball, Washington plunged into a full-fledged acting career. His initial roles were those typically given to Black performers, that of a mansion's butler, a porter at the train station, a native, a doorman. More experience, though, brought parts with more breadth. He played a cowboy with John Wayne in *Haunted Gold* and performed alongside Wallace Beery in *Beggars of Life*. If Washington wasn't always recognized in the credits, it may have been because he often used the nickname "Blue," rather than his given name. The nickname came from a school chum, Francesco Capra, who by now was known as Frank and enjoying success as a director in Hollywood.

When payday came, Blue Washington would often vanish, lured by a fondness for parties, women, and alcohol. His frequent absences left a parental void at home. With Marion Washington not exactly a homebody either, Susie Washington and her youngest son, Roscoe, stepped into the parental chasm.

Susie Washington unfailingly took on a maternal role to raise her grandson. Roscoe—"Uncle Rocky" to his nephew—became a father figure. Challenges stressed their good intentions. Susie, by now in her mid-fifties, continued to work multiple jobs, each of which entailed fatiguing manual labor. Roscoe was by now married. Together with his wife Hazel, he moved to a house 200 yards south of his mother's home on Avenue Nineteen. Theirs became a second home for their nephew.

In the absence of his grandmother and uncle, Kenny Washington found himself gravitating to the homes of neighbors, the D'Agostinos on one side and the Schiarras and Gusarios on the other. Mothers would take him to morning mass, then send him on his way to school in dress shirt and tie, the only boy in his elementary school thusly attired. The amount of time Washington spent in the homes of these immigrant neighbors was soon apparent in the lilt of his speech, which became tinged with an Italian accent.

Sports was a passion, if not an obsession, for many of the boys in the neighborhood. Baseball was the game of choice. When not playing in the street or at Downey Playground, Kenny Washington would throw a rubber ball in solitude. He threw daily and for hours. Every toss was made with aim and purpose. In time, the youth's arm strength grew. As it did, he increased the distance of his throws until he achieved remarkably consistent accuracy from a distance of 20 yards.

Football entered Washington's world a bit later than baseball. He was nine when he first tossed a football. Pushed was more like it. The oblong spheroid was much too big for hands of one his age. Keen to improve, Washington pestered the playground supervisor, Marion Sparrow, to teach him how to throw and kick a football properly. When Washington joined the Boy Scouts at thirteen, his Troop 143 from Lady Help of Christians entered its members into a youth football league. With Washington's swift and shifty running as well as long passing skills, Troop 143 went undefeated.

Through his early teens it was clear that Kenny Washington was athletically gifted. His size, throwing arm, running speed, and powerful baseball-hitting skills developed to a level far superior to those of everyone else in the neighborhood. Tales reached the ears of his grandmother. Her pride grew. One day Susie Washington gushed, "Watch and see what I tell you. Some day that boy's name is going to be in headlines."[3]

2

A MEA CULPA

The fat, leather football zipped through the air with a velocity rare for a thrower of his age. Even more astonishing was the distance the ball traveled. Scattered about the high school football field were teenagers in hot pursuit. Their eyes were wide, mouths agape at the unfolding play. With each step taken in a chase for the football, amazement heightened at what each was seeing. The ball's flight came to an end 50 yards away, in the hands of the thrower's intended target and in the end zone for a touchdown. The pass bespoke a gifted talent, albeit one which Kenny Washington held at just fifteen years of age.

The idea of such a supremely gifted player at Lincoln High School was a novel one. The school was more sports minnow than powerhouse. Lincoln was the only high school in Los Angeles that didn't have a football stadium. Its football team practiced on the side of a hill with no space for a full-sized field. Large numbers of the 2,100-member student body were either immigrants or American-born children of recent arrivals to the country. Some lacked understanding of American sports, while others held after-school work responsibilities and were needed to either bring income to their household or assist in family stores or restaurants. Lincoln High was rarely able to field teams of a championship caliber.

The reputation that Lincoln High clung to was one of academic success. A label of ruffians also painted the image of the school's student body. This was born of achievements by two of its most successful former athletes, boxers. One, a dropout, Jacob Finkelstein, and the other, Fidel LaBarbas. Finkelstein, under the stage name Jackie Fields, won an Olympic gold medal in 1924 and later the world welterweight title. LaBarbas also brought home an Olympic gold medal from the Paris games and later won the world flyweight championship. Such was the perception of Lincoln

High that during his first week at the school a new teacher stood before his pupils for the first time and proclaimed, "I'm the toughest guy in this vicinity. If there are any of you who don't think so, now is the time to step up."[1] None did.

In the fall of 1933, the makeup of the Lincoln High football team was young, heavy on underclass players and light in the senior class. There was little in the way of expectation for success. None of this was new to the school's football coach, Jim Tunney. But it failed to diminish either his enthusiasm for coaching or his passion for teaching. A tall, lean family man, Jim Tunney was approaching thirty. He rarely missed mass each morning at 6:30. His coaching drew from experience, having quarterbacked the 1926 Loyola College team to an undefeated season.

Preseason practice in September 1933 brought the promise of future changes. Tunney was exposed to exceptionality, a new enrollee in the school possessing a powerful throwing arm and fleet, shifty running skills—Kenny Washington. In a rare move, the coach assigned Washington to the varsity squad. Never mind that Washington was just five weeks past his fifteenth birthday, measured 6 feet in height yet weighed only 122 pounds or that his football skills were raw. His inclusion was meant to serve as a sort of football apprenticeship. Not only would Washington learn by observing but also improve his skills from practice and scrimmages against the older boys. Tunney too could invest time to teach and polish his raw gem.

A loss to Franklin High School in the fourth game of Lincoln's 6-game season left the Tigers with a 2–2 record and ended any hope of a trip to the playoffs. The Tigers' fifth opponent, Jefferson High, was talented—called a juggernaut by sportswriters—having won the City League title in 1932. They were in the thick of the chase for a repeat crown and represented, perhaps, Lincoln's toughest foe of the season.

It was the week before Thanksgiving when the schedule maker brought the two teams together at Belmont High School's stadium. Vigorous enthusiasm filled the air. By the fourth quarter, however, the fervor was trumped by surprise. Lincoln's defense managed to hold Jefferson to only 6 points. Elation at the play of the Tigers' defense was tempered by an inability on the part of the offense to score. In the waning minutes of play, Jim Tunney threw caution to the wind. He inserted his third quarterback of the afternoon, the sophomore Kenny Washington.

With little time left in the game, Lincoln High took possession at its own 35-yard line. Suddenly, behind their new quarterback, near magnificence would burst from the moribund. With shifty runs and deft passes, the Tigers began a drive that would amass 50 yards. As more and more of the 65 yards that separated Lincoln High from a chance to tie the game was erased, the Jefferson defense was put on its heels. Spirits rose among the Lincoln faithful. Optimism grew on their sideline. As Lincoln reached the Jefferson 15-yard line, only one thing evoked worry—the clock. It was a serious concern. The players scurried to complete another play, but before they could, the timer's gun went off. The game ended. Lincoln High lost, 6–0. Still, there were encouraging signs amid the defeat and, most of all, optimism generated from the play of underclass players.

Whatever elation Washington held after his first varsity performance was doused days later when his grandmother, Susie Washington, died. The teenager packed his things and moved in with his mother. Marion Washington had matured. She secured regular work as a maid and earned enough to rent a small home on Twenty-Second Avenue for $40 a month.

When practice began for the 1934 season, Tunney greeted a bigger and more talented Kenny Washington. Now sixteen, Washington had grown to almost 6 feet 2 inches in height. He was still thin, but his size 13 feet and large hands portended shifty running skills, swift foot speed, and an immensely strong throwing arm. Tunney installed Washington as his quarterback. When asked what offense he planned to run, the coach smiled and said, "Just give the ball to Kenny."[2]

In actuality, Tunney's offense consisted of five plays. Four involved his young quarterback. Little more was needed. Washington's combination of running and passing skills gave the coach a lethal weapon.

Lincoln High's season began inauspiciously. A win in a nonleague game was followed by a tie and then a stinging defeat, 19–6, to Roosevelt High. In the loss, Washington intercepted a pass at the Lincoln High 5-yard line and dodged would-be tacklers over the ensuing 95 yards for his team's lone touchdown. While defeat stung, it would be the last time Kenny Washington would experience it. After the Roosevelt game, he was never again on a losing side in a high school football game.

Through the remaining games of the 1934 season, the Tigers' quarterback was nothing short of sensational. His touchdowns were marvels—the 95-yard return of an interception against Roosevelt, scoring passes of 50 and 37 yards in the Fremont game, a 70-yard run in the win over Franklin. Washington's running style was both confusing and terrifying to defenders. His misshapen legs and feet left would-be tacklers to wonder about his path. Leather helmets were little defense against contact with a Washington knee, as many a woozy or concussed defender would testify.

The 1933 Lincoln High Tigers managed only 6 touchdowns during their 6-game season. Going into their final 2 games, the 1934 edition Tigers had doubled that total and Kenny Washington, via either interception, the run, or the pass, had been responsible for every one of them.

Perhaps the most dramatic game of the season came against Beverly Hills High School. Late in the fourth quarter, Lincoln High trailed, 12–6. That's when Washington unleashed a performance that sent the stadium abuzz. With 1 minute left on the clock, the Tigers regained possession of the ball 53 yards from the end zone. Washington took control. He first rifled a pass to Joe Garofolo that gained 22 yards. On the next play, the strong-armed quarterback connected on a pass to Lawrence Cancellieri, who was tackled at the 15. All in the stadium fretted at what little time was left. Chased by pursuers back to the 30-yard line, Washington managed to unleash a throw that Pete Torreano caught at the 5-yard line. The receiver was then knocked out of bounds at the 1. On the next play Washington plunged over the goal line for a touchdown to tie the game. His kick then gave Lincoln High the extra point it needed for a thrilling 13–12 victory.

Such drama vaulted Kenny Washington into the spotlight. On that afternoon both the *Times* and *Daily News* had sportswriters in the stadium, which was a rarity. Each wrote of Washington in glowing terms. Lee Bastajian of the *Los Angeles Daily News* wrote that Washington "sparkled brilliantly in the Lincoln victory."[3] Jack Singer issued a mea culpa in the *Los Angeles Times*. "This is both an apology and a eulogy for Kenneth (George) Washington, Lincoln High's colored and colorful quarterback who has been sadly neglected in the public prints."[4]

Lincoln High completed its season the following week with a 40–0 romp past Franklin High. In the rout, Washington scored the Tigers' first 2 touchdowns. When he found a seam off left tackle and dashed 70 yards for his third score, Tunney substituted him in a show of sportsmanship.

One year later there was no need for any sportswriter to apologize. The fall of 1935 saw Kenny Washington erupt into a full-fledged phenom. Saturdays frequently saw large newspaper headlines trumpet his Friday afternoon play. Adjectives flowed throughout game stories. An occasional photo of Washington in action would grace the front page of a sports section.

Washington's talent turned the fall of 1935 into the ride of a lifetime for the Lincoln High School football team. The seventeen-year-old didn't just amaze, he evoked wonder. Tales of his arm strength flushed disbelief. Never had a quarterback with such a strong and accurate throwing arm graced Los Angeles high school football fields. Tunney told of a day in practice where he placed Washington on one goal line, then put a receiver on the opposite goal line. Once the ball was in the air, the receiver had to step out to the 4-yard line to make the catch after the ball had traveled 96 yards in the air. Teammates routinely joked with Washington about his throwing accuracy. One afternoon in practice, Pete Torreano challenged Washington. "I betcha can't hit me in the eye with a pass from where you're standin'." The quarterback laughed and replied, "Which eye?"[5] In a split second Washington raised his right arm, cocked his wrist, then let loose with a pass that seared through the air with such might that 30 yards upfield, it snapped his teammate's head back.

The Tigers plowed through their schedule by winning high-scoring, lopsided games and posting defensive shutouts. Their touchdown total was more than triple that of 1933. Of the 19 that Lincoln High scored, Washington ran for 11 and threw for 5 more. He achieved all that while being substituted at halftime in half of his team's games, so great were their leads. With each week the adjectives grew. From outstanding in September, Washington was being hailed the greatest by December. When he scored four times on a muddy, sawdust-covered field to beat Garfield High, 27–0, and claim the Northern League title, the *Los Angeles Times* heralded the quarterback "one of the greatest backs to flash across the Los Angeles High School heavens in many years."[6]

The first round of the playoffs matched Lincoln High with Fairfax High. For Lincoln, the game put the school on a bigger stage—in Gilmore Stadium, a year-old, 18,000-seat bowl located on the fringe of Hollywood. Before 11,000 fans, Lincoln High put on what one sportswriter called "the greatest show staged by a high school team in many, many years."[7] Tunney directed Washington to use almost every trick play imaginable: reverses, double reverses, a double reverse and pass. The Tigers employed laterals, even double laterals. By the end of the game, Kenny Washington had run for 3 touchdowns, caught a fourth, and thrown for a fifth. The outcome was never in doubt. Lincoln High romped, 31–6.

Victory launched Washington and his teammates into the city championship game. Their opponent would be the longtime area powerhouse, Fremont High, owner of three city titles in the previous five seasons. Conversely, Lincoln High had never won a city championship.

Throughout the week leading up to the game, sportswriters heaped praise on the Lincoln High sensation. "Washington is perhaps the greatest, and the most unorthodox back that has ever performed for a Los Angeles high school," wrote Jack Singer in the *Times*.[8] Columnists urged fans to see the talented quarterback in his final high school game.

For the first time ever, the Los Angeles City Football Championship was played in the mammoth Los Angeles Memorial Coliseum. Neither

Lincoln nor Fremont could score in the first half. Two minutes into the third quarter, however, that changed. Kenny Washington got his mitts on an errant Fremont pass at the 35-yard line and ran it back to the 8. Two plays later he streaked around right end. Just as a Fremont defender grabbed two fistfuls of his jersey, Washington crossed the goal line for a touchdown. He booted the extra point through the uprights for a 7–0 lead.

On the first play of the fourth quarter, Washington scored again. He had orchestrated a 52-yard drive in the final minutes of the third quarter. The Lincoln High quarterback finished the drive with a 4-yard run around the left end to extend the Lincoln advantage to 13–0. An errant snap from center became a safety and gave Fremont its first points of the game. With 2 minutes left in the game, Fremont High scored to narrow the gap to 4, 13–9. While the narrow margin heightened hope among the Fremont High fans, it was as close as the score would get.

In the waning moments of play, eyes darted from the action on the field to the large hand on the scoreboard clock. Once it showed time had expired, jubilant Lincoln High fans ran onto the field in celebration. For the first time in the school's history, Lincoln High had achieved an undefeated season and claimed a city football championship.

A tally of the game's statistics gave startling testament to Washington's brilliance. Of the 173 yards Lincoln High amassed on offense, Washington gained 169 of them. Not once all afternoon did he take a breather, playing all 48 minutes. During those minutes he scored all 13 of his team's points.

Readers who opened their morning paper on December 1 saw a large spread that recognized the All-City Dream Team. The *Los Angeles Times* enlisted twenty-nine high school coaches to select the 1935 high school football all-stars. Their quarterback selection was no surprise: Kenny Washington. Two weeks later Washington was named to the All–Southern California team as well. Wrote the *Times*'s Jack Singer, "In any constellation of stars, there is always one star that shines more brightly than all the others. This year it is Kenny Washington. The greatest passer to grace a high school gridiron in many years."[9]

However, as gifted as he appeared to be in the sport, football was far from Kenny Washington's preferred sport. It was actually baseball. And he may have been even more talented on the diamond than he was on the gridiron.

Washington's baseball skills first showed themselves to followers of the high school game on Tuesday, May 22, 1934. It coincided with Lincoln High School's ascension from that of a middling baseball program to a Los

Angeles city power. Similar to the rise of the school's football team, it centered on the talent of one particular player, Kenny Washington.

On the May afternoon in question, the Tigers traveled from their campus to Fremont High School in south Los Angeles for their third game of the five-week season. The hosts were not only the defending city champs but an area baseball juggernaut. Fremont High had sent several alums into professional baseball. There was a feeling that Fremont's next star would be their sixteen-year-old sophomore third baseman, Bob Doerr.

Both schools pitched their ace. A scarcity of hits resulted. Lincoln High scratched out a run in the second inning. In the third came a blow that would signal a transition in high school baseball power. Lincoln's own sophomore talent came to bat. With a mighty swing, Kenny Washington tore into a pitch and sent it high into the air and well beyond the Fremont High outfielders. From the Lincoln High bench, players raucously celebrated. Washington's home run put his team in front, 2–0. It wasn't until the sixth inning of the seven-inning game that Fremont got on the scoreboard. It was Doerr who did it with a home run. His blast, however, would be the only run Fremont High managed. Lincoln High, the heretofore league lightweight, toppled the defending city champs, 2–1.

By the end of May, Washington was hitting over .500. Lincoln High had stormed through the first round of league play without a defeat. The Tigers were unquestionably the surprise team of the City League. It was then that two events shattered Lincoln High School's dream of a championship season. One was self-caused; the other was entirely out of the team's control.

On Friday, June 1, the Tigers were beaten in an upset, 3–2, by Los Angeles High. The loss knocked Lincoln High from first place and allowed Fairfax to assume the league's top spot. Three games remained before the playoffs. Of the top three contenders for the City League title—Lincoln, Fairfax, and Fremont—the Tigers were considered to have the easiest remaining schedule.

Four days later, the title hopes of Lincoln High and every other high school baseball team in Los Angeles were quashed. On Tuesday, June 5, before the afternoon games could be played, the Board of Education brought the 1934 high school baseball season to an immediate halt.

A public health crisis had broken out in Los Angeles. A drastic rise was reported in poliomyelitis cases, or as the disease was more commonly known, infantile paralysis or polio. Among many measures instituted, the city and county Health Departments ordered that large public gatherings be stopped. Their edict covered high school sporting events. The high school baseball season was declared over. Fairfax High was awarded the City League title. Washington finished second in the race for the batting title to Fremont's Doerr.

Once the 1935 high school baseball season began, longtime baseball minnows, Lincoln High and its power-hitting shortstop, Kenny Washington, stalked Fremont High for city bragging rights. In 5 of their first 6 games, the Tigers won while scoring in the neighborhood of 10 runs per contest. Washington was the team's hitting star. He carried a batting average of over .500, and one attained with frightful power.

Fruits of the Tigers' success was an April 25 matchup with Fremont High. The prize up for grabs was the 1935 city championship trophy. Even though Bobby Doerr had left school to sign a professional baseball contract, many sportswriters still pegged the Pathfinders as the championship favorite. They were wrong. When Washington smashed a decisive blow, a home run, Lincoln High toppled the local baseball giant and seized the crown with a 7–5 victory.

When the spring of 1936 arrived, the Lincoln High baseball team was so overpowering it had the opportunity to clinch its second consecutive league title with two weeks still to play. In the decisive game against Franklin High, Lincoln prevailed, 4–2. The margin of victory came from a long 2-run home run that Washington belted off Franklin's ace pitcher, "Lefty" Phillips.

Anticipation was high for the playoffs. A rematch with Fremont High seemed a certainty. But for Washington and his teammates, championship aspirations would be crushed and in fast and stunning fashion. The Department of Education simply ordered the season done. There would be no playoff. No city champion for 1936 would be crowned. Washington led all players in the city with a batting average over .400. He was named the shortstop on the All-City team. But for the second time in three seasons, individual honors would be small consolation.

The surprising end to the baseball season pushed the Lincoln High track coach into action. He persuaded Washington to join his squad. Washington's specialty event would be atypical for that of a quarterback and shortstop—the shot put. Heaving the twelve-pound lead-and-steel ball was usually done by someone more muscular, if not hefty, in stature, such as a football lineman. Despite having no prior experience, Washington quickly adapted to the new event. In a dual meet against Roosevelt High, he came away victorious. That was followed by wins in meets with Garfield High and Franklin High. Washington's winning mark improved at each meet until he entered the league championship with a best mark that was a full foot farther than when he began.

Washington's continued improvement led to one of the biggest successes in Lincoln High's sports history, one more shocking than ever achieved in the city. The school had been a nonentity on the track-and-field scene in Los Angeles. Leading up to the 1936 Northern League championship meet, Lincoln High's coach, John Fox, made the decision to utilize his new team member in more than just his usual event. The coach entered Washington in four: the half mile, low hurdles, and long jump, as well as in his specialty, the shot put. The move would pay enormous dividends.

In each of his events, Washington produced valuable points—almost half those scored by his team. He finished second in the half mile, second in the long jump, fourth in the low hurdles, and earned second in the shot put. Powered by Washington's success, Lincoln High edged out Belmont High by a single point, 46–45, and won the league title. It was hailed as the greatest upset in Los Angeles high school track-and-field history.

The result was the final achievement in an unprecedented string of sports success for Lincoln High School. In 1935 and 1936, the school earned league titles in football, baseball, and track and field. It celebrated its first ever outright city championships in football and baseball. While all of it involved teams and teamwork, at the core of each was the talent of one player, Kenny Washington. So distinct were his skills that the feats would not be replicated by the three Lincoln High teams for decades.

3

ANTICIPATION AND
ANIMOSITY IN WESTWOOD

The nonstop smile was noticeable to everyone at the field. Two dozen boosters, a half dozen newspapermen, and a couple of pro football players who ringed the sidelines were surprised to see it. A smile was something few expected to see from Bill Spaulding during spring football drills, but every time his freshman left halfback touched the football in drills, the result painted a large grin on the coach's face.

Consternation, even a bit of ire, and not a smiling coach was what the onlookers expected to see. After all, Spaulding's 1935 and 1936 UCLA teams raised the expectations of the school's fans with second- and third-place finishes in the Pacific Coast Conference. Yet many of the players responsible for that success were now gone. Ten starters in all, not to mention three reserves who received considerable playing time, had graduated. The offensive line was most worrisome. Two inexperienced freshmen, a sophomore, and a junior had the inside track to be starters. Forty players drilled, scrimmaged, and otherwise trained in Spaulding's effort to mold his 1937 UCLA football team. Almost every observer agreed that the players showed a noticeable drop-off in talent from the previous season. All, that is, but one.

Bill Spaulding had waited more than a year for this opportunity to add Kenny Washington to the UCLA varsity. He was keen to see how Washington would respond to tougher competition. The coach was also eager to see just what Washington's talents could bring to the Bruin offense.

In the fall of 1935, there was no bigger recruiting target for the UCLA head coach than Kenny Washington. All it took was for Spaulding to see Washington in a high school game and he became infatuated. Spaulding wasn't alone with his enamoration, however. Numerous schools sought the Lincoln High standout. Recruiting at times became nasty. There were coaches who tried to scare rivals off Washington's trail with claims his grades would not pass scrutiny, and he was unlikely to be admitted to their institution. Lincoln High's principal refuted each and every such charge. He stated unequivocally that Washington was an excellent student, whose high school grades would guarantee entry into almost any school in the country.

For a time, it appeared "Slip" Madigan would lure the talented prospect to his mighty program at St. Mary's College in Northern California. Oregon State made a strong pitch, and there was a feeling Washington was giving the school strong consideration. To showcase its acceptance of players of all races, Loyola College invited Washington to its football awards banquet, at which Alpheus Duvall, a hulking African American lineman, was named the team's outstanding player. Washington spent a weekend in Berkeley and expressed interest in playing for the University of California. The Bears had just enjoyed a 9-win season and were champions of the Pacific Coast Conference.

Once news of Washington's Berkeley visit reached the newspapers, UCLA's coaches stepped up their pursuit. A car, a Ford Model T, was added to previously promised inducements of a $100 a month stipend, an allotment for meals on the campus, and free clothing from the Desmond's Department Store branch in Westwood. Three weeks after Washington was named the best back on the All-City team, he confirmed to Spaulding that he would indeed enroll at UCLA.

As ecstatic as the successful recruitment was, Spaulding would have to wait a year to gain Washington's talents for the UCLA varsity. First-year students were prohibited by National Collegiate Athletic Association rules from participation in varsity sports. The NCAA rule relegated Washington to the UCLA freshman football team for the 1936 season.

Each week during the 5-game freshman season, raves abounded for one remarkable feat or another by the sensational yearling. A 68-yard touchdown run was the game's lone score in a 6–0 win over Santa Monica Junior College. A 38-yard touchdown run as time expired beat Bakersfield College. A 33-yard run in the final 3 minutes of play set up a game-winning touchdown against Stanford. In the final game, against Santa Ana Junior College, Washington rifled a touchdown pass that sailed 50 yards in the air.

During his first year on the UCLA campus, Washington struck up a friendship with another football newcomer, Woody Strode, the only other Black player on the team. Almost three years Washington's senior, Strode's arrival on the campus came after more than two years in a UCLA extension program to improve his grades in order to gain eligibility to play football. Strode was chiseled from thousands of daily push-ups. His physique brought $25 payments from artists who sought to sketch and paint his form.

Once April arrived, Washington received his first opportunity to make an impression on the varsity coach. Spring football was a time when colleges were permitted to conduct practice sessions over a nine-week period. Teaching was paramount. Experimentation was also involved. Players were tried at different positions. New plays were installed, or as was the case at UCLA, new wrinkles added to existing plays. Spring football was as time consuming and mentally taxing for the coach as it was for players. "Until I get through this spring practice business my golf isn't going to improve much," Spaulding muttered to a friend.[1]

Under Spaulding, UCLA operated out of a single-wing offense. The scheme was originally designed by legendary coach "Pop" Warner at Carlisle Indian Industrial School in 1907 to utilize the talents of his star player, Jim Thorpe. In the single wing, one of four backs was deployed as a wingback and positioned 1 yard beyond the end and a yard behind the line of scrimmage; hence, the name "single wing."

In the single wing the quarterback was situated 2 yards behind the tackle and utilized primarily as a blocker. The two halfbacks lined up 5 to 7 yards behind the guards. If one of the backs was a fullback, he then would stand 1 yard closer to the line than the other back and function as a blocker. Other variations simply employed a right halfback and a left halfback. The snap from center would be made to either back who, depending upon the play call, had the option to run with the football or throw it.

One particular area of emphasis during UCLA's spring drills was the passing game. Previously mocked by fans as "pass and pray," there was optimism that the Bruins now had the talent to make the forward pass an effective weapon. Throughout drills and in scrimmages, more pass plays were called. Lateral passes were added to existing plays.

Privately, Spaulding liked the progress he saw. Publicly, the coach made a concerted effort to be reserved in his assessments of the team. A half dozen sportswriters were in attendance at almost every practice. They saw firsthand the coach smile broadly each time Kenny Washington rifled a long pass or ripped off a scintillating run. Yet when queried, Spaulding would reply with no emotion and insist the freshman was just one of a half dozen players in competition for playing time at left halfback.

On Saturday, May 13, Bill Spaulding lost the ability to conceal the truth any longer. That afternoon, the school concluded spring practice with an intrasquad game. Spaulding and his assistant coaches divvied their players into two squads and named each with the school colors. Washington was placed on the Bruin Blues. Play had barely begun when the new varsity member made chins drop and eyebrows rise. Washington was playing safety on defense. Bob Chambers of the UCLA Golds heaved a long pass. Washington reacted quickly. He dashed into the ball's path and snatched the football at his own 40-yard line before it could be caught by the intended receiver. Like a flash he pivoted and dashed down the sideline. No one was able to lay so much as a finger on the streaking Washington, who raced 60 yards with the theft to score the game's first touchdown.

Twice, Washington gave a glimpse of the potential the passing game held come fall. Playing left halfback, he took a snap from center, dropped back to almost midfield, then rifled the ball to Merle Harris at the 20-yard line. Harris spun free of a defender and scampered into the end zone for the Bruin Blue's second touchdown of the afternoon.

During the second half Washington intercepted his second pass of the game. He snared this one at midfield and returned it to the 33-yard line. On the next play, Washington hit Johnny Baida with a pass. He then watched his teammate stiff arm several tacklers over the final 18 yards for the third touchdown of a 19–0 Bruin Blues triumph.

Before Washington could play his first college game, the *Pasadena Post* proclaimed him the greatest football player to ever set foot on the UCLA campus. A columnist in the *Oakland Tribune* took the praise a step further. He hailed Washington the best player in the country. Even UCLA's own publicity director, Ben Person, said, "He's superb, colossal."[2]

The attention, however, was like a match head to flint. While many Bruins were enthusiastic at the prospect of such a talented teammate, several simmered with resentment. Upperclassmen with two and even three years of hard work under their belt grew irritated by the almost nonstop praise for the untested new player. There was undeniable jealousy in the ranks. Bruised egos also contributed to some of the animosity. "Izzy" Cantor's was one. A standout halfback on the 1936 team, Cantor seethed when told he would be relegated to the bench behind Washington.

And then there was "Slats" Wyrick. For all of the headaches the problematic team chemistry doled out to UCLA's coaches, in the leadup to the 1937 season none matched that dispensed by Celestine Moses Wyrick. Coaches considered the strong, 6-foot-4-inch, 218-pound junior to be their best tackle. He was agile, a hard worker, and excelled at making his initial block at the line of scrimmage, then releasing to swiftly get downfield. Babe Horrell, the UCLA line coach, was optimistic that Wyrick and Jack "King Kong" Cohen, whose Herculean feats included lifting 300 pounds, would sustain blocks and give Washington time to pass or holes he could run through. Therein lay the problem. Slats Wyrick loathed Kenny Washington.

A week before the Oregon game, Spaulding took his team to the Rose Bowl in Pasadena. With the upcoming game slated for a Friday night, the coach wanted his players to get used to playing under bright floodlights. It was during the scrimmage that the festering problem grew worse. The ire of Wyrick had spread. While coaches were intent on fine-tuning the offense, plays repeatedly broke down. It was not hard to see why. Neither Wyrick nor the Bruins' fullback, Walt Schell, sustained their blocks. Onrushing defenders had almost unrestrained access to the ballcarrier and flattened Washington repeatedly with hard tackles. Coaches knew full well the reason. It wasn't from a lack of ability, poor blocking skills, or bad technique. It was entirely malicious, done intentionally, and only when the ball was in the hands of Kenny Washington.

Days before the Oregon game, Wyrick and Schell finally went public with their feelings. Each vowed they would not block when Washington had the football. To some fans and reporters, it confirmed their negative opinion of Spaulding. They saw him as a player's coach, lax in the discipline department. Others envisaged Spaulding a taskmaster, an impression gleaned from the man they saw Saturday afternoons on the sidelines—he of furrowed brows, chomping a cigar and using a pocketknife to clean his teeth. In truth, Bill Spaulding was neither, and he was both. To Wyrick and Schell's proclamation the coach seethed. Rather than discipline the players, Spaulding vowed to deal with them quietly and in his own way.

It didn't take long into the season-opening game with Oregon for Washington to set the Coliseum crowd abuzz. In the eyes of many, his 58-yard touchdown run confirmed every laudatory word written over the summer. It was in the third quarter, after Washington scored on a 5-yard run, that Spaulding enacted his long-pondered plan.

The Bruins' coach motioned for his new star to come out of the game. As UCLA lined up to kick the extra point, many assumed that removing Washington was a gesture of sportsmanship. After all, the sophomore had run roughshod through and around the Oregon defense. The outcome of the game was no longer in doubt. But in truth, Spaulding put Washington on the bench to watch the rest of his players fail.

Over the final quarter of play, the UCLA offense sputtered. It wasn't just unable to score; the Bruins couldn't manage a single first down without Washington in the backfield. The contrast was glaring. "It was a Dr. Jekyll and Mr. Hyde football team," wrote Claude Newman in the *Hollywood*

Citizen-News. "Potent and fast-stepping with Washington, just another ballclub without him."[3]

While Spaulding was pleased with the victory, he was equally pleased by the fourth-quarter impotence of his offense. As he would observe the following week in practice, his lesson combined with the team's rousing win worked. By removing Washington, the coach drilled into his team a very loud and clear message, that without the standout sophomore, winning would be out of the Bruins' reach.

4

DO WE PLAY?

The platform was a flurry of activity. All about the Glendale Railroad Depot was commotion but not that of usual clock-watching travelers or the emotional partings of lovers. On this night, the throng that passed through the station's carved wooden entry doors and beneath the ornate Spanish mission façade carried frivolity with their luggage. It was a far larger crowd than what the station was used to seeing.

Thirteen days earlier, excitement over UCLA football had erupted into fervor. Just one win, the Bruins' season-opening defeat of the University of Oregon, had propelled sportswriters to call this the best football team UCLA had ever fielded.

Disappearance of the evening sun and nearing of eight on the station clocks moved the merriment from platform to train. Such was the outpouring of fan interest in UCLA's impending game at Stanford that the school had to accommodate a throng. The usual single car added to handle the forty-six Bruin players became an entire train, the "Bruin Special," in order to carry both the team and fervent fans who were offered $9.25 round-trip tickets.

Only once before in the history of the school had such excitement for an away football game burst forth. During the previous fall, almost 10,000 traveled to Berkeley to witness the Bruins' 17–6 thumping of their rivals, the University of California. University administrators estimated 7,500 fans would make this trip to Palo Alto for the Stanford game.

As the train pulled out of the station, all around Southern California many more fans were beginning their travels by different means. Santa Fe had prepared a fleet of twelve chartered buses to carry fans north. The airlines received larger than usual bookings for flights north as well. Even bigger still were the expected numbers of fans who would travel north on the 101 in their own cars. UCLA administrators guessed that number could exceed 2,000.

Among the multitude of fans with travel plans were three Los Angeles firefighters and a female friend. The group met up outside Station House 30 at Fourteenth and Central Avenues just after 10:30 p.m. High-spirited and excited for the game the following afternoon, George LaVigne, Archie Woodyard, and Bessie Hood climbed into the relatively new Packard parked outside the station house. It was 10:40 p.m. when the car pulled away, driven by its owner, Lawrence Washington, who was eager to watch his nephew Kenny play.

While enthusiasm swirled all around him, Bill Spaulding fretted. The UCLA coach felt his players were sloppy in their win over Oregon. He worked his team hard in the days leading up to the Stanford game. Preparation included scrimmages with full contact. Reporters from the local newspapers turned up to watch. Their reporting did little to bridle the almost zealous fervor that was sweeping fandom. Kenny Washington, they wrote, scored almost at will in the scrimmages against a defense made to mimic Stanford's tactics. Hiking confidence was the news that a week after losing to the Bruins, Oregon defeated Stanford, 7–6.

The reports of Washington's practice frolics masked a major source of Spaulding's consternation. Eight of the Bruins' top players spent the week hobbling to and from class, unable to practice. Their injuries ranged from bruised shins to a broken hand, and worse in one case, an injured knee. As if things couldn't get worse, during a scrimmage Washington rushed from his position in the defensive backfield to try to make a tackle. On contact the Bruins' star frantically shook his hand and winced in pain. Blood gushed from the little finger of his right hand.

Washington felt pain in the days that followed. The injury would impair his grip and ability to throw a football. The next day, Washington appeared at practice with his right pinky and ring fingers taped together. All it took was one attempt at throwing a football for Spaulding to send him to the locker room. "Let us pray," the coach muttered to reporters.[1]

Consternation grew three nights later when Spaulding learned Washington was in the campus hospital. He had a bad head cold, and the team doctor ordered bed rest. Spaulding was assured that his star would be able to play once kickoff arrived Saturday afternoon at 2:00.

Throughout the evening and into the night of Friday, October 8, the northbound lanes of the Golden State Highway were dotted with enthusiastic UCLA fans. Each was making a Herculean journey. The drive from Los Angeles to Palo Alto was long, both in distance, 360 miles, and duration, eight hours. Drivers traversed steep mountain passes then cut through the expansive farmlands in the center of the state.

Just after 2:30 in the morning, Lawrence Washington and his friends reached the midpoint of their drive, the central California town of Tulare. Where the highway passed the northwest corner of Tagus Ranch, the largest fruit ranch in the world, a large truck and trailer was parked by the side of the Golden State Highway. Its driver and another man were engrossed in conversation. The sound of a car traveling at a high rate of speed interrupted their discussion. The men turned, saw the Packard, and commented with admiration. In the beam of the expensive car's headlights, a slower car grew large.

Lawrence Washington pressed his foot to the accelerator. The speed of his car climbed from seventy to eighty miles an hour. He jinked the steering wheel to the left. His Packard responded to pass the slower vehicle. Ahead was a section of highway, only recently resurfaced. So recently, that new center lines had yet to be painted. Also, there was no sign to warn that an S curve lay ahead. Once he had passed the other car, Washington guided his Packard back to the right. Suddenly, out of the darkness a large truck with a trailer hauling fourteen tons of grapes came around the bend. The truck was two and a half feet over where the center line should have been. Washington had but a millisecond to react. He fiercely tugged the steering wheel to the right. Avoiding a collision was impossible.

The impact was violent. The left side of Washington's Packard and the car's roof were sheared off. The force of the collision embedded the driver's door into a corner of the truck's trailer. Both passengers in the back seat of the Packard were thrown from the car. George LaVigne's skull was crushed, and he was killed instantly. Archie Woodyard lay on the side of the road with several broken ribs. Bessie Hood, who sat in the front seat, had only a scratch on her face.

The sickening sound of the high-speed, metal-on-metal impact reverberated about the vast farmland. It was soon replaced by the screech of brakes. One by one, passersby stopped to help. One sped off to retrieve aid. In the mangled wreckage, Lawrence Washington screamed for help. His left leg and arm were badly broken. So too was his neck. Pain coursed from internal injuries. Blood poured from a deep cut over the man's left eye and covered his face.

As minutes lapsed, Washington's cries faded. By the time an ambulance arrived he had lapsed into unconsciousness. The ambulance attendants realized very quickly they were in a race against time. Lawrence Washington's condition was grave. The wail of the siren pierced the pitch-black night with its sound of despair. Before rescuers could reach their destination, however, Lawrence Washington died. The county coroner would attribute his death to severe trauma to the chest.

News of the crash spread fast. At daybreak, word of mouth shot news throughout the town of Tulare. From the newsroom of the local newspaper, the *Tulare Advance-Register*, a report about the fatal accident reached the wire service office in Fresno. Soon teletypes in newspaper newsrooms across the country were clattering out news that the uncle of football star Kenny Washington had been killed in a car crash. Morning brought gawkers to the garage where the wrecked car had been towed. The town's curious grew to large numbers throughout the morning. Everyone was astonished by the sight of the horribly mangled Packard.

Two hundred miles north of Tulare, daybreak painted a picture that foreshadowed what would soon beset the UCLA football team and, in particular, its star player. The sky was gray. Rainfall pelted and puddled. None upon awakening could know that a challenge far more difficult for some to tackle than an opposing football player lay ahead.

It was late morning when the Bruins football team left the President Hotel for Stanford Stadium. The team had arrived by train late the previous night, greeted by a newspaper headline "U.C.L.A. Features Non-Aryans." Spaulding kept his team busy throughout the morning with breakfast, then a lengthy strategy session. On arrival at the game site, the coach led his players off the bus and toward the visitors' locker room. By now sportswriters had begun to arrive. Many knew of the tragedy. Kenny Washington still did not. It was mulled whether to tell the player immediately or wait until after the game. Members of the coaching staff argued both options. After listening to their points, Bill Spaulding spoke up. Washington, he said, had to know.

After wrestling with what he would say, the Bruins' head coach summoned his player. He ushered Washington to a private place away from the eyes and ears of teammates. Somberly on a quad outside the visitors' locker room, the tragic news was delivered. An assistant coach who witnessed the exchange grimaced at the sight of Washington, badly shaken by the news.

No one was close enough to hear what the coach said or whether his words were of a consoling or inspiring nature or both. But when the game began almost twelve hours after the accident, Kenny Washington burst forth with a performance greater than he had ever produced before.

Throughout the first quarter, Washington darted through and sprinted around Stanford's defenders with ease. Twice he was on the verge of breaking long runs for touchdowns, only to be thwarted by near-miraculous shoestring tackles. One sportswriter typed that the Bruin sensation made Stanford's defenders look like "high school boys."[2] In fact, the writer observed that Washington "looked like an All-American to your correspondent in that first quarter."[3]

One-third of the fans at Stanford Stadium were UCLA rooters. Washington's play made their rhythmic claps and encouraging cheers drown the support of the home crowd. But during the final minutes of the first quarter, two plays brought their exuberant noise to a deafening silence. Injury hit Kenny Washington. First was a knock to the knee at the end of a run. It hobbled the sophomore and would hamper the UCLA run game for the rest of the afternoon. Then Washington came out of a scrum with two broken fingers. X-rays would later expose three fractures in the right pinky and ring fingers. His ability to grip a football to throw a pass was almost nil. By halftime, the Bruins trailed, 12–0.

In the locker room, Spaulding excoriated his players. In his anger he refused to let any of them sit down. His loud voice echoed off the walls. "They kicked the hell out of us," he screamed while berating the effort.[4]

With Washington unable to throw effectively, and the offensive line repeatedly overwhelmed by their rivals, Spaulding resorted to trick plays in the second half. None worked. UCLA could muster little in the way of offense. The Bruins fumbled the football away 3 times and threw 7 interceptions. Their only points in a 12–7 defeat came on a runback of an interception.

In the aftermath, sportswriters pecked criticism of Spaulding into their press box typewriters. Play calling was challenged, but almost every writer had a different slant. For those who complained that UCLA should have run Washington up the middle more there was another that claimed the left side was vulnerable to the sweep all afternoon. Only one UCLA player was singled out for praise. Curley Grieve, sports editor of the *San Francisco Examiner*, called Kenny Washington a defensive demon. Speaking to reporters after the game, the Stanford coach, "Tiny" Thornhill, said of Washington, "There's a great ballplayer for you. That kid's G.R.E.A.T!"[5]

Four days later, on a Wednesday night at 8:00, twenty-nine of the thirty players who made up the UCLA travel squad boarded a northbound train for the next game at Oregon State. The lone absentee was Kenny Washington. The grief-stricken nineteen-year-old had been away from classes and missed practices during the preceding days. While his teammates departed for Oregon, Washington was gathered with family to prepare for his uncle's funeral.

On Thursday, October 14, 1937, more than 100 firefighters, both Black and white, representing companies and houses from throughout

Southern California, assembled at Angelus Funeral Home on Crenshaw Boulevard to honor Lawrence Washington. Eulogists included the mayor of Los Angeles, Frank L. Shaw. A color guard and honor guard involved men solemn and attired in Class A dress uniform. Captain J. L. Taylor, a Black pioneer in the department, cried and shook from grief. When the service ended, Washington dashed to the train station to join his teammates in Oregon.

The gray skies over Corvallis, Oregon, extended a week of gloominess. The Bruins' play against Oregon State, a 7–7 tie, failed to make sunny the disposition of their fans. What little excitement the Bruins enjoyed in the game happened when Washington intercepted a pass in the first quarter, then proceeded to evade a half dozen tacklers over 48 yards before he was brought down. It was a run one local sportswriter called "one of the prettiest runs ever witnessed on Bell Field."[6] A 3–0 loss to Washington State followed and spawned rancor in the lead up to homecoming.

When homecoming arrived the last weekend in October, enthusiasm for the Bruins was nil. They hadn't won since the opener against Oregon. Injuries, academic suspensions, and players driven to quit by heavy class workloads wreaked havoc on Spaulding.

Homecoming involved UCLA's chief rival of the day, the University of California. Antagonism in the rivalry came from the history of the two campuses. It was sibling in nature. UCLA was begun in 1919 as Southern Branch, a division of the University of California in Berkeley. By 1927 growth of Southern Branch was such that the decision was made to turn the school into an entirely separate university and call it the University of California at Los Angeles. After the change, alumni of the Berkeley school remained dismissive toward UCLA. Students and alums were chided as little bears and little brothers.

When preparation for the California game began, the team's routine changed. Bill Spaulding locked the gates to the UCLA practice field. With the prying eyes of sportswriters and, possibly, spies from the opposition kept away, the Bruins' coach set about to implement radical change. The biggest involved Kenny Washington. Spaulding announced to the team that Washington would call all the offensive plays. This was not just for the Cal game but the remainder of the season as well.

The idea did not belong to Spaulding. It came from players, a group of whom went to their coach with the suggestion. Those who played with him said Washington's play calling was a big factor in the freshman team's success the year before. Spaulding was told the players had full confidence in the sophomore's leadership skills as well as his football knowledge. The coach himself noticed a growing fondness for Washington. Players had taken to rubbing his hair for good luck when they left the locker room before games. While sportswriters and fans tagged Washington with the nickname "Kingfish," players on the UCLA offense called him "General."

The UCLA-California matchup offered a deep disparity. In the bookie dens around Los Angeles, UCLA was a 15-to-1 underdog. The city's largest newspaper considered UCLA's chances of victory to be "infinitesimal."[7] One newspaper columnist went so far as to suggest UCLA should forfeit, not play the game at all.

As was predicted, the outcome was one-sided. UCLA lost 27–14, but they succumbed to the best team in the nation, Washington's effort was Herculean. Of the 280 yards UCLA gained on offense, 200 were amassed by the brilliant sophomore, 110 via the run and 90 by passes. The performance smothered Washington in praise. The *Berkeley Gazette* called Washington remarkable. Frank Finch of the *Los Angeles Times* called Washington's play an All-America performance. Harry Borba of the *San Francisco Examiner* wrote, "Because of his color, Washington has to be twice as good as the ordinary athlete. And he is."[8]

The following week against the University of Washington, UCLA plummeted from its most spirited performance of the season to the worst. The performance had far more to do with conditions than playing skills. Heavy rains fell on Seattle the night before the game. When the Bruins took the field, it was not only cold, but mud was ankle deep. By the second half, it was snowing. The muddy playing surface became slick from ice. Almost every time Kenny Washington tried to run with the football he slid, slipped, or fell. His fingers were made numb by the freezing temperatures. Throwing the football became impossible.

Washington could hear fans laugh loudly whenever he fell. Frustration grew and morphed with embarrassment into anger. He heard the University of Washington coach, Jimmy Phelan, mock him with words laced with racial epithets and laughter. Such was the sting from the coach's behavior that as Washington left the field after the 26–0 defeat, he angrily vowed that one day he would get revenge.

The kind of hateful derision the Bruins' standout endured in Seattle paled in comparison with the disdain he received in the following game. The seventh of UCLA's 9 games brought Southern Methodist University to the Coliseum. The SMU Mustangs held a rich football tradition. Twice in the previous five years they were Southwest Conference champions. Their 1935 team amassed a 12-win season, ranked third nationally, and culminated its stellar season with a trip to play in the Rose Bowl.

There was another side to the SMU tradition, however, and it put Washington and Strode in the middle of something far more ugly than a simple game of football. SMU was located in the heart of a Jim Crow state. Texans adhered to laws that enforced strict racial segregation. Blacks were not permitted to attend SMU, let alone play on its football team. In fact, none of SMU's thirty players had ever been on the same playing field with a Black player. Mack Saxon, the football coach at Texas College of Mines in El Paso, explained, "The practice of allowing Negroes to play football against white boys in Texas is unheard of."[9]

In the days before SMU was to board a train to Los Angeles, SMU's coach, Matty Bell, sensed consternation among his players. He called a team meeting. The coach pointed out that he played pro football with Fritz Pollard and Paul Robeson. "I don't believe in drawing the color line in sports," he said. "Every boy should have his chance to participate regardless of color."[10] Bell put the matter to a vote. Would his players agree to play against Kenny Washington and Woody Strode, or would they insist that the two UCLA players be held out of the game? Would Bell's players go even further and vote to cancel the game altogether? "We polled the team," Bell said after the meeting. "They said they wanted to meet the strongest team that UCLA could put on the field, regardless of who was on it."[11]

The decision was not entirely well received in Texas. One sports columnist warned, "The negro star Kenny Washington, had best stay on the sidelines."[12] When the first administrator from SMU arrived in Los Angeles two days before the game, he was asked if the Mustang players planned to rough up Washington and Strode. The man declined to answer.

A small crowd, half that of the Cal game, was indicative of how fans felt about UCLA's losing ways. Those who instead chose to stay home and listen to the game on radio heard either Mel LeRon on KFAC, Frank Bull on KHJ, or Ken Frogley on KRKD exclaim with excitement on the very first play of the game. Washington intercepted an SMU pass. He dodged would-be tacklers over 60 yards, then crossed the goal line for a touchdown. Before the Bruins could erupt into celebration, a yellow penalty flag was spied lying on the green grass. The UCLA left end had been offside, and the points from Washington's gallop were removed from the scoreboard.

Minutes later Washington put up points that would not be removed. With UCLA on offense and at the SMU 32-yard line, the brilliant back took the snap from center and back pedaled to almost midfield. Seeing Woody Strode running wide open, he rifled a throw that Strode caught in the end zone for the game's first score.

During the second quarter, Washington engineered an 82-yard drive that culminated in UCLA's second touchdown. He first broke a run for 11 yards, then another for 7. A 17-yard dash put the ball on the SMU 35-yard line. Washington then hit Walt Schell with a pass at the 25-yard line, and the fullback rambled until he was brought down at the 4. Billy Bob Williams then replaced Schell and scored to push the UCLA lead to 13–0.

Almost from the opening kickoff, Washington and Strode were pounded and pummeled. Racial slurs spewed almost nonstop. Tackles carried far more than the usual aggression. In piles punches were thrown, elbows were jabbed, and even kicks with hard leather, cleated football shoes were landed. Washington and Strode were subjected to a level of hostility and display of outright hatred that far exceeded what they had experienced before.

In the second quarter, an SMU lineman leveled Washington with folded forearms to the back. At halftime, the UCLA team doctor was the busiest man in the locker room. Almost his entire attention was reserved for Washington's badly scratched face. The doctor worked to stop the bleeding from a cut lip and tended to Washington's right eye, which was swollen almost completely shut.

After making changes at halftime, the SMU offense erupted in the third quarter. Before the Bruins could react, their lead was gone, and they trailed, 26–13. Late in the third quarter, the battering took a toll. Exhausted and in excruciating pain from a back injury, Washington hobbled from the field. All 35,000 fans—UCLA and visitors from Dallas—rose simultaneously to applaud his play. Observing this, a reporter with the *Dallas Times Herald* typed,

> In that moment you forgot that he was black. He was of no color at all, he was simply a great athlete. But all you could see coming off the field to the tunnel that led to the dressing room was a pigeon-toed boy, swinging his helmet slowly, his shoulders drooped, the tears streaming down his face. It was a long walk—but for years to come in Kenny Washington's ears will ring what for him must be the sweetest music he has ever heard—Texans cheering for him.[13]

In the locker room after the 26–13 defeat, Washington brushed aside questions about dirty play. "They hit me hard, but they played me square," he said.[14] In the SMU locker room, the Mustangs were effusive in their praise. "Kenny Washington is one of the best football players I have ever seen," said Bell. His team captain, Charlie Sprague, gushed, "He is a treat to watch. But a terror to play against."[15]

So bruised and battered was Washington's body, he was unable to practice at all the following week. Whether at the forefront of his thoughts or in the back of his mind, Washington knew he would be subjected to more in UCLA's next game. The opponent was the University of Missouri. It was a school that, like SMU, did not permit enrollment by nonwhites.

The Missouri game was the first time all season that Washington was not on the field at kickoff. Persistent back pain made Bill Spaulding revise his lineup. A small crowd, one that filled less than a quarter of the Coliseum seats, saw sluggish play. Minus Washington, the UCLA offense was listless. Missouri was too but for an entirely different reason. Only forty-eight hours earlier they had played their rivals, the University of Kansas, in a Thanksgiving Day game. The Tigers then boarded a train and arrived in Los Angeles only five hours prior to kickoff.

Once Washington did enter the game, a ruthless assault began. Missouri players scooped handfuls of chalk from the sideline. When they tackled Washington, they smeared the lime powder in his face. Racial insults were spewed from the Missouri sideline. If Washington didn't get up quickly enough after tackles, he received forearm shivers, punches, and blows from elbows. Through it all the Bruins' standout remained unfazed. "Kenny was terrific at just playing on through it. He was amazing," said Bruin Don MacPherson, who called the Missouri players "a bunch of rednecks."[16]

For three full quarters neither team could score. On the last play of the quarter, Strode recovered a fumble on the UCLA 44-yard line. The turnover would prove a turning point. The Bruins would mount a 15-play drive. It culminated with Washington's plunge behind left tackle from the 2-yard line for a touchdown and a 7–0 lead.

In the game's final minutes, Missouri sent the Coliseum into the depths of drama. The Tigers drove to the UCLA 12-yard line and threatened to tie the game. Fans nervously switched their gaze from the large clock atop the scoreboard to the action on the field. The red second hand showed 30 seconds remained when the Missouri quarterback unleashed a pass. Washington darted into its path. He reached with his left arm and speared the football. Cutting sharply to his right, Washington sprinted down the sideline in front of the Missouri bench, its players and coaches silenced by shock. As Washington reached the 3-yard line, a Missouri pursuer caught him. While being wrestled toward the sideline, Washington heard a teammate call to him. "Throw it, Kenny. Throw it!"[17] With a quick glance he saw Johnny Ryland and pitched the ball in his direction. Ryland snatched it out of the air, then danced across the goal line. As the referee raised his arms to signal touchdown, only 1 second remained on the clock.

In the press box, Tom Hanlon shouted and bounced about with such excitement that the broadcaster broke his chair. Don Faurot, the Missouri coach, raced onto the field after the referees, convinced Washington had been downed before the lateral. All around the Coliseum UCLA fans danced with delirium, able to celebrate victory for the first time since the season-opening game with Oregon. Winning meant the victory flag could be unpacked. The 12-foot-by-31-foot flag, a gift from the local Rotary Club, was traditionally hoisted after victories and flown beneath the American flag on the UCLA campus flagpole.

One game remained on the 1937 football schedule. It involved UCLA's crosstown rival, a team that had beaten the Bruins in humiliating fashion in years past. Many worried the USC Trojans had the firepower to do just that again.

5

THE PASS

The fans who trudged the steps of the Coliseum carried with them a mixture of anger and disgust. For two hours, 76,000 had watched UCLA put forth one of the worst displays of football execution they had ever seen. With 9 minutes left in the game and their Bruins trailing cross-town rival USC, 19–0, these fans had enough. Never mind that this was the last game of the year, that there would be no more football to watch for another nine months. These fans could not stomach another play, so they headed for the exits.

UCLA fans weren't the only ones complaining. From their perch high atop the Coliseum, newsreel cameramen groused at the dull game. Each hoped to capture a spectacular play and receive accolades for a highlight that could be shown in cinemas around the country. The game, however, wasn't able to provide any such moment of fanfare.

For those in the press box, statistics gave credence to the opinion of the fans and cameramen below. In 51 minutes of play, UCLA managed to cross the 50-yard line into USC territory only once. A fierce rush contained UCLA to a mere 25 yards rushing and only 46 via the air.

So disgusted were the departing fans that few, if any, were tempted by a mighty roar to change course and return to their seats. Even on finding that a bad snap from center hit USC's fullback Roy Engle in the head, and the fumble was recovered by UCLA at the USC 44-yard line, there was little confidence the Bruins would capitalize.

UCLA's first play after the fumble recovery proved them right. Hal Hirshon's pass sailed incomplete, another example for the postgame discourse on the Bruins' ineptness. But that is when, as Braven Dyer wrote in the *Los Angeles Times*, "black lightning struck the desolate scene."[1]

After UCLA recovered the USC fumble, the remarkable began to take shape. On second down, Kenny Washington received the snap from center. He dropped back, five or six steps across the 50 into UCLA territory. Then, catching sight of Hal Hirshon running past a USC defender, Washington whipped a pass. Hirshon peeked over his right shoulder and saw the ball streak toward him on a line. At the 10-yard line, 41 yards from where Washington released the football, the USC defender leaped. His attempt to swat the pass missed. Instead, the football landed in Hirshon's outstretched arms, and he dashed the remaining 7 yards untouched into the end zone for a UCLA touchdown. The extra point made the score 19–7.

Rules of the day allowed USC to decide whether it wished to receive or kick off. Having seen his defense dominate the UCLA offense all afternoon, Howard Jones told his players to kick. It was a decision that left some in the large stadium perplexed.

Oncoming nightfall threw dusk about the stadium. The newsreel cameramen fretted with their aperture settings while UCLA returned the kickoff to the 27-yard line. As the Bruins moved toward the line of scrimmage, Hirshon told Washington he was confident he could get past the USC safety just as he had before. "Okay," Washington replied. "You just keep running, and I'll stall around back here as long as I can."[2] On taking the snap from center, Washington retreated, all the while angling to his right. From what appeared to most to be the 10-yard line, he took two steps forward then unleashed a mighty throw.

Indeed, Hirshon had been able to run past the USC defender. His head turned to the right. He glanced upward. Hirshon feared Washington's throw would sail over his head. Hirshon continued his sprint. At the 12-yard line he extended his arms and was surprised to feel the ball smack hard against his palms. Hirshon never broke stride and amid the sounds of bedlam scored once again. It was a play that, from the line of scrimmage to the goal line, covered 73 yards.

The Coliseum became awash in pandemonium. Fans screamed and howled in a mixture of amazement and delight. "The greatest play I have ever seen," marveled former Bruins halfback Bert LaBrucherie.[3] In the press box, reporters debated the length of the pass. Many wondered aloud whether they had just witnessed the longest completed pass in the history of the sport. At issue was where Washington released the ball. Some claimed it was the 10-yard line; others insisted the 17. A cameraman with Fox Movie Tones was confident he captured the play on film. Reporters were eager to see it and settle the raging debate.

Figure 5.1   Washington's powerful throwing arm amazed fans and set passing distance records. *Photo courtesy of* Los Angeles Daily News *Negatives, Library Special Collections, Charles E. Young Research Library, UCLA*

Below, chaos surged through the UCLA side of the stadium. Panic gripped its rival's rooters across the way. After a failed extra point attempt, the score was 19–13. For UCLA, victory was within reach. Unlike before, Howard Jones opted to receive the kickoff. The UCLA defense looked and played nothing like it had to that point. Bruin players flew about the field and repeatedly thwarted USC play calls. Soon the Bruins had the football once again, this time at their own 43.

A Hirshon pass to Woody Strode brought the Bruins across midfield and into USC territory. Washington then carried and punched through a hole off left tackle. He shirked several would-be tacklers until he was brought down 9 yards upfield at the 40. Then came a trick play, something Spaulding had installed during a secret closed-door practice weeks before. It was more, however, than just a trick play. Its seamless execution was a symbol of sorts of the respect and camaraderie that had grown within the UCLA football team.

The play Washington called was a tackle-eligible play, one designed for, of all people, Slats Wyrick. When the ball found Wyrick's hands, USC was completely fooled. The nimble tackle lumbered 40 yards for a touchdown that on appearances tied the game.

Amid the raucous celebrating, few heard the toot of a referee's whistle. Early on his run, Wyrick had slipped as he shook free of a would-be tackler. One of the officials ruled that his knee touched the turf at the 32-yard line. In a bad break for the Bruins, Wyrick's touchdown was nullified.

The crowd remained frenetic. Three minutes remained in the game. Washington was fighting fatigue and the effects of playing both ways in an intense contest. He limped about the field and occasionally doubled over in pain. In spite of his physical condition, throws by the Bruins' halfback carried remarkable crispness, were strong and accurate. He again sparked another dramatic drive, first with a pass to Johnny Baida, which put the ball at the USC 24, then another that gained 10 yards more.

After three quarters of ineffectiveness, the UCLA offense could suddenly do no wrong. Two more throws gained only a single yard. On third down, Hirshon became the passer. In a defensive lapse, not a single USC defender noticed Washington slip out of the backfield as a pass receiver. Hirshon caught sight of Washington wide open in the end zone. Near exhaustion from his long touchdown runs, Hirshon put all his might into a throw. Seeing the football was underthrown and lacked zip, Washington tried to compensate. He pivoted, changed direction, and dove toward the goal line in an effort fueled by desperation. With arms extended, Washington strained for the oncoming pass only to hear the large crowd groan as the ball bounced off the grass incomplete, mere inches in front of his hands.

With only 1 minute left on the clock and in need of a touchdown to tie the score, UCLA chose to go for it on fourth down from the USC 16. Washington took the snap from center. USC brought a ferocious pass rush. With no choice but to release the pass to avoid being tackled, Washington fired a bullet for Woody Strode, who was open at the 4. It came at

Strode quickly—too quickly, it turned out. The ball whistled through the receiver's hands and thus ended the Bruins' final hope.

On the crack of the timekeeper's pistol, fans rushed the field. The sea of postgame revelers prevented the two coaches from being able to find each other for a customary handshake. Spaulding, instead, veered toward the tunnel and the USC locker room in search of his counterpart, Howard Jones. When he reached the USC locker-room door, a guard blocked entry. "Howard," Spaulding shouted at his golfing buddy. "Come out Howard, we've stopped throwing passes!"[4]

As fans left the stadium, USC's 19–13 victory was far overshadowed by talk of Washington's Herculean pass. Reporters continued to debate just how far the ball had sailed. Rube Samuelson of the *Pasadena Post* was insistent Washington released the ball from the UCLA 13 and that Hirshon caught it at the USC 15, making it a 72-yard heave. Bill Henry of the *Times* was convinced Hirshon was not at the 15 but the 12. Henry McLemore of the *Hollywood Citizen-News* claimed the pass traveled 76 yards in the air.

The reporting throng was certain Washington's pass eclipsed a record and was the longest completed pass in college football history. Within the game, the consensus gave Harold "Brick" Mueller of the University of California the record. In the 1921 Rose Bowl game with Ohio State, Mueller had a touchdown heave of 75 yards. Mueller, however, insisted for years that the ball only traveled 56 yards in the air.

Reporters scurried to the referees' dressing room. Bobby Morris was closest to Washington when he released the pass. He put Washington at either the 15 or 16 when he threw the football. In the UCLA locker room, sportswriters happened across Washington and Strode, naked and just out of the shower. "Sorry, Kenny. But that potato was too hot to handle. It went right through my hands," Strode said. "It's okay, buddy," Washington replied. "I just had to open up on that one. They were charging too fast."[5]

The following morning, Sunday, December 5, newspaper headlines from coast to coast heralded Washington's pass:

IT'S A NEW RECORD! KENNY PASSES 72 YARDS.
    KENNY WASHINGTON ASTOUNDS COAST FANS WITH
SUPER TOSS.
    WASHINGTON'S PASS AMAZES COAST GRID FANS.

Still one big question remained unanswered: Just how far had Washington's pass traveled? It took twenty-four hours for the question to be answered. A Sunday screening was arranged to view the Fox Movie Tone film. When the projectionist began the showing, the men saw a remarkable throw, one that shot over the heads of the USC defenders on a line with very little arc. The film was conclusive. Washington was at the UCLA 15-yard line when the football left his hand. Hirshon caught it at the USC 23-yard line. Washington's pass traveled 62 yards in the air. The majority of the men who witnessed the screening left adamant that Washington had eclipsed Brick Mueller's throw and was, in fact, a new football record.

In his syndicated column, The Sportlight, which appeared in hundreds of newspapers, Grantland Rice stated categorically that the record now belonged to Washington. Culling notes from an earlier interview with Bill Spaulding, Rice shared with readers the coach's insights about his star player. "Washington can cock his wrist about two inches and hit you in the eye at 50 yards. He can throw the longest pass with less effort than anyone else I ever saw. I've seen him throw the ball from 70 to 75 yards more than once. And without taking a windup." In comparison with the celebrated 1921 Rose Bowl pass by Brick Mueller, Rice wrote, "The Washington pass was many yards longer."[6]

Around Los Angeles, Washington was thrust into celebrity status. Eight days after the USC game, he was honored at a Los Angeles Winter Baseball League game between the New York Colored Giants and Detroit Stars. Among the players to extend congratulations was Negro League star "Cool Papa" Bell. When the governor of California, Frank Merriam, learned Washington was in the same building, he diverted from a chamber of commerce function to meet the UCLA football hero. The local Elks club feted Washington at its New Year's Eve dance. Media clamored too. Norman Hartford had Washington on his interview program on KGFJ radio. The Reverend Fenwick T. Fowler invited Washington to his Baptist church, where the sermon topic was "The Swivel-Hipped Halfback."

At the team awards banquet, a highlight of the night was the presentation of the American Legion trophy to the Bruins' outstanding player. The award was voted on by local sportswriters. In a first, its recipient earned the honor by unanimous vote. Unique too was that it went to a sophomore. Applause filled the room as the large trophy was handed to Kenny Washington.

It was two months to the day of the final football game that preseason baseball training was to begin. When the anticipated day arrived, heavy rain kept the Bruins off the diamond. One rained-out day of practice turned to two, then three, and many more. Before Bruins coach Marty Krug knew it,

Figure 5.2   When the governor of California learned Washington was in the build-ing, he changed plans to meet him. With Governor Earl Warren in May 1946. *Photo courtesy of the* Los Angeles Times *Photographic Archive, Library Special Collections, Charles E. Young Research Library, UCLA*

unrelenting rain had delayed baseball preparations by ten days. When rain finally subsided and Krug was able to welcome his charges, Kenny Washington was among the players, the first of his race to play baseball at UCLA.

Krug had little time to assemble a team. Just three days stood between the Bruins' first practice and their first game of the season. Washington's baseball skills were rusty. UCLA had been unable to gather enough players to field a freshman baseball team in 1937. Washington instead joined the track team and set a freshman record by heaving the shot put 50'9".

When Marty Krug scheduled an intrasquad game, he would soon realize he had a unique talent on his team. That realization came in the second inning, when a moment of marvel erupted into unabated awe. It happened when Washington came to bat against a left-handed pitcher. From the hurler's hand spun a curveball that sank and hooked toward the inside corner of home plate. Washington, a right-handed batter, whipped a mighty swing that shot the pitch quickly over the left-field fence for a home run. When Washington came to bat a second time, a right-handed pitcher tried to fool him with a curveball too. Washington caught the low, outside pitch with the meat part of his bat and again drove it over the left-field fence.

Washington's performance was lauded by *Daily Bruin* sportswriter Milt Cohen "as rare a slugging fest as seen in many a day."[7]

Washington's power hitting wasn't all that impressed his baseball teammates. Al Martel called Washington's throwing arm a howitzer. Whenever a potential close play at first base forced Washington to put all he had into a throw, the end result often saw the Bruins' first baseman, Bill Gray, hop about while shaking his right hand in pain.

After only three days of practice, UCLA plunged into its schedule. Its opponent, Loyola, a small Jesuit College from a nearby community, scored 4 times in the first two innings to put UCLA in a hole. UCLA put its first runs on the scoreboard in the fourth inning, when Kenny Washington doubled, then scored on a teammate's subsequent double. They did little else and lost, 12–3.

Three weeks into the season, UCLA began its 15-game schedule of league games. It was then, playing California Intercollegiate Baseball Association (CIBA) foes, that Washington's dormant baseball skills blossomed. Against the University of California, he had 3 hits, a double, 2 singles, and drove in 3 runs. In the field, Washington handled 6 chances without an error and turned an impressive double play. When Stanford came to town, Washington fueled the Bruins' offense with both speed and power. In the first game the UCLA shortstop started a 2-run rally with a daring bunt single. The next afternoon fans left talking about the long 2-run home run Washington sent over the center-field fence, which narrowly missed striking the scoreboard.

An early April trip to the San Francisco Bay Area meant playing 4 league games over six days. The first game drew considerable attention, largely because it pitted two standout football players who were also sensations on the baseball diamond. University of California right fielder Sam Chapman had earned All-America football recognition the previous fall. Now he was coveted by big-league baseball scouts. No less an authority than Ty Cobb, the twelve-time American League batting champion, urged his old team, the Philadelphia Athletics, to break the bank and sign Chapman.

When UCLA and Cal met on the diamond, scouts from the New York Yankees, Cincinnati Reds, and Cleveland Indians sat shoulder to shoulder with fans in the stands. Chapman was cheered on each of his 2 hits. Washington had 2 hits as well. In the fifth inning, UCLA loaded the bases only for a line drive to the Cal second baseman to turn into a triple play. In the ninth inning, Washington came to bat with the bases loaded and UCLA trailing, 4–0. He lined a single to bring two runners across the plate with runs. But they would be the only runs UCLA could muster in a 4–2 defeat.

Two days after the game in Berkeley, Washington produced a feat of legendary proportions. Friday, April 9, brought the Bruins to the Stanford campus for a game in Sunken Diamond. The park was in a bowl created when dirt was dug to form the berms for the school's football stadium. Sunken Diamond was a large park, with a fence bordering the outfield that scaled twenty feet in height. From home plate to the fence in both right and left field measured 360 feet; center field was 400 feet away. It was a rarity for a home run to be hit out of the park.

In the seventh inning, Washington sent a pitch sailing far beyond the wall in right-center field. Teammates were astounded. Several insisted the ball was still rising as it cleared the wall. Some were even adamant that it traveled at least another 100 feet before falling to earth. Teammates were in awe. Locals were aghast. Al Martel, the Bruins' third baseman, called Washington "one of the most powerful hitters I've ever seen, college or pro."[8] Observers claimed it was the first time a right-handed batter sent a baseball out of that area of the five-year-old ballpark. None of the Detroit Tigers, who used the park for spring training in 1932, managed to achieve the feat. Stanford coaches and fans were unanimous that Washington's was the longest home run ever hit out of the Stanford campus ballpark.

Through UCLA's first 7 league games, Washington had 16 hits in 33 times at bat. One-fourth of his hits were home runs. After 10 games he was the runaway leader in the race for the league batting title with a .454 batting average.

By the time the season concluded, Washington was the undeniable shining star of a fourth-place team. When statistics were published in the *Daily Bruin*, Washington boasted a sterling .397 batting average. Tabulations by the league's secretary, Arnold Eddy, showed in CIBA games Washington was the fourth-leading hitter in the league, with a .409 batting average. Coaches chose Washington as the all-CIBA shortstop.

For all of Washington's prolific play, however, the true spoils of such success remained off limits. "Leading Hitter, best shortstop in the college baseball out our way is Kenny Washington of U.C.L.A. Coaches of other teams say he has major league ability, but big-league scouts aren't interested in him. Washington is a negro," explained Prescott Sullivan in the *San Francisco Examiner*.[9]

In the days that followed the 1938 college baseball season, Washington's former Lincoln High School teammate, Alex Petrushkin, signed a contract with the Boston Red Sox. His UCLA teammate, Bill Gray, was

Figure 5.3   In the 1939 film *$1,000 a Touchdown*, star Joe E. Brown (pictured with costar Martha Ray) wore a UCLA uniform with the number 13 in tribute to Kenny Washington. *Photo courtesy of the author*

in negotiations with the Brooklyn Dodgers. Sam Chapman, the University of California's standout, got the biggest deal of all. Chapman, who hit .321, 76 points below Washington's season batting average, accepted a bonus of $8,500 from the Philadelphia Athletics and was immediately made the team's center fielder.

While Chapman stepped straight off the Berkeley campus and into the flannels of the Athletics, Washington donned an entirely different kind of uniform for his summer job—a white waiter jacket and black slacks. At UCLA, football coaches used connections to place their players in jobs around town. Washington, along with Woody Strode, joined the stage service crew at Warner Brothers Studios. There, they were assigned to a soundstage and tasked to fulfill the needs of the cast and crew.

Around the Warner Brothers lot, Washington was a magnet to the more sports crazed of the actors, producers, and directors. Whether on the soundstage where *Jezebel* was being filmed or the set of the *Adventures of Robin Hood*, Washington found Erroll Flynn, Pat O'Brien, George Brent, and many others to be fans. "I just love watching you guys play," said Flynn to Washington and Strode.[10] Such was Joe E. Brown's admiration that in the film *$1,000 a Touchdown*, he wore a replica UCLA football jersey with Washington's number 13.

In early August, Washington left the studio job to prepare for the 1938 season. Each day he got together with Strode and worked on passing drills. By September, the bright studio klieg lights and the energy that was a motion picture soundstage would pale compared to what lay ahead. Washington's play during his sophomore season built enormous expectations for his junior year. Not only would Los Angeles be watching, but the rest of the country would have a keen eye to see just how good Kenny Washington truly was.

6

THE MOST DANGEROUS
PLAYER IN THE GAME

An air of frivolity filled the large banquet room. Laughter spilled out into the hallways of the opulent Hotel Biltmore in downtown Los Angeles. The annual football day luncheon of the Los Angeles Advertising Club packed the room with club members, newspaper sportswriters, head football coaches, and college publicity men. The tenor about the room was that of hilarity, all of which one would expect of an event emceed by none other than the popular comedic actor Joe E. Brown. Question-and-answer sessions featured a main dish of embellishment sprinkled with a dash of deception.

What was undeniable amid the sea of humor was the underlying topic of almost every head coach in the room: the remarkable season and the unleashed skills of Kenny Washington. The subject was amplified when Brown graduated from gentle prodding to resolute skewering. "Is it true that you will sign a petition to bar all colored players from football in the Pacific Coast Conference?" Brown asked of the USC head coach, Howard Jones. "If Bill Spaulding will bring it around to me, I will sign it alright," Jones answered as the room erupted in laughter.[1]

Brown's biting humor was a reflection of the impact Kenny Washington's success was having on West Coast college football. Spurred by Washington's remarkable effort in their December meeting, several of USC's strongest supporters railed at the school for failing to recruit talented Black football players. Pressed about it by reporters from the *Los Angeles Sentinel*, Will Hunter, the USC athletic director, answered that none had come out for sports at the school.

There were sportswriters who felt Washington and Strode would create change. Gene Coughlin of the *Los Angeles Examiner* wrote, "Let Bill Spaulding come up with a football team of championship caliber next fall,

47

with Kenny Washington and Woodrow Strode being important factors and the movement to quit playing Negroes in intercollegiate games will take definite shape."[2]

In the fall of 1938, only fourteen colleges in America fielded integrated football teams. On those teams were twenty-five Black players. By 1938, most of the schools in the Pacific Coast Conference had at one time or another fielded integrated football teams. In contrast to UCLA, however, their approach was one of reticence. The University of Washington, University of Oregon, and USC integrated in the mid-1920s. In Stanford's very first season of football, 1891, a Black was a member of the team. The player chose, however, not to play after the inaugural season, and the Stanford football team would remain all white for the next sixty years. Walker Gordon joined the football team at the University of California in 1914 and was All-America in 1918. When Stub Allison became the Bears' coach in 1931, it was said that he was reluctant to integrate his teams. Only Washington State and Oregon State resisted integration and would do so for more than fifty years.

Within these programs indifference, if not outright detest, prevailed. One such example was displayed in the days prior to Stanford's 1937 game with UCLA. A Stanford player was tasked with mimicking Kenny Washington in practice. The player arrived on the practice field with his face darkened by burnt cork. "I'm Kenny Washington," he said with a laugh. "See what you can do to me."[3] Washington State players thought it a humorous prank to assign the role of Kenny Washington in a scrimmage to their lone player from the South.

So talented were Washington and Strode, particularly on defense, that opposing ballcarriers would not have been faulted for thinking the two were responsible for almost every tackle during games. In one game, an opposing ballcarrier was tackled on several successive plays by either Washington or Strode and sometimes both. After being tackled by a Caucasian UCLA player, the ballcarrier said with a smirk on his face, "Doctor Livingston I presume."[4]

Players weren't alone as purveyors of ignorance, let alone an appalling lack of sensitivity. Even under the guise of praise, there were newspapermen who succumbed to atrocious stereotypes to make a point. An Oregon newspaper referred to Washington and Strode as UCLA's "darkies." Another such case involved a columnist for a San Francisco newspaper who, while expressing raves for Washington's talent, suggested the player carried the football "like a watermelon going somewhere with someone who really cares—about watermelon."[5]

And then there was the way Washington was referenced in newspaper write-ups. While Caucasian players were never identified by their race, mentions of Washington often carried the prefix "negro," "dusky," or "colored." Where a strong teammate might be labeled the Redondo Rhino, Washington was given nicknames such as "Chocolate Soldier," "the Sepia Slinger," "the Sepia Cyclone," "Black Lightning," or "Brown Bomber." One reporter called Washington and Strode "The Gold Dust Twins," a twist on Fairbank's Gold Dust Soap, which featured caricatures of two Black children on the box. It was a nickname that stuck and would appear in numerous newspaper and magazine articles about the players.

For a Black student, UCLA was a dichotomy. Among a student body of 7,911, in 1938 less than 3 percent were Black. While the school was welcoming and Blacks were accepted members of several sports teams, once those students strayed off campus things were different. UCLA was situated in Westwood, a toney area west of Los Angeles and bordered by exclusive communities, Beverly Hills and Bel Air. Residents of all three areas had housing covenants written into their deeds of trust, stipulations that expressly forbade the homeowner to sell to Blacks.

Not only could the players not live in the area surrounding the campus, but barbershops in Westwood refused to cut the hair of Blacks.

As Kenny Washington entered his junior year at UCLA, turmoil enveloped Bruin football. Furor raged among boosters over the losses in the previous year. Cries grew for Spaulding to be replaced as head coach. In answer to the complaints, a panel was commissioned to evaluate coaching, recruiting, and other important aspects of the football program. Prior to the start of spring football, Bill Spaulding announced his resignation. Findings from the evaluation were never made public, but Spaulding confided to friends that they prompted his decision.

Coach and administration reached agreement. Spaulding would lead the Bruins for one final season. He would then move into the role of athletic director until he reached UCLA's mandatory retirement age.

Bill Spaulding's final season as a collegiate coach presented one of his biggest challenges. Spring and summer preseason drills had again exposed the Bruins' offensive line as the team's Achilles heel. The unit was lacking in size, strength, experience, and skill. What made this worse was that the veteran coach had on his hands "the most dangerous offensive ace in football in the person of Kenny Washington," as Sid Ziff wrote in the *Los Angeles Evening Herald*.[6]

In Washington, Bill Spaulding had a generational talent. This was the kind of player a coach, if lucky, has on his team once in a career. Physical

Figure 6.1   Washington was a well-liked and popular figure on the UCLA campus. He was also known for being a dapper dresser. *Photo courtesy of New York Public Library*

maturity had taken Washington to 190 pounds. It made him unafraid to take on defenders, many of whom he simply ran over. Washington too had another weapon, one unmatched by rivals—a powerful stiff arm that made him difficult to tackle. The thrust of one of his strong arms and a punch from the base of his palm to an opponent's chest or head dropped many a would-be tackler to the turf and left them frustrated, if not simmering with anger.

One big headache from the same time a year earlier was now alleviated. That was the attitude of fellow players toward Washington. The span of a year had taken Washington from pariah to messiah, a well-liked character away from the field and highly respected leader on the gridiron. "Kenny is the finest of good sports," one Bruin said. "They don't make them any better. Gosh, when he has the ball, we just have to give him all we've got. We couldn't let him down."[7]

UCLA's first game presented a measuring-stick opportunity for Washington. The opponent was the University of Iowa. The Hawkeyes featured a back, Nile Kinnick, whom many considered to be the top back in the Big 10 Conference, if not the entire Midwest. The matchup offered opportunity for fans and the media to compare the two and determine if Washington was more than just the best back on the West Coast.

All 40,000 who turned up to the Coliseum probably agreed that neither player was impressive. UCLA won, 27–3, but Washington fumbled 3 times. One of the UCLA touchdowns came on a head-scratching faux pas by Kinnick. The Iowa standout intercepted a pass in the end zone. He was promptly trapped and tried to lateral the football to a teammate. The ball, however, fell to the ground, where Woody Strode alertly pounced on it for a UCLA score.

In the next two weeks Washington more than atoned for his poor first-game performance. He scored 1 of the team's 2 touchdowns in a 14–13 upset loss at Oregon. Against the University of Washington, he scored on spectacular runs of 45 and 17 yards to highlight a 13–0 UCLA win.

During the fall of 1938, Washington's attentions came to involve more than just studies and football. The previous winter, he accompanied a friend to Los Angeles City College. While sitting on a bench, the two men were approached by a group of coeds. Introductions were made. One of the women, June Bradley, somewhat sarcastically chastised Washington for not standing as a gentleman should. Washington sprang to his feet. "I'm sorry. I'm not a gentleman," he said with a smile.[8] It wasn't long after their introduction that a first date became a second, and by the fall of 1938 Washington and Bradley were an inseparable couple.

The season's fourth week sent UCLA north to Berkeley for a game with its rivals, the University of California. The Bears were a team brimming with confidence. They were undefeated and able to boast of being defending conference and Rose Bowl champions. Play was physical. The hosts dished out a beating that was unquestionably punishing to the Bruins but also malicious and abusive to UCLA's star player.

During the first quarter, Washington made local fans nervous with a series of long runs and long passes. In the second quarter, Washington's play deteriorated. Few had seen him so inconsistent. His short passes were wide of the mark. His long passes appeared to be heaved with no effort at accuracy. After UCLA was defeated 20–7, criticism, if not outright blame, was thrust in Washington's direction.

When reporters arrived for Monday afternoon practice, they were surprised when Washington failed to turn up. It was then that Spaulding revealed that Washington was in the hospital. During the game in Berkeley, he had been kicked in the head. He had complained of dizzy spells and had been taken to a hospital where two days of bed rest and complete quiet were ordered.

When he recovered and did return, his play was markedly improved. Over the next three weeks, few could argue that there was a better player in college football. The week following the humbling by California, bettors were apprehensive about the Bruins' chances against the University of Idaho. In bookie dens the game was rated a toss-up. Washington, however, made it a rout. He rushed for 123 yards and scored 2 touchdowns. UCLA won, 33–0. In a 6–0 win over Stanford, Washington rushed for 104 yards. A week later he totaled 137 yards rushing and also scored twice as UCLA romped past Washington State, 21–0.

As eye popping as Washington's rushing and touchdown numbers were, some coaches insisted his best performances were on defense. Washington played safety in the Bruins' defensive backfield. Such were his instincts and coverage skills that some foes thought he was a linebacker. If opponents thought he was all over the field, well, he often was—in some cases, by intuitiveness while in others by design. Spaulding liked to start Washington on the left side. But anticipating certain plays, he would shift him to the right side. When down and distance might dictate a tendency for a particular play, Washington could thoroughly confuse the opposition and line up as a defensive end. Bruins assistant coach Babe Horrell called him "the greatest defensive back I have seen in many years."[9]

Riding high with 3 consecutive wins and 5 victories in 7 games, UCLA was eager to test its mettle against Wisconsin in the eighth week of the season. The Badgers were coached by Harry Stuhldreher, he of Notre Dame fame, one of the legendary Four Horsemen. It was in the second quarter that Washington got the chance to impress. He scooped up a teammate's fumble and dashed over and around several would-be tacklers. Cheers serenaded a run that culminated in the end zone. However, the touchdown was nullified by a holding penalty.

Fumbles would repeatedly thwart Bruin drives throughout the afternoon. UCLA players called Wisconsin the hardest-hitting team they faced all season. Those hits produced 10 fumbles, 6 of which the Badgers managed to recover.

With 4 minutes to play and Wisconsin leading, 14–0, Washington engineered an impressive drive. Using precision passing and a trio of acrobatic pass receptions, he helped the Bruins chew up 88 yards. There were mere seconds left on the scoreboard clock when Washington leaped for a pass at the 34-yard line, spun, and sprinted for the goal line. At the 2 he was pulled down and seemingly piled on by most, if not every, Wisconsin defender on the field. Once the pile was unstacked, Washington remained down. He was assisted to the UCLA sideline, where the team doctor determined he'd had the wind knocked out of him and suggested to Spaulding he be checked further in the dressing room.

As Washington made his way toward the tunnel, fans groaned. Some pleaded for his return. Across the field, Harry Stuhldreher heard the commotion and saw Washington on his way to the locker room. The coach left the Wisconsin bench to intercept Washington in the west end zone. As UCLA scored a touchdown with 2 seconds remaining in the game, Stuhldreher and Washington were shaking hands at the opposite end of the field. "That Washington is a sweet football player," the coach told writers after the 14–7 Wisconsin triumph.[10]

The Bruins were no match for a USC team with Rose Bowl aspirations. Washington's touchdown pass to Woody Strode accounted for the lone UCLA score in a 42–7 loss. Similarly, his touchdown pass to Jim Mitchell produced UCLA's only touchdown in a 6–6 tie with Oregon State a week later.

While the card section in the Coliseum spelled out tributes to Bill Spaulding on the occasion of his final home game as UCLA coach, it would not be the Bruins' last game. Losing actually brought the invitation to play in a bowl game.

Organizers of the inaugural Pineapple Bowl in Honolulu had secured USC as a participant. However, by beating UCLA the Trojans claimed the Pacific Coast Conference title and with it, an invitation to play in the much more prestigious Rose Bowl. Pineapple Bowl organizers turned to UCLA. Bill Ackerman, who oversaw the UCLA athletic department, accepted the invitation to spend Christmas and New Year's in Hawaii. The school was guaranteed $10,000 to cover a thirty-person travel party, plus the chance to share a percentage of gate receipts should they exceed projections. UCLA would play 2 games, 1 on the day after Christmas against a local semipro club, and the Pineapple Bowl game on January 2, in which the opponent would be the University of Hawaii.

On December 21, twenty-six UCLA players and their coaches disembarked the SS *Matsonia*. During the five-day cruise many of the players battled seasickness. No sooner had the Bruins stepped onto the dock in Honolulu when young girls draped fragrant floral leis, six in all, around each player's neck. Washington was coaxed to attempt the hula and shook his hips to loud laugher, the loudest of which was his own. Organizers of the game handed every player a pineapple. Among the welcoming committee was island legend Duke Kahanamoku, the Olympic swimming champion and now sheriff of Honolulu. Amid the hoopla a sportswriter broke news to Kenny Washington that he had just been named to the Associated Press' All–Pacific Coast first team.

The Bruins were treated like royalty. UCLA was housed at the lavish Moana Seaside Hotel on Waikiki Beach. Players were taken sightseeing to Koko Head, treated to a luau complete with hula dancers, and given tickets to a professional wrestling match. Bill Spaulding continually had to remind his players that their goal was to win 2 football games. He imposed an 11:00 p.m. curfew and put the beach and swimming pools off limits until after the games.

No sooner had the players arrived on the island when Spaulding ordered them to suit up and be ready to scrimmage. He wanted his players to shake off their sea legs. As for the coach, he reacclimated to dry land at the local golf courses, where he could be found whenever not on the practice field.

At the center of all the attention in Hawaii was Kenny Washington. Each day the local newspapers carried large pictures, column notes, articles, and headlines about the UCLA star. "Honolulu fans certainly have a treat in store—seeing Kenny (the Kingfish) Washington in action. One of the greatest backs in the nation," wrote Red McQueen in the *Honolulu Advertiser*.[11]

While children played with toys unwrapped the day before, and parents cleaned up after Christmas Day, the Bruins clobbered the semipro club, Hawaii Town, 46–0. Spaulding substituted liberally. Despite playing just half the game, Washington scored 3 touchdowns and rushed for 136 yards.

When it was all over, the UCLA standout found he had been thrust into the national spotlight by, of all people, Walter Winchell, the most prominent reporter in America. Winchell's Sunday night radio broadcasts were a collection of scoops, news, and gossip. The program drew the largest audience of any show on the air. When his Christmas broadcast began with its traditional "Good evening, Mr. and Mrs. America, from border to border and coast to coast and all the ships at sea. Let's go to press," Winchell reported his latest scoop—that Kenny Washington was secretly convalescing in a Los Angeles hospital and had been there for three weeks recovering from a brain injury.

In newspaper newsrooms, particularly in Los Angeles, howls greeted Winchell's so-called scoop. For the next two days following Winchell's announcement, columnists throughout the country tore holes in his report. Newspapers gleefully pointed out that Washington was not in a hospital but in Hawaii, where he had scored 3 touchdowns in a game on December 26.

Emotions ran high on January 2, when the Bruins entered the field at Honolulu Stadium. Every one of the 18,000 seats was filled. Outside, hundreds more were left frustrated, turned away at the box office and turnstiles.

Hawaii's defense focused its attention on Kenny Washington. Theirs was not a malicious intent, but rather strategic. Shut down the Bruins' most prolific offensive threat and give your team a chance to win. What read well on a chalkboard was not realistic. It merely freed up UCLA's right back, Chuck Fenenbock, who rushed for 131 yards and scored a touchdown. Washington tallied 111 yards even while being shuttled in and out of the game by Spaulding, who doled out playing time to every Bruin who made the trip.

When the game ended and UCLA had won, 32–7, fans poured onto the field. They rushed toward Washington. Hundreds surrounded him and tried to hoist him onto their shoulders. "Fenenbock's your man," Washington shouted. "He was the star of this game. I'm not Fenenbock!"[12] Police ran to the player's aide. They pushed the mob aside, clearing a path so Washington could escape to the locker room.

While Hawaiians showered Washington with adoration, acclaim was absent back home. When the eight recognized All-America teams were announced, Washington's name was conspicuously absent. It did not appear on any of the eight first or second teams nor the lone third team chosen by Grantland Rice for *Collier's Magazine*.

The omission rankled sportswriters. One from Wisconsin who had only seen Washington play in person one time wrote, "Let no one omit the highest praise for Kenny Washington. He's a star in any league. If they have better backs than Washington, the teams should have better records."[13]

When the team returned to Los Angeles, Bill Spaulding set about to pack his things and vacate his office. He was asked about the best players to ever play for him. Said the now ex-coach, "If you ever see a better player than Kenny Washington was for us, let me know."[14]

7

JACKIE JOINS THE TEAM

The day after UCLA's bowl game in Hawaii, a new head coach was installed. Unsuccessful in trying to pry Buck Shaw from Santa Clara, the school heeded the pleadings of its players and promoted Bill Spaulding's assistant, Babe Horrell.

Though only thirty-six, Edwin Chilion "Babe" Horrell brought vast experience to the job. As a collegian he was an All-America guard and center on the last two of the University of California's three consecutive undefeated national champions. A quiet man, who neither smoked nor drank, Horrell possessed a tireless work ethic. Upon being given the top job, Horrell wasted no time implementing change. The most visible was to the uniforms. Horrell replaced the school's gold-and-blue uniforms with a silver-and-blue combination, silver-colored leather helmets and pants. The blue jerseys were emblazoned with silver numbers.

While Horrell remained committed to the single-wing offense, he pondered tweaks to make it more effective than that which Spaulding ran. Ditching the huddle, having his quarterback call plays, using fewer power plays, and incorporating more elements of the spread offense to widen alignment spacing and take advantage of his players' speed were discussed. One of the biggest improvements Horrell hoped to make was the addition of a mercurial junior college back by the name of Jackie Robinson.

Jackie Robinson possessed astounding talent. He led Pasadena City College to an undefeated season and a state football title. His play brought crowds of such magnitude that the school moved its home games into the Rose Bowl Stadium. On the basketball court he was the leading scorer in the league. In baseball, Robinson set stolen-base records at Muir Tech High School and was key to Pasadena City College winning a league baseball title. In May 1938, Robinson sailed 25'6½" at the West Coast Relays in Fresno to eclipse his brother Mack's national junior college record in the long jump. Such was his speed and quickness that he was nicknamed "Jackrabbit Jackie."

Of the colleges pursuing Robinson, most felt certain he favored the University of Oregon. His brother Mack, a silver medal winner in the 1936 Olympic Games, attended the school. But in early December rumors surfaced that Robinson was having second thoughts. It was said he wasn't happy with how his brother was treated. Whether that was the reason or not, Jackie Robinson reversed course and decided to keep his options open.

During the first week of December, a coach at the University of Oregon received an alarming phone call. "Spec" Keene, the football coach at Willamette College, was on the line. Keene had just returned from Los Angeles. While there, he had seen Jackie Robinson driving a brand-new car. Bill Hayward, Oregon's track coach, hurriedly traveled south. On his return to campus, he was prodded about Robinson. When asked if the car had come from UCLA, Hayward simply raised his eyebrows.

Once classes resumed following the holiday break, Jackie Robinson enrolled at UCLA. Babe Horrell's celebration was tempered. Robinson had academic deficiencies. He had neglected to take algebra, French, and geometry in junior college. Passing each was required for admission to UCLA. Administrators placed him in the school's extension division. That meant learning the UCLA offense would have to wait. Participation in spring football practice was out.

When preseason practice began, Horrell kept the gates to the field shut and locked. Security guards were positioned one at the gates, another on the sideline, and a third on a nearby hill. The coach was installing trick plays and did not want spies or scouts to see them. Expectations rose. The Bruin quartet of Washington, Robinson, Bill Overlin, and Ned Mathews was heralded as the best backfield in the country. Late summer heat, strong competition for positions, and new plays made frustrations rise too, particularly in the newest Bruin, Jackie Robinson.

Teammates saw a temperamental side to Robinson. He became annoyed easily. Slights, real or perceived, would ignite volatility. Washington recognized the problem. He invited Robinson to join him on walks. The two would talk things out. Washington's message was both simple and direct: "If you haven't the right attitude, you'll soon find yourself walking alone."[1]

While the general circulation newspapers carried stories that touted this as potentially the best team UCLA had ever fielded, publications such

Figure 7.1 **The 1939 UCLA backfield, left to right, of Jackie Robinson, Ned Mathews, Bill Overlin, and Kenny Washington was heralded as the best in college football.** *Photo courtesy of the* Herald-Examiner *collection, Los Angeles Public Library*

as the *Los Angeles Sentinel, California Eagle, Chicago Defender,* and *Pittsburgh Courier* lauded the team for an entirely different reason. During their first two seasons with the Bruin varsity, Washington and Strode had been the only members of their race on the team. The 1939 Bruins' varsity counted five Black players among its sixty-one. In addition to Robinson arriving from Pasadena City College, his close friend and teammate Ray Bartlett transferred from the junior college as well. Bartlett would play end on both offense and defense. Johnny Wynne, a rugged fullback, joined from the freshman team and impressed during spring practice. One sportswriter called the five "Dark Angels of Destruction."[2]

While many considered the Bruins' roster of players to be the most talented in school history, the schedule those players would face was tougher than any UCLA had ever met before. Four of the eight opponents played at the elite level of college football. Santa Clara, a late addition to the schedule, was two years removed from an undefeated season and a number 9 ranking in the final Associated Press poll. Traditional rival California won 10 of 11 in 1938. Heading into the season, USC was ranked number 1 in the country. But first, the Bruins had to get past their season-opening opponent, Texas Christian, the reigning national champions of college football.

More than 65,000 fans roared with delight as the kickoff to open the 1939 season hurtled through the night air. During the first quarter it was clear that UCLA's new offense confused TCU. Jackie Robinson lined up in a different spot and went in motion on almost every play. He might exit the backfield toward an end, then turn upfield as a pass receiver, or line up as a wingback and go in motion behind the halfbacks. Washington added to the confusion. When Robinson went in motion, Washington might hand the ball off to him or on other plays fake a handoff, take a step or two toward the line, then stop and throw a pass.

Still, there were hiccups. This was the first game in which the new scheme was employed. On occasion, assignments were missed, timing was off, handoffs and passes were flubbed. TCU quickly improvised a defensive strategy. Defensive ends angled their run pursuit to pinch Robinson while an interior push was employed to try and stifle Washington. Throughout much of the first half, as UCLA worked out rough spots, the TCU plan was successful.

It wasn't until early in the second half that a big break brought the throng to its collective feet. Using a series of fast sweeps, TCU took the opening possession of the half and drove 48 yards to the UCLA 29-yard line. As quickly as fans could conjure the word "unstoppable," a fumble brought UCLA a stroke of luck.

It was then that new facets to the UCLA offense paid dividends. In this instance, Washington, and not Robinson, lined up as a wingback and went in motion. As he reached the backfield, Washington received the direct snap from center and dashed around the left side for 12 yards. Next, it was Robinson's turn. He streaked around the right end and gained 16 more. After a fullback dive up the middle picked up 3 yards, Washington again carried the football. This time his run took him around the left end and gained 17 yards. The Washington–Robinson combination electrified the field. Following Washington's big gain, Robinson flew around the right end to pick up another 9 yards. When Washington on the next play blasted past the left guard, he ran for 7 yards before being tackled at the TCU 9-yard line.

In six plays, UCLA's dynamic new offense marched 62 yards through a thoroughly confounded TCU defense. On first-and-goal, the eleven TCU defenders spread out, fearful of what Washington or Robinson might do. Instead, the Bruins called for a fullback dive. Woody Strode shoved

Figure 7.2 Washington runs to set up the game's only touchdown as UCLA opens the 1939 season by defeating the defending national champs, TCU. *Photo courtesy of the* Herald-Examiner *collection, Los Angeles Public Library*

defenders out of the way to clear a path into the end zone for Bill Overlin, and UCLA took a 6–0 lead.

An anxiousness reverberated about the Coliseum throughout the nighttime fray. Nine times TCU threatened UCLA's lead. In the fourth quarter, a mishandled punt turned into a safety and made the score a baseball-like 6–2. Over the final minutes of play, TCU surged forth with a worrisome drive. Its quest for a game-winning touchdown reached the UCLA 9-yard line. It was there that Ned Mathews got his hands on a TCU pass and intercepted it. An ear-deafening roar went up from the Coliseum crowd. Serenaded by the horde, Mathews picked his way through pursuers and would-be tacklers. He dashed 61 yards before he was brought down. Excited teammates leaped upon his shoulders in celebration.

The 6–2 upset win sparked a revelry rarely seen around UCLA football. So many boosters and alums pressed into the locker room that players had barely enough room to change. Eager handshakes left Horrell's right hand painfully sore. Surrounded by a group of Southern California and Texas sportswriters, TCU coach Dutch Meyer exclaimed that Washington was "the best halfback a team of mine ever played against."[3] The coach added, "Oh how he can pass."[4]

Over each of the next four weeks, excitement grew into zeal. Kenny Washington was responsible for both touchdowns in a 14–7 win over the University of Washington, one by run and the second on a toss to Woody Strode.

The Bruins tied Stanford, 14–14, an effort fueled by anger. The night before the game Washington, Robinson, Strode, and Ray Bartlett along with several white teammates entered a Palo Alto restaurant. The group was told Washington, Robinson, Bartlett, and Strode would not be served. "If they don't fit, we don't fit. Let's go," said Ned Mathews, as the UCLA quarterback led the group out of the establishment.[5]

Washington scored all 3 touchdowns in UCLA's third win, a 20–6 triumph over the University of Montana. Further impressive, Washington rushed for 164 yards. "That fellow Washington is even better than Red Grange," praised the Montana coach, Doug Fessenden, a college teammate of the University of Illinois legend.[6]

A highlight of a 16–6 win over the University of Oregon was a touchdown pass from Washington to Robinson that whistled 52 yards in the air. The win concluded an undefeated October. It raised the stakes for the sixth game on the UCLA schedule, the traditional rivalry game against the University of California.

Enthusiasm gave way to panic when, three days before the game, Jackie Robinson was injured in practice. During a scrimmage Robinson, who had just caught a pass from Washington, was tackled hard by two reserve players. He needed assistance to get off the field. The doctor's diagnosis was a badly sprained right ankle, which meant he would not play in the Cal game.

Game day pulled a crowd of more than 65,000 into the Coliseum. Ticket takers noticed the numbers of Black fans coming to watch UCLA play grew each week. When the Bruins and Bears kicked off, more than 9,000 were in the stands. Among them was orchestra leader Count Basie and his new singer, Helen Humes.

The game was midway through the first quarter when Washington struck. He took a handoff, darted past the left tackle, then shook off two tacklers at the line. Certain that their teammates had Washington wrapped up, the Cal defensive backs abandoned their pursuit. Washington took advantage by dashing 35 more yards to score a touchdown.

Not long before halftime, Washington rifled a pass over the middle. It was intended for Woody Strode, but a Cal defender managed to get a finger on it and deflect the pass. The football then fluttered into the arms of another Bruins receiver, Don MacPherson, who turned and ran 17 yards into the end zone for UCLA's second touchdown.

In the third period, Washington's passing produced yet another score. This came on a throw to Strode that covered 21 yards. The California offense would never pose a serious threat all afternoon. The 20–7 triumph was the worst beating UCLA had ever given its rivals. More importantly, it raised the Bruins' record to 5 wins, 1 tie, and no defeats, which kept them in the thick of the chase for a conference title and berth in the Rose Bowl.

Beating California thrust UCLA onto a national stage. Voters in the Associated Press college football poll made the Bruins number 19 in the country. This was no longer a tiny Southern Branch but a legitimate college football power.

The Bruins had no time to bask in glory from the California win. The next opponent was even better. Santa Clara was ranked 14 in the same Associated Press poll. In each of the previous three years, the Broncos finished the season ranked in the top 10.

Fierce defense was on display the afternoon the two schools met. Both teams fought mightily to crack the enemy shield and score. Neither could. With Jackie Robinson sidelined by injury, Kenny Washington found himself a marked man. Santa Clara defenders swarmed him relentlessly.

In the third quarter, Santa Clara made the strongest threat to break the scoreless deadlock. A pass found an open receiver at the UCLA 9-yard line. The play had all the makings of a touchdown before Washington caught the receiver from behind, wrapped him in a bear hug, and wrestled him to the turf. On third down, Washington swatted a pass away at the goal line. The UCLA defensive stand was capped when Johnny Wynne stuffed a run that denied Santa Clara the chance to put points on the scoreboard.

With 6 minutes to play, UCLA put together an impressive drive. When Washington tore through the Santa Clara defense on an 18-yard run, the Bruins had driven 59 yards to reach the Santa Clara 19. On second down, Washington loped to his right and looked for an open receiver. When he found none, he tucked the football and ran. His quick cuts and shifts of speed moved one Santa Clara player to say he didn't know whether to tackle Washington or stop and admire his talent. One finally pushed the Bruins' sensation out of bounds at the 9-yard line.

Washington was tired. He had been on the field all afternoon and would play all 60 minutes. In the closing seconds, the wear and tear of an intense and brutal afternoon showed in the UCLA star. Washington tried a pass into the end zone that sailed incomplete. On the play, a UCLA lineman was detected holding, and 15 yards was marched off. The penalty was costly. With time for only one play, UCLA tried a field goal. The kick fell 2 yards short.

Despite the 0–0 tie with Santa Clara, regard for UCLA swelled. Sportswriters pushed the Bruins up to 11 in the Associated Press poll. In the race for the Pacific Coast Conference title, only two teams remained undefeated: UCLA and its crosstown rival, USC.

The following Saturday 50,000 fans were left aghast, worried that the excitement and the Rose Bowl dream were about to evaporate. With 4 minutes to play against Oregon State, defeat seemed almost certain. A touchdown pass by Kenny Washington in the second quarter accounted for UCLA's points on the scoreboard. As time ran down, the Bruins trailed Oregon State, 13–7.

With 61 seconds to play, UCLA regained possession of the football at its own 18-yard line. Washington hit Strode with a pass that gained 16 yards. The next play, a pass to McPherson, picked up 20 more. Washington fed Jackie Robinson with a lateral, and the fleet Bruin back zipped through and past defenders until being tackled at the Oregon State 23-yard line. A pass was called for the next play, but when Washington couldn't find an open receiver, he took off running. With powerful stiff arms, he pushed aside four would-be tacklers until he was driven out of bounds at the 7-yard line.

Three subsequent runs gained nothing. On fourth down, with the game on the line, the Oregon State defenders expected Washington to carry the football. They were caught completely off guard when the hand-off went instead to Leo Cantor, who scored easily. A beaming Washington lifted Cantor, his broad smile and unbridled zeal celebrating the remarkable comeback and 13–13 tie.

After the game in the locker room, Washington's train of thought was broken by a commotion near the door. He was surprised, as were his teammates, to see Oregon State defensive players enter the room. They had asked their coach if they might go and congratulate Washington. Lon Stiner, the Oregon State coach, was taken aback. "It was the first time it ever happened in my experience," he said. "I can think of no finer compliment to a great ballplayer."[7] One by one, the opposing players approached Washington to shake hands. "We have never seen a finer player or a better sport," one said.[8]

The Bruins closed out November with a 24–7 win over Washington State. Celebrating, however, was overshowed by an atmosphere of nastiness. Much of it was stirred by the demonstrative Washington State coach, Babe Hollingbery. Hollingbery was an emotional man. Histrionics and temper tirades were common from him. Fans and sportswriters howled when he would slam his fedora to the ground at a referee's call he disagreed with.

Throughout the game, hits on Washington and Robinson were especially hard. In the second quarter, Washington was cracked on the forehead by a Washington State player. He was left dazed by the blow and, to some, didn't seem right for the remainder of the half. In the third quarter, the nastiness escalated. Racial epithets were spewed from the Washington State bench. Woody Strode slapped a Washington State player and was kicked out of the game. Officials claimed they did not see what made Strode react.

As he did often, Hollingbery ran along the sideline, gyrating and gesturing. After Washington completed a particularly long run, he heard the opposing coach shout a racial slur. In it was a single odious word that made controlled restraint crumble and rage erupt. Teammates came to Washington's defense. Several confronted Washington State players. A punch was thrown. Washington's ire, however, was directed at one man. He took several steps toward the Washington State bench, raised his right arm, pointed a finger, then shouted, "Mr. Hollingbery, neither you nor anybody on your football team can lick me."[9]

When the game ended, the 35,000 fans who remained in the darkened Coliseum applauded the UCLA players on their walk to their locker room. The next game, the last game of the season, would match the two remaining undefeated teams in the Pacific Coast Conference: rivals UCLA and USC. The winner would claim the Pacific Coast Conference title and go to the Rose Bowl. Never had a UCLA football program been so close to such a coveted prize.

8

AN UNPARALLELED OVATION

The group strode through the Farragut Hotel in downtown Knoxville, Tennessee. Such was their concentration that none, not even the hungry, paid any attention to the ornate dining room with its white linen tablecloths, chandeliers, and high-backed chairs as they walked past. The group was a football team. General Bob Neyland and his University of Tennessee players had only hours earlier completed a 7–0 win over Auburn. It was a victory that concluded an undefeated regular season. Now their minds were on another game, albeit one 2,200 miles away, It had yet to be announced publicly, but Tennessee was on its way to the Rose Bowl. The players, their coaches, and several sportswriters headed toward a banquet room in the hotel where they planned to gather around a radio, listen to UCLA's game with USC, and learn which of the two would be their opponent in the Rose Bowl.

The excitement of the meeting of undefeated Los Angeles rivals was not without controversy, however. It was first broached a month earlier in a column in the *Kansas City Star*. The paper's sports editor raised the question of whether a team from the South would play in the Rose Bowl should the opponent be UCLA with five Black players. The local paper in Knoxville and the *Birmingham Post* followed up similarly. Tennessee players, they reported, would balk at playing an integrated team. The threat that Tennessee would renege on its agreement to play in the game was very real, and the Pacific Coast Conference was concerned.

Odds in the various bookie dens around Los Angeles gave Tennessee reason for optimism. All rated USC the favorite. Coaches whose teams had played both made USC a 2-touchdown favorite. Still, USC was taking nothing for granted. "UCLA is the most dangerous team in the country," said Howard Jones, the Trojans coach.[1] A big reason for his respect was

Kenny Washington, who entered the game averaging more than 5 yards every time he touched the football.

When game day arrived, a festive atmosphere encircled the stadium. It was noon when the stadium box office opened. Within minutes, the 600 tickets that remained were gone. The game was officially a sellout. Scalpers around the stadium commanded twice face value. The magnitude of the game was amplified when NBC opted to broadcast it from coast to coast and sent their top play-by-play broadcaster, Bill Stern, to call the action. Grantland Rice, the dean of college football writers, traveled from the East. Associated Press sent not one but three photographers to capture pictures.

The game was homecoming for USC, whose campus neighbored the Coliseum. Pageantry raised the level of frivolity higher than that at a normal game on the schedule. Yet some, in an effort to support their school, crossed a line of decency and descended into disgracefulness. Members of Phi Kappa Psi erected three grass huts on the lawn in front of their fraternity house on West Twenty-Eighth Street. In the foreground was the replica of a ship. It bore the sign "S.C. Slave Ship." Nailed to a nearby palm tree were three black figures, their features distorted in minstrel effect. Each wore shirts emblazoned with the uniform number of Kenny Washington, Jackie Robinson, and Woody Strode.

Noise many decibels louder than what any of the Bruins had heard before greeted the team as it emerged from the tunnel. Every seat in the massive stadium was filled. The crowd count—103,303—was the largest ever to see a college football game.

Jitters plagued productivity during the early going. Both teams fumbled the ball away. USC was first to pose a scoring threat. It came in the first quarter; the Trojans reached the UCLA 11-yard line. Their quarterback, Grenny Lansdell, shot through a hole in the line and made a dash for the goal line. As he reached the 1, two Bruins hit him—Jackie Robinson low, and Ned Mathews high. The force launched the ball from Lansdell's arm and into the end zone. Woody Strode alertly snapped up the football for a touchback to avert the USC scoring threat.

Later, a Washington interception brought consternation to the USC sideline. Howard Jones was unusually anxious and uncharacteristically demonstrative throughout the game. When his quarterback came to the bench after throwing the first quarter interception, Jones implored him to avoid throwing to Washington's side of the field for the rest of the game.

The Coliseum crowd was a cornucopia of celebrities. F. Scott Fitzgerald was an unabashed Bruins football fan and never tired of telling people that his favorite player was Kenny Washington. Same with the boxing champ and actor "Slapsie" Maxie Rosenbloom. Douglas Fairbanks and his wife, British-born Lady Ashley, never missed a Bruins home game, and Bing Crosby cheered with vigor. When the actress Marlene Dietrich emerged from an entry portal to a loud cheer, she blew kisses to what she thought was a welcome by adoring fans. It was moments after when she was told the cheers were for Kenny Washington.

Physical play reflected the stakes. The level of intensity begat its importance. No play was a greater example of the game's ferocity than a run play in which Washington made up his mind to run straight at USC's best player. Harry Smith, a strong, 215-pound defensive lineman, had All-America recognition on his résumé. Washington drove as hard at Smith as the USC standout drove toward Washington. Their resulting collision was loud and forceful and shot awe throughout the large stadium. For a brief moment the two were static before Smith drove Washington onto his back. It was the last time all day that Smith got so much as a finger on the UCLA sensation, who left the lineman frustrated thereafter with a bevy of shifty moves.

Throughout the second quarter, UCLA chewed up yardage with laterals to Robinson and passes by Washington. None, however, produced points, and the players went to the locker room tied, 0–0, at halftime. Through the second half, back and forth the two teams went. Fumbles and interceptions contributed to play that made hopes fluctuate much like the sky overhead, bright one moment, cloudy the next.

It was the fourth quarter and the closing minutes of play when drama set in and anticipation grew. UCLA took possession of the football at its own 20-yard line. Cheers rose from UCLA's fans, who had seen just this sort of scenario produce miraculous drives throughout the season.

On the Bruins' first play, Jackie Robinson gained 14 yards on a reverse. Next, Washington went around the left side for 9 more. Leo Cantor picked up the yard needed for a first down and put the ball on the UCLA 44-yard line. That's when Kenny Washington took to the air. His first pass went to MacPherson for an 18-yard pickup. He then threw to Robinson, who got to the USC 26 before he was tackled.

USC frantically called time-out to reset its defensive strategy. Once play resumed, Washington continued his wizardry. After an incomplete pass to Strode, the pair connected to move the football to the USC 15. A pass to Ned Mathews gained 5 yards, and runs by Washington and Cantor gave the Bruins their sixth first down of the drive and put the football at the USC 3-yard line.

On first down, Mathews called for a run. Washington tried to burst through a gap next to the left guard but was stopped for no gain. On second down, Cantor too was stopped at the line. Again, Cantor got the call on third down. This time the UCLA line opened a big hole. Cheers that vocalized hope rose. But just as the Bruins' halfback began to bull through the opening, a USC defender dove forward to stop his charge dead in its tracks.

Mathews gathered his teammates in the huddle. Less than 3 minutes remained in the game. He had 10 seconds in which to call a play. The football was placed in the middle of the field, ideal for a field goal try and no farther in distance than a normal point after touchdown. John Frawley had been inconsistent on kicks throughout the season, but Washington had converted when called upon. Jackie Robinson rarely missed while at Pasadena City College.

Horrell left the decision up to his quarterback. Mathews asked his teammates whether to kick the field goal or go for the touchdown. Five players urged the field goal option. Five were adamant they should go for the touchdown. Mathews broke the tie. The Bruins would go for it all.

The UCLA quarterback called a pass play, a quick toss to Don MacPherson in the back of the end zone. The ball was snapped to Washington. Amid the sea of chaos, the receiver was open. As quickly as the ball was released, the Trojans reacted. MacPherson reached for the football. A USC defender turned just as the ball arrived, swatted with both arms, and batted the pass to the ground. Groans filled the air from one side of the big stadium while loud cheers burst from the other. The incomplete pass meant a standstill, a 0–0 tie. Both teams would conclude their season undefeated. Based on league tiebreaker rules, however, USC would claim the Pacific Coast Conference title and go to the Rose Bowl.

In the Farragut Hotel, no sooner had Washington's pass been batted to the turf when loud yells filled the large banquet room. Tennessee's players broke into jubilant celebration. Neyland hurriedly left the room. Several reporters chased after the coach. They hollered questions, hoping for official confirmation that the Vols were Rose Bowl bound. Once safely away from prying ears, Neyland was on a phone with the athletic director of USC to confirm that his team was committed to playing in the game.

With scant seconds left on the scoreboard clock, Babe Horrell motioned for Kenny Washington to come off the field. It was a rare sight. In the ten 60-minute games that made up the 1939 season, Washington had been on the field for 580 of those minutes. In the press box, statisticians tallied Washington's rushing and passing yardage for the day. The tabulation showed 1,365 yards rushing and passing for the season, 9 more than Tom

Harmon of the University of Michigan. It meant Washington would finish 1939 as the nation's leader in total yardage gained.

From his position on the field, Bobby Morris, the referee, noticed Horrell summon Washington to the sideline. Morris was savvy enough to understand not only the coach's motive, but the magnitude of the moment as well. The referee blew hard into his whistle and signaled for time-out. Sight of the referee waving his arms above his head and Washington heading for the sideline triggered fans to react. One by one, in various sections of the enormous stadium, fans stood. By the time his teammates moved toward Washington, patted him on the shoulder pads, and shook his hand, 103,303 people were on their feet. Everyone in the stadium applauded and cheered Kenny Washington.

Grenny Lansdell, the USC quarterback, ran from his huddle toward the UCLA sideline to shake Washington's hand. The cheers continued in far greater volume than any cheer for any play or player all afternoon. Every palm clap, every whistle, every decibel of noise was a representation of gratitude, appreciation, adoration, and most of all, respect.

Horrell wanted his star player to enjoy the deserved ovation and nodded for Washington to head for the locker room. As the Bruins' star trotted toward the southwest corner of the stadium, he paused twice. Each time he turned, first toward the fans in the east stands then next to face those seated at the north side of the large stadium. With each step the applause and the cheers continued. Morris, the referee, held up play to allow the outpouring to continue. Continue it did for almost ten full minutes, until Washington reached the entrance to the tunnel and disappeared from view.

The scene was emotional. "You felt that something had been won that no score could ever record," wrote Helen F. Chappell in the *Chicago Defender.*[2] Particularly moved was the *New York Daily News* columnist Ed Sullivan. Two days after the game, Sullivan devoted his entire Listen Kids column to the unprecedented ovation given Washington. In what was reprinted by newspapers throughout the country, Sullivan wrote:

> On Saturday afternoon I saw a wonderfully thrilling thing happen at the Los Angeles Coliseum during the spectacular scoreless tie played between the teams of the University of California Los Angeles and University of Southern California. Late in the game 103,000 people stood up without urging and cheered a boy who was leaving the field. . . . Marlene Dietrich, Bing Crosby, Priscilla Lane, Walter Pidgeon, Lewis Milestone, were in our section and they kept applauding until the boy disappeared into the tunnel leading to the dressing room. It was deeply moving, this unparalleled ovation for a boy, because he was a Negro.

I have never been so moved emotionally and so proud of my country, because there are not many countries in which such a thing could happen. A moment such as this one, with a vast stadium acclaiming a boy, comes as close to perfection as we are privileged to know it in this funny old world.[3]

Alone as his teammates slugged out the final few plays of the game, it was then, and only then, that Kenny Washington reacted to the magnitude of what had just been expressed. Walking up the grade toward the UCLA locker room, he was overcome by feelings. The young man's knees buckled; his body crumpled under the weight of emotion. In the darkened tunnel beneath the giant stadium, the solitary figure, Kenny Washington, broke into tears and wept.

9

UNADULTERATED HOKUM

A s the ferocity of the UCLA–USC game was building toward a peak in
Los Angeles, the future of several players on the field in the Coliseum
was being dictated halfway across the country. Owners, coaches, and publicity men who represented the ten National Football League teams were
gathered in a ballroom of the Schroeder Hotel in Milwaukee. Each would
leave at the end of the evening with exclusive negotiating rights to twenty
college seniors procured through a draft lottery.

Selections were made in reverse order to the 1939 standings. The
Chicago Cardinals, who finished with the worst record, chose first. Conversely, the league champions, the New York Giants, had the final selection
in each round.

Affixed to one wall of the room were long strips of paper. Each carried the last name and school of several of the 350 draft-eligible seniors on
college football teams across the country.

Presiding over the draft was Carl Storck, the newly elected president
of the league. A jovial, rotund man with a penchant for black cigars and a
weakness for chocolate bonbons, Storck juggled running the league with
an executive position for an automobile manufacturer as well as ownership
of a minor-league baseball team. Storck was a cofounder of the NFL. He
pushed team owners to be progressive and stressed that the league should
provide "the country's most spectacular type of football."[1]

Once selecting commenced, the Cardinals announced the name of
the first pick, George Cafego, a halfback from the University of Tennessee.
Team after team subsequently cried out their pick. With each selection it
became evident that a new trend was about to take shape in professional
football. The game, previously centered around the run, was transitioning
to a more pass-oriented offense. The Detroit Lions displayed their intention

to adopt this change with their choice, the sixth in the first round. Gus Henderson, the Lions' coach, pressed for and got a passer from a college in Los Angeles—Doyle Nave, the quarterback at the University of Southern California. Another USC back, Grenny Lansdell, was selected tenth by the New York Giants. In all, nine members of the USC team were chosen in the draft.

But when the twenty-two rounds of selecting had concluded and the last of the 200 names of top college seniors was called out, one was conspicuously missing. It was not an accidental omission either. The player in question did not appear on the preproduced list that hung from the wall of the 350 top prospects for consideration. The player was Kenny Washington. No amount of praise or on-the-field success was about to print Washington's name on the NFL's prospect list or persuade a team to call out his name as its selection. The reason was simple. It had nothing to do with football talent. The sole reason Kenny Washington was omitted by the owners and coaches of the ten National Football League teams was purely the color of his skin.

Furor erupted once the omission became clear, none more forceful than that of NBC sportscaster Sam Balter. On his *Inside of Sports* radio program, Balter excoriated Storck and the ten NFL team owners for their failure to select Washington. "You have scouts—you know this better than I—you know their unanimous reports: he would be the greatest sensation in pro league history. He was No. 1 on all your lists—None of you chose him," Balter railed. "What you did Saturday was a source of bitter disillusionment."[2] Balter invited Storck to appear on his show and explain Washington's exclusion from the draft. He never received a reply.

To the masses, the blind eye cast by National Football League coaches and owners to Kenny Washington was hardly a surprise. The NFL had been made up solely of white coaches and white players since the Chicago Cardinals cut Joe Lillard in 1933. It was an action that led to an unwritten eligibility policy.

Joe Lillard was no stranger to controversy. In 1931 he became immersed in it. Lillard was a heralded newcomer on the Oregon University football team. His running and passing skills drew the nickname "Midnight Express" and propelled his team to three straight wins to begin the 1931 season. It was then that an accusation was made that put Lillard's continued eligibility in question. Lillard, it was charged, played semipro baseball with the New York Colored Giants. Further, to avoid detection and retain his amateur standing Lillard played under an assumed name, George Gilkerson.

When confronted, Lillard denied the claim. Specifically, though, he only asserted that he did not play under an assumed name. About the rest he confessed. "I worked as a chauffeur driving the players' car. Whenever anybody was sick or crippled up, I would play as substitute. I did not think it affected my standing as an amateur in the coast conference."[3] On the eve of Oregon's game with USC in Los Angeles, Lillard was ruled ineligible and kicked off the team. Oregon's coach, Dr. Clarence W. Spears, said he was "pretty sick about the development."[4] The next afternoon without their star halfback, the Ducks were trounced, 53–0.

The following season Lillard became a full-fledged professional in both baseball and football. He pitched for the Chicago American Giants in the Negro National League. In 1932, Lillard was signed to a contract with the NFL's Chicago Cardinals that paid $185 per game. By 1933, Lillard was considered the Cardinals' best player. He was the team's biggest passing threat, its top rusher, and a leading scorer. Lillard returned punts, kicked field goals and extra points. But along the way he often found himself at the center of trouble. Opposing players, particularly those who hailed from the South, taunted Lillard. They goaded him into fights. Twice during the 1933 season Lillard was ejected from games for fighting.

Many in the media were surprised when the Cardinals let Lillard go at the end of the season. "I felt sorry for Lillard. He was a marked man," said his coach, Paul Schissler. "After a while whole teams, Northern and Southern would give Joe the works, and I'd have to take him out. It got so my Cardinals were a marked team because we had Lillard with us. We had to let him go, for our own sake, and for his too!"[5]

The on-field hostility endured by the Cardinals was noticed by every coach in the league. It shaped the thinking of coaches and team owners alike. "The owners contend that the reason colored stars are not playing in the National Football League is because there are too many southern players in the league," said the former University of Iowa All-America Ozzie Simmons.[6] Fritz Pollard, the first of his race to become a head coach in the National Football League, added, "It's the odd ideas of a few men who bring about this condition."[7]

Not only would his ethnicity preclude Washington from plying his skills at the highest level of football, but it would also bar him from the sport that was his first love: baseball. One Los Angeles sportswriter sought to change that. Dave Farrell made a plea on Kenny Washington's behalf to Larry MacPhail, president of the Brooklyn Dodgers. MacPhail was a frequent visitor to Los Angeles. He liked to attend horse races with friends, such as St. Louis Browns manager Fred Haney. MacPhail was an innovator.

He brought night baseball to the big leagues and was in the midst of lobbying for interleague play and a 16-team postseason playoff. Farrell seized the opportunity to put a challenge to MacPhail:

> You have been looking for a heavy hitting outfielder. I don't know how much you've put out to get one. Let me tell you about Kenny. He hit the longest ball I've ever seen. Up at the Stanford Field in Palo Alto the right-field fence is 500 feet from home plate. A ball has only been knocked over that fence three times. Twice it has been done by left-handed hitters. The other time, Kenny reached out, caught a high hard one on the outside corner and belted it over the fence by some 20 feet. Our Pacific Coast Conference in baseball is the equal of any B-League in America. Kenny hit .400 in the loop. You certainly can use him, and he has the kind of an arm that can throw forward passes 60 yards. Baseball needs new vitality—new faces. Let's stop being ostriches and face a few facts. How about just being sensible.[8]

Farrell's newspaper column question received no reply from the Brooklyn Dodgers president.

As December 1939 turned to January 1940, anticipation grew for the announcement of All-America teams. In all, more than a dozen All-America teams were chosen each winter by an equal variety of media. News distribution services—Associated Press (AP), United Press (UP), Central Press (CP), Newspaper Enterprise Association (NEA), and William Randolph Hearst's International News Service (INS)—produced All-America teams. Publications such as *Collier's Weekly*, *Collyer's*, *Life*, *Sporting News*, and *Liberty Magazine* offered All-America teams that were chosen through a variety of methods: polls of coaches, sportswriters, and even players.

Before any of the 1939 All-America teams could be announced, the first award presented racked the UCLA Bruins with consternation. The Downtown Athletic Club of New York awarded the Heisman Trophy, indicative of college football's player of the year, to Nile Kinnick, the University of Iowa quarterback. Washington's teammates were perplexed. "We played against him last year," said UCLA center Whitey Matheson. "He wasn't in Washington's class. How can he have improved so much in one season?"[9]

Three days after the Heisman announcement, the first of the All-America teams was made public. It brought dramatic change to the mood within the UCLA football program. NBC sportscaster Bill Stern liked to be first with the All-America team he selected for *Life Magazine*. His 1939 team brought a milestone—the first ever first-team football All-America from UCLA, Kenny Washington.

Over the next two weeks, the other services and organizations one by one announced their All-America choices. Each announcement brought a level of disbelief, if not dismay, to those who admired Kenny Washington. NEA, UP, AP, and INS each put Washington on its second team.

The INS selection, in particular, brought outrage. It was chosen by a panel of college coaches and involved a plethora of backroom deal making. In one such instance, USC coach Howard Jones lobbied fellow coaches to vote for his back, Grenny Lansdell. In each case Jones would offer to vote for the other coach's player. That generated several votes for Lansdell but only single votes from Jones for the other coaches' players. As a result, when Hearst announced its INS All-America team, Lansdell was a first-team selection. The far superior Washington was on the second team.

With each announcement Los Angeles newspaper columnists bristled. "If ever there was an All-American it's Kenny Washington," wrote Bob Ray in the *Times*.[10] His colleague Dick Hyland typed, "I regret that Washington was not given the credit he deserved and earned on the football field before our eyes. If it means anything, to him or anyone else, may we conclude this yarn with the remark that one who has in former years picked and placed on All-American teams' various boys, thinks that Kenny Washington, the football player, is as worthy of that honor as any man in uniform for the past 15 years."[11]

Perhaps the most anticipated of the All-America teams was the one selected by the heralded sportswriter Grantland Rice. When the designated Friday evening arrived and his announcement sounded from radio speakers, listeners in Los Angeles, at the very least, were dumbfounded. Washington was ignored. Instead, Rice placed Banks McFadden of Clemson on his All-America team. Of the twelve nationally recognized All-America teams, the *Collier's Weekly* team chosen by Rice was the only one to name McFadden a first-team All-America. Sportswriters excoriated the exclusion. A *Los Angeles Daily News* columnist editorialized, "Naturally the boys down south wouldn't want a colored boy on their selection."[12] The *Pittsburgh Courier* called Washington's omission "unadulterated hokum." Even a columnist from Rice's home state criticized the omission. "If Kenny Washington had been a white man," suggested Fred Russell in the *Nashville Banner*, "he would have been the most talked about player of the year. There is just nothing he can't do brilliantly."[13]

Of the myriad All-America teams, one was distinctly unique. *Liberty Magazine* employed a complex poll of voters—college football players,

1,659 in all, from ninety-one colleges throughout the country. A sports-writer, Norman Sper, organized the poll. He asked players to vote for the best player at each position they faced during the season. He also asked each to select one they considered to be the absolute best they faced. From the results Sper produced all-opponent and all-region teams. For *Liberty Magazine* his tabulations created its All-America football team.

Two days after Christmas, the 1939 *Liberty Magazine* All-America team was revealed. Its first team, chosen by fellow players, featured Kenny Washington. Of the recognized All-America teams, Washington was honored by nine. On one he was a third-team selection. Six named him to their second team. NBC and *Liberty Magazine* recognized Washington as a first-team All-America, the first in UCLA's history.

In addition to his work for *Liberty Magazine*, Sper's data was used in the selection of another prestigious award, the Fairbanks Award. The Fairbanks Award was actually the first college football player of the year trophy, initially awarded in 1931. It carried the name of its benefactor, the famous Hollywood actor and avid sports fan Douglas Fairbanks. While the Heisman Trophy represented the opinions of members of the media, Sper's tabulations formed the basis for awarding the Fairbanks Award. When the vote was tallied for the 1939 Fairbanks Award, Kenny Washington was not only the winner, but all 103 players polled who played against Washington named him the best they had faced. It was the first and only time the winner of the Fairbanks Award was a unanimous choice.

News of the honor moved Washington. When asked which of his many awards meant the most, he did not hesitate. "The one when the players chose me unanimously for the All-American team."[14]

Amid the flurry of All-America announcements came an announcement that wrought greater explosive fury than any of the previous snubs. The East–West Shrine Game was an envy of top college players throughout the country. Played New Year's Day at Kezar Stadium in San Francisco, the game matched twenty-two top players from schools east of the Mississippi and twenty-two from schools in the West, each of whom had just completed their senior season.

The game was staged and sponsored by the Shriners, a 340,000-member fraternal organization that in many communities included their most prominent citizens. Proceeds from the game went to the Shriners Hospitals for Crippled Children. When the forty-four players for the January 1, 1940, game were revealed, the announcement spawned outrage. Kenny Washington was not selected.

As if the outrage was anticipated, the game committee included a statement in its player selection announcement. "It is the unanimous opinion of the committee that the best possible team has been chosen."[15] Few if any bought it. They pointed out that never in the fourteen-year history of the East–West game had a Black player been chosen to participate and accused the game of racial bias. "Kenny Washington won't get to perform in the San Francisco shrine game on New Year's Day simply because his pigmentation happens to be several shades too dark!" wrote Ron Gemmell in the *Statesman Journal* in Salem, Oregon.[16] In the *Oakland Tribune*, Art Cohn chastised organizers, "It's fifteen years old now, the Shrine game, old enough to know better. Old enough to be above all prejudice, more so at a time in history as this."[17]

Outrage spread. A San Francisco labor union, the Maritime Federation, added its voice to the critics. "He was left off the all-star team solely because he is a Negro," said Revels Cayton, the organization's secretary.[18] His and other organizations pressed the governor of California to intervene. When Culbert L. Olson replied, it only fanned the flames even higher. Olson's secretary issued a statement saying Washington would have turned down the invitation in order to play baseball at UCLA. Clearly unbeknownst to the governor's office, Washington had previously declared he had no intention of playing baseball.

Hundreds of letters poured in with complaints. A boycott was threatened. Members of the Shriners were taken aback at the outrage. "I'd like to see Kenny Washington in the game. At least 90 percent of the Shriners themselves are heartily in favor of him," said Don Elliott, the past potentate of the organization.[19] Members of the organization's hierarchy distanced themselves from the controversy. They stressed that it was a committee of coaches, and not Shriners, who were responsible for choosing the players. Almost instantly, ire was shifted to Babe Hollingbery.

The Washington State coach along with Percy Locey, coach at the University of Denver, was responsible for selecting players who would make up the game's West squad. Reporters pressed Hollingbery for an explanation of Washington's omission from the all-star game. The coach was tight lipped. As pressure built, Hollingbery finally relented. He admitted race was behind the decision. "It would jeopardize our standing among the southern colleges," he explained.[20]

In Los Angeles, Washington was showered with awards. He was feted by the Los Angeles Fellowship League, celebrated by the local Masons, and the Helms Athletic Foundation named him Los Angeles Athlete of the Year over Wimbledon champion Alice Marble and welterweight boxing champ

Henry Armstrong. Bigger still, during the holidays Washington and June Bradley found time to break big news to their families. They planned to marry. Few were surprised by the revelation.

At the end of January, once classes resumed and students returned to campus, the UCLA Alumni Association held the annual awards banquet for the football team. It would hardly come as any surprise that the majority of the large trophies on display were taken home by Kenny Washington. Ed Sedgwick, who directed most of Buster Keaton's movies, presented Washington with the Most Valuable Player Award, a gold watch. The American Legion awarded Washington a second MVP Award in the form of a large perpetual trophy. Amid loud applause, Norman Sper handed Washington the gleaming Fairbanks Award. The presentation came with a somber tinge. Only two weeks before Washington was named the 1939 winner, the iconic actor for whom it was named suffered a heart attack and died.

The night culminated with a first-of-its-kind presentation. The university announced the ultimate tribute to a UCLA athlete. It was one which no Bruin athlete had ever received before. The number 13, Kenny Washington's number, would never be worn again by a UCLA football player. At UCLA, it was the first time an athlete's number was ever retired.

Sportswriters added an exclamation mark to the night of tribute. The campus newspaper, the *Daily Bruin*, lauded, "His running, his passing, his blocking, and his great defensive work. The statistics are available if you want them, but they will soon be forgotten. The name of Kenny Washington, however, will never be forgotten."[21]

10

BING, BOXING, AND BRIGHT LIGHTS

In December 1939, two of the most influential men in America set their sights on new sporting endeavors. For each man the goal was to manage a potential champion in a favored sport. The sport was boxing. The talent both men viewed as a potential champion was Kenny Washington.

The opportunity to earn a living in professional baseball, as with football, was off limits to Washington. Boxing, on the other hand, meant opportunity to Black athletes. The ascension of Joe Louis to the heavyweight title in June 1937 increased the popularity of the sport among African Americans. It pulled many athletic Blacks into the sport. Henry Armstrong was one. When he read in a St. Louis newspaper that Kid Chocolate was paid $75,000 for his win over Al Singer, Armstrong moved to Los Angeles and took up the sport. Actors Al Jolson and George Raft underwrote his contract, and in 1937 Armstrong claimed the world featherweight championship.

Boxing was popular in and around Los Angeles. Every other Friday night, fight cards brought throngs to the 10,000-seat Olympic Auditorium south of downtown. Jack Doyle's arena in Vernon was a mecca for fight fans, as was Hollywood Legion Stadium. Promoters and matchmakers clamored for talented fighters who could lure crowds. Trainers sought marketable talent. The boxing team at UCLA and the campus boxing championships proved a fertile recruiting ground.

Boxing and Kenny Washington had been inescapably linked since his freshman year at UCLA. His freshman football coach, Norm Duncan, oversaw the boxing program. In April of that year, Washington agreed to take part in a school-wide boxing tournament. In his first bout Washington's skills astonished onlookers. A blow to the head separated his opponent from a front tooth. Another smash to the midsection sent the rival into the ropes. The referee waved his arms to stop the fight before even 2 minutes were completed in the very first round. Washington's speed and power drew raves. His boxing prowess was heralded as being as unique to the sport as his passing and running skills were on the football field.

In the all-university heavyweight final, Washington's opponent was an upperclassman with far more boxing experience. Washington, in contrast, was raw—though with greater natural talent. Almost immediately Washington took command of the fight. A right cross left his opponent staggered, knees buckled, and on his heels. The opponent drew on his experience. Many previous bouts had taught him how to hang on and to regain his senses. Once he had, the more experienced fighter moved Washington from corner to corner. As the end of the second and final round drew near the tactic worked. Washington was tired, unable to unleash the sort of power punch necessary to put his opponent away. Once the bell sounded to end the round and the bout, it was left to the judges to decide a winner. They sided with the upperclassman. Several students heckled the decision. They hollered that Washington had it all the way and jeered the referee as he left the ring.

Twice, once in his sophomore year and again after football season during his junior season, Washington was the recipient of more recruiting by Duncan. The coach wanted Washington to join the UCLA boxing team. Both times the invitation was declined. As a sophomore, Washington chose to play baseball in the spring. As a junior, the football team did not return from Hawaii in time for the start of the boxing season. Washington chose, instead, to work at Warner Brothers.

In each instance, though, Washington agreed to serve as an emergency member of the team and worked out with the squad. In the spring of his junior year, Washington was approached to spar with a visiting fighter in need of a workout. The opponent was bigger, 6 feet 5 inches, much more experienced, and four years older. Once the gloves were laced on and the two men assumed positions in the ring, Washington promptly flattened his rival with one punch. It was only after apologies were extended and Washington was confident his opponent was all right that he learned he had just knocked out Johnny Paycheck, the 1935 Chicago Golden Gloves champion and a popular heavyweight fighter at the Olympic Auditorium.

On the weekend of Washington's final college game, *Los Angeles Sports Weekly* set the city further abuzz with an exclusive copyrighted story. In it, the country's biggest fight promoter, Mike Jacobs, announced his intention to sign Kenny Washington to a boxing contract. The New York–based

Jacobs was the exclusive promoter of the heavyweight champion Joe Louis. He was influential and used to getting what he wanted.

In the *Los Angeles Sports Weekly* article, Jacobs expressed confidence that Washington would succeed Louis as heavyweight champion. Following the college football season, Jacobs conveyed an offer to the football star—$500 per fight. He pointed out that Joe Louis had received $50 a fight when he began his career. Newspapers across the country picked up the story. The *Pittsburgh Courier* wrote that Washington "is considered by experts who have seen him box to be ready to step right into the ring and hold his own with the best. He has a tremendous kick in either hand, is clever, fast, shifty, and way above the average intelligence."[1]

When an interviewer pressed Washington's girlfriend about the offer, June Bradley replied, "He isn't going to fight!"[2] When Washington was asked about it, he laughed and said he had turned Jacobs down.

Still the push to get the football star into boxing continued with the strongest emissary yet, Bing Crosby. Bing Crosby was not only the highest-paid entertainer in the country, he may have also been America's most ardent sportsman. He was an incessant golfer who, in 1937, put up $500 of his own money as first prize, offered participants a beachside clambake, and launched what would become a popular professional golf tournament. Crosby owned the Del Mar Turf Club, a spectacular horse track on the shores of the Pacific north of San Diego. His own stable included Ra II, one of the top three-year-olds of 1939. He made frequent deep-sea fishing trips to Mexico and was part owner of a minor-league baseball team, the Hollywood Stars.

The revered crooner and actor was a fan of Kenny Washington. He proposed a tempting offer to the football star. Should Washington choose to take up boxing, the entertainment idol wanted to manage him. Figures were bandied about, $1,000 a fight. Crosby asked Washington if he would consider going to George Blake's gym for a bit of sparring and an evaluation. Washington agreed.

George Blake was held in high regard in the sport. He was considered unique in the fight game, a man of impeccable integrity. His teaching skills were second to none. Blake served as coach of the United States' boxing team in the 1920 Olympic Games in Belgium. During World War I he was chief boxing instructor for the United States Army. Throughout a stellar career Blake guided a bevy of Southern California boxers to world titles, among them Fidel LaBarba and Pete Sanstol.

Behind closed doors in Blake's private gym, the veteran trainer put Washington in the ring with Johnny Petry, then turned the two loose.

Petry was a veteran who, at one stretch of his career, had gone sixteen fights without a loss. All but two of Petry's wins came by either knockout or technical knockout. When it was over, Blake was impressed. "I think well of Washington's chances," he said. "He showed speed and punch. He is a very intelligent fellow and picks it up quick. He looks way above the average for one of his limited experience. In my opinion, he might be heard from as a fighter in less than a year."[3]

Glowing praise and rosy predictions could not sway Washington. He told Blake and Crosby that he was considering offers for far more money. Then there was his mother. Marion Washington was fearful, more fearful than she was about her son being injured on a football field. "I have to think of my mother," he said. "My goal in life is to see that she is happy for the rest of her days, and I'll do anything to bring that about."[4] He declined Bing Crosby's offer and never again gave thought to a career as a professional boxer.

Kenny Washington had vowed that he was finished with football. It was a vow that did not make it to three weeks. It ended in the way most strong positions crumble, overpowered by a force far more powerful, in this case an opportunity that was too good to pass up.

It came days after the USC game from a promoter, Larry Sunbrock. The man had a proven business track record. Sunbrock was keen to recognize popularity and turn it into a fast buck. Sunbrock's ideas and promotions were varied. He toured the country with a team of fiddlers and staged world championship contests. His rodeo shows in Los Angeles turned away twice the 25,000 he could jam into Gilmore Stadium and Wrigley Field. Sunbrock convinced the actor Mickey Rooney to play drums for a swing band that played at his jitterbug dance championship and drew 300 contestants. He pulled 85,000 to the Coliseum for a Wild West show that featured a blind woman on the back of a horse jumping from a high dive into a tank of water. Sunbrock promoted races—races that involved airplanes, races that involved automobiles, even races that involved elephants.

In the fall of 1939, Larry Sunbrock set his sights on a new promotion, one that involved football. This was not just any football promotion. His idea was to build a series of games around the biggest football star in Southern California, Kenny Washington.

Sunbrock's idea was to build an all-star team around Washington. The team would feature players who, like Washington, had just finished their final college season. They would play two exhibition games, one on December 31, in Los Angeles and another two weeks later in San Diego.

In time, a third game would be arranged, this one on January 21, in Los Angeles.

Roscoe Washington extracted a lucrative deal for his nephew. Kenny Washington would receive a $1,000 bonus for signing the contract with Sunbrock and $1,000 per game. It was more than the average salary being paid in the National Football League and much more than the average American household income of $1,368.

Sunbrock found a willing opponent in the Los Angeles Bulldogs, a minor-league team with big ambition. At 2:15 p.m. on December 31, Gilmore Stadium reverberated with excitement. Only 500 of the 18,000 seats weren't occupied. The crowd was the largest to turn out for a professional football game in Los Angeles that season. It was almost twice what had come to see the Bulldogs play an NFL foe in September. Ticket takers estimated one-third of the crowd were Blacks who eagerly came to watch Kenny Washington and Woody Strode.

The Bulldogs began the game with a 56-yard drive that concluded with a 1-yard touchdown plunge. The first time Washington handled the football, he burst off tackle and gained 9 yards. Throughout the half he enthralled fans with slashing runs, accurate passing, and timely plays on defense.

Late in the first half Washington raised the noise level in the wooden oval. From their own 46-yard line he rifled a pass to Vic Bottari that covered 36 yards in the air and gave the All-Stars a first down at the Bulldogs 18-yard line. Two plays later, Washington took the snap from center and moved to his right as if to pass. When two defenders closed in from either side, he darted forward to avoid them and found plenty of open field ahead. Washington stiff-armed two would-be tacklers at the 5 and wound up in the end zone to even the score, 6–6. Keen to celebrate, a hastily assembled band fumbled their music selection. They played the USC fight song rather than that of Washington's alma mater to celebrate the touchdown.

With 16 seconds left in the half, the Bulldogs regained the lead on a 60-yard pass play, then added a third touchdown in the third, when a Washington pass was intercepted and run back 70 yards into the end zone. A field goal made the final score 22–6.

When the game ended, hundreds of fans dashed onto the field in pursuit of Washington. Many implored him for autographs. Others slapped his shoulder pads, while most were elated to offer a vocal well done. Sportswriters used words like "classy" and "outstanding" to describe his play. The *California Eagle* emphasized the crowd. "Why did so many people attend the game? We'll tell you. Kenny Washington is the answer."[5]

In the days that followed, another suitor came calling, also taken by the widespread public appeal of Kenny Washington. Harry Popkin was an avid sports fan who owned several local theaters. He was the son of immigrants from Poland whose father served in the Russian army alongside the Cossacks. Popkin was a natural-born entrepreneur. As a youth he pedaled a bicycle through his neighborhood selling yeast that his father had made.

In 1929, Popkin bought his first theater. By the winter of 1939, his holdings had grown to more than thirty cinemas. To ensure his theaters had quality films that would attract customers, Popkin established his own motion picture production company. His concept met with success. The first two films released by his company, Million Dollar Productions, were well received and profitable.

Popkin's focus differed from those of other Hollywood production companies. He seized upon the growing Black community with films that featured all-Black casts to become a leader in the genre. It was a film type that had struggled to grow through the 1930s. Banks were reluctant to finance such films, which, on average, cost between $10,000 and $15,000 to make. Among their concerns was the limited number of all-Black movie houses, 430 around the country in all. There was uncertainty at the number of white cinemas willing to show all-Black films, and then there was the lack of star power. Big-name Black entertainers—Bill Robinson, Duke Ellington, and Louis Armstrong—were reluctant to perform in all-Black films. Their sights were on Hollywood instead.

Popkin had the capital to finance his own films. As a theater owner he knew that the limited appeal for all-Black films was changing. Motion picture houses in the South, once segregated, were opening balconies to Black customers. In one-cinema towns in the South, all-Black films were being shown at the end of the day to attract a new customer and grow revenues. As 1939 drew to a close, Popkin also had a plan to address the star system void as well. He had an idea for a film, one with a football theme, and knew the perfect person to be its star—Kenny Washington.

In the week after Washington's pro football debut, the player and his uncle Rocky accepted Popkin's invitation to meet. A proposal was laid out. Popkin envisioned a football story, one with a romantic angle. Washington was to be a quarterback fending off overtures from gamblers. Popkin proposed filming in February. The finished product would be released in March. It was then that Popkin and Roscoe Washington negotiated salary. When the men emerged, a $2,500 figure was agreed to. If all went well, two more films with Kenny Washington in the starring role were proposed.

Success of the first All-Star game sparked work to stage a fourth. Promoters in San Francisco floated the idea of a game at Kezar Stadium on February 4. Rather than a pro team as the opposition, an all-star team of pro players was raised. A deal was struck for a game that would be called the Golden Gate Bowl. It would match the Kenny Washington All-Stars against a team headed by the former Stanford star and coach of the NFL's Chicago Cardinals, Ernie Nevers.

Two weeks after his professional football debut, Kenny Washington put on a dazzling performance in his second game. Against a team of college all-stars from Northern California, Washington scored 2 touchdowns and passed for a third. His first left the 10,000 fans spellbound. He took the football 2 yards deep in his own end zone and managed to evade pursuing defenders over 102 yards to reach the opposite end zone. Washington's second touchdown was a dive from the 1-yard line. A 23-yard pass to Ralph Stanley broke a 13–13 tie and helped orchestrate a 26–13 win for the Kenny Washington All-Stars.

A week later the Kenny Washington All-Stars took on the Los Angeles Bulldogs for a second time. The 8,500 fans who pressed through turnstiles recognized a much different atmosphere. Large motion picture cameras were positioned around Gilmore Stadium. Harry Popkin had seized on the opportunity to film the game and give his movie a sense of real game action.

During the four weeks since they were first assembled, the All-Stars had become a bit more organized. The offense, in disarray in the first meeting with the Bulldogs, was now a cohesive unit, as was exhibited in the opening minutes of play. Washington produced an electrifying touchdown run. Near-flawless blocks by two of his linemen, Harry Smith and Bob Fisher, opened a huge hole. Washington darted through, then to the cheers from the fans ran 44 yards to score.

The game was a far cry from the one-sided affair on New Year's Eve afternoon. In the fourth quarter, Washington orchestrated a 59-yard drive with pinpoint passes and evasive runs. On a scamper around the right end from the Bulldogs 2, he scored to give the All-Stars a 14–12 lead. Only 2 minutes were left on the scoreboard clock when the Bulldogs took the ensuing kick. With a series of runs they penetrated All-Star territory. With mere ticks on the clock, the Bulldogs attempted a 48-yard field goal. Despite kicking from a difficult angle, it sailed through the uprights to give the pro team a 15–14 triumph.

Washington's play against the professionals made believers out of his few remaining doubters. "I wasn't sold on him," said All-Stars assistant coach Bill Howard. "But when we met the Los Angeles Bulldogs and they leveled off on him, then I had to agree that he's one of the greatest backs of all time."[6]

When Kenny Washington arrived at the practice field in San Francisco, he was beseeched by both well-wishers and autograph seekers. The voracity of the adoration left the All-Star's coach with no choice but to cancel the practice he had scheduled.

The night before the game, Washington drove across the bay to Berkeley to watch the college basketball game between UCLA and California. He was anxious to see his friend Jackie Robinson play for the Bruins. When Washington was recognized, fans rose with applause. Their ovation lasted a full five minutes.

Organizers had fingers crossed that a large crowd would flood the 59,000-seat Kezar Stadium. When game day arrived, the flood that occurred was not of the large-crowd kind, but one of weather. Heavy rain drenched San Francisco and made the field unplayable. It was decided rather than waste the Herculean promotional work, the game would be pushed back one week.

Bright sunshine greeted players and 8,500 fans the following Sunday. Like the weather, Washington's play was brilliant. In the second quarter after an interception gave his side the ball at the opponent's 27-yard line, Washington raised his right arm as if to pass, then darted off left tackle to the 6, for a gain of 21 yards. On the very next play Washington shot through the same gap and scored a touchdown.

In the third quarter, Washington intercepted a pass on his team's 18-yard line. He then darted and cut until he was tackled at the 29. On the first play from scrimmage, he threw a pass that gained 13 yards. Mixing up plays, Washington ran for a gain of 16 yards. A pass put the ball at the opponent's 31-yard line before Washington found Vic Bottari open at the 5. Washington concluded the drive by running the final 5 yards for yet another touchdown.

When statistics were tabulated after the Kenny Washington All-Stars defeated the Ernie Nevers All-Stars, 21–0, Washington had run the football 14 times and gained 110 yards. Reporters suggested fans had just watched Kenny Washington play football for the last time. The player said nothing to dispel the idea, saying he was anxious to return to Los Angeles, complete his studies, and embark on a career in law enforcement.

While Washington was in San Francisco, more scenes were shot for his upcoming movie. Back in Los Angeles, Popkin assembled a cast of experienced performers to surround Washington in the film. Jeni Le Gon, who enjoyed success in films at Paramount and Fox, would play the part of Washington's girlfriend. Mantan Moreland, a comedic entertainer with many years in vaudeville and a half dozen motion pictures under his belt, was cast as "Pop," the team trainer.

For Washington, the opportunity was both significant and groundbreaking. Never before had the motion picture industry sought to parlay the popularity of a Black sports star into success on the big screen. Paul Robeson, the two-time football All-America at Rutgers University, had been a success in movies. But Robeson first began in theater, having worked his way through law school by acting on the New York stage. His charisma and rich baritone voice brought opportunities in Hollywood, such as a starring role in *Song of Freedom* and a half dozen other films in the 1930s.

Popkin held off additional filming until Washington completed his final exams. Once concluded and attentions returned to shooting, a brouhaha developed. It involved the script. Washington took offense at having a character who was to be his brother depicted as a drunk. He voiced concern to Popkin. The two went back and forth before the screenwriter, Joe O'Donnell, relented and agreed to make a change. The rewrite involved seventy-two pages of script.

Filming moved to the farming areas of central California. Scenes were shot in two small towns. Chase scenes with Jeni Le Gon behind the wheel featured cars speeding over ninety miles an hour on Highway 99. In Los Angeles, a casting call went out for burly extras. A week later those who were chosen gathered for a fight scene in a building on Sunset Boulevard. But the fighting got out of hand. What was supposed to be a staged brawl escalated into the real thing. By the time brawlers were pulled apart, one was lying on the floor with a broken leg. Several more had to be treated for cuts and swollen eyes.

Popkin sent letters to cinema owners. He raved that *While Thousands Cheer* would be his biggest production yet, "written around the most famous figure in the world today, Kenny Washington."[7] Many responded to urge delay of the film's release until fall. By bringing out a football film during football season, theater operators said they would have better opportunities for effective advertising and promotion. One went so far as to suggest the timing would double their audiences. Popkin agreed to the request and by September 1 had more than 500 cinemas around the country lined up to show the film.

On Thursday, November 14, 1940, *While Thousands Cheer* premiered at Popkin's Million Dollar Theatre at Third and Broadway near downtown Los Angeles. It opened opposite an enormous marketing push for Charlie

Figure 10.1 Washington's popularity brought opportunity outside of football. He starred in the 1940 motion picture *While Thousands Cheer* with Jeni Le Gon. *Photo courtesy of the Edward Mapp collection/Margaret Herrick Library*

Chaplin's political satire, *The Great Dictator*, and the ever-popular James Cagney's latest film, *City for Conquest*. Neither had much effect on crowds for *While Thousands Cheer*. In fact, such were the crowds that Popkin ordered the film's start time be pushed up one hour so a second showing could be played afterward.

Reviews were largely favorable. *Variety*, the industry trade publication, pronounced, "It rates high in entertainment value and with Kenny Washington as the box office lure should prove profitable for managers everywhere."[8] *Los Angeles Times* sports columnist Bob Ray wrote that Washington "has turned in another fine performance in his debut as a movie actor."[9]

Following a successful one-month showing in Los Angeles, *While Thousands Cheer* was released to cinemas around the country. Washington received praise for his work. "He shows the same intelligent ability on screen that he mastered in becoming one of the immortals of the football field," wrote the reviewer in the *New York Age*.[10] In the *Pittsburgh Courier*, Earl Morris complimented, "I liked Kenny Washington, better as an actor than I did Joe Louis," then added, "Put Kenny Washington, and his film, 'While Thousands Cheer,' on your must list."[11] Still another writer, J. Cullen Fentress, wrote in his syndicated column that Washington "establishes himself as an All-America actor as well."[12]

By the time *While Thousands Cheer* completed its run, it was one of the highest-grossing all–Black films of 1940. Profitability, though, wasn't Popkin's only goal. He wanted the film to carry a social message and felt he achieved that. "We tried to show the world that Black football players could be very good and they were," said Popkin's brother Leo, who directed the film.[13] The Popkins hoped to make two more films with Washington, but before they could do so, another endeavor got in the way.

11

THE STAR AMONG STARS

As Kenny Washington arrived in Chicago, he did not just step from the train onto a platform at the station but onto a stage the likes of which he had never been on before. The Super Chief deposited Washington into a new world. Chicago was the farthest he had ever ventured from home. He was here for the most prestigious game in which any college football standout could play.

Washington was selected to play in the College All-Star Game. The event matched the best of the just-graduated college seniors against the reigning National Football League champions, the Green Bay Packers.

Scanning the platform, Washington found Bernie Jefferson, the former Northwestern back, who had volunteered to be the UCLA standout's host. Within a day and one practice Jefferson would tell a reporter, "I used to think I could play football, but Kenny makes me look like a beginner."[1]

When the All-Stars assembled on the practice field at Northwestern University, many were happy to see Washington. "After three years of playing against Washington, you can bet I'm glad that he's on our side this time," beamed USC All-America Bill Fisk.[2] "You folks in Chicago haven't seen anything until you see Washington play football," said Santa Clara All-America John Schiechl.[3]

But it would be a day or two before Washington could display the skills that generated such praise. The Bruin great had the dubious distinction of being the first player to be sidelined during practice week. Doctors diagnosed a scalp infection, likely from a helmet used during the filming of *While Thousands Cheer*. A visit to a physician for treatment kept him from the first practice session, but he was back in earnest the next day.

Throughout the week Washington was a man in demand. Almost daily he was the target of fans who formed a gauntlet from the practice field to the locker room, each hoping to receive an autograph. Media sought him out almost constantly. The enthusiastic reception from onetime rivals on the West Coast impacted other teammates. Soon, even those from the South recruited Washington for their card games. He brought levity to tense strategy meetings. In one, the All-Stars' coach, Eddie Anderson from the University of Iowa, was explaining punt return plans. He instructed that two men were to be deep in the safety position. Anderson wanted them spread out. "I don't want you holding hands," the coach barked. He then turned, looked toward Washington, and asked, "Now, Kenny, why don't I want two of you back there in the safety position holding hands?" Washington grinned and said, "Well coach, that's no time for romance."[4]

Four days into All-Star Game preparations, Anderson divided his team and put the players through a gamelike scrimmage. It was during this intra-squad tussle that anyone who thought tales of Kenny Washington's football exploits were strictly hyperbole learned otherwise.

When the blue team took possession, Washington carried the foot-ball on almost every play of an 80-yard drive that culminated in a touch-down. His elusiveness wrought frustration. His speed evoked excitement. Moments later Washington again scored, this time on a long run. When he wasn't impressing with his running, he gave coaches pause for play-calling ingenuity with a series of pinpoint passes. Washington's practice perfor-mance buoyed confidence and raised expectations for success against the NFL champs.

When evening turned to night on Thursday, August 29, Chicago was a city abuzz. Cars poured into the city's Grant Park as their drivers and pas-sengers sent turnstiles at Soldier Field into a rare spinning frenzy. Overhead, searchlights pierced the dark sky, telling those miles away of a special event taking place in the stadium.

By kickoff there were 84,567 packed tightly into seats and grand-stands. Brooklyn Dodgers owner Dan Topping and his wife, the ten-time world figure skating champion turned actress Sonja Henie, occupied seats near the playing field. NFL coaches Jock Sutherland and Jimmy Conzel-man swapped notes. The turnout was the largest in the seven-year history of the game.

The eleven starters Eddie Anderson sent onto the field to begin the game were players chosen by a national fan vote. In some parts of the country, the local newspaper was aggressive in promoting its hometown player. In Indiana, polling stations were placed in factories and Purdue's Lou Brock received 200,000 more votes than Kenny Washington. But nine days of practice had taught the All-Stars' coach that Washington was his best player. Brock's start was limited to just one play; then Washington ran onto the field.

Beneath bright floodlights the collegiate standouts shone like never before. It took just 6 plays for them to puncture the goal line and score. For only having a week of practice under their belt, the Packers displayed a remarkably polished passing attack. It wasn't long into the game that they had countered the All-Stars' opening score with 2 of their own and held a 14–7 advantage.

Late in the first quarter the collegiate stars drove, finally reaching the 1-yard line. Anderson sent Washington on. On the first play of the second period, Washington took the snap and charged toward the goal line. Buckets Goldenberg, Green Bay's All-Pro standout, met Washington head-on and was bowled over. Washington plowed his way into the end zone and the score was tied, 14–14.

The NFL champions resumed their precision passing to score 2 more touchdowns. The high-scoring contest thrilled the large crowd. By halftime, after a rushing touchdown by the college standouts, the score was 28–21. Late in the third quarter, Green Bay scored again. Don Hutson leaped between two All-Star defenders to extend the pros' lead to 35–21. The Packers point tally was the highest total ever scored by a team in the game's history.

If fans expected the All-Stars to ease up or even quit, they were mistaken. Their coach shifted the offensive emphasis to Kenny Washington. Following Hutson's touchdown, it was Washington who generated the loudest roar of the night from the enormous throng. He gathered in the Packers' kickoff at his own 4-yard line and proceeded to sprint through, maneuver around, and run past all eleven members of the Green Bay kickoff unit. Just as he had crossed midfield, however, Washington was tripped from behind at the Green Bay 47-yard line. High above in the press box, reporters noted his 48-yard runback was just 1 yard shy of equaling the game record.

It was then that the collegians resorted to the pass to try and close the gap on the pros. Three straight throws by Washington took the ball to the Green Bay 12. With the electricity in the stadium rising, Washington took the snap from center and darted through would-be tacklers for a gain of 10 yards and a first down. Amby Schindler, the back from USC, took the next snap and followed his center into the end zone to cut the deficit to just 35–28.

While drama was rising on the field, catastrophe struck from an origin miles away. The Mutual Radio Network, which was carrying the broadcast of the game to stations all around the country, suddenly and unexpectedly cut away. At that moment, Henry Wallace was accepting the Democratic nomination to be Franklin D. Roosevelt's running mate as vice president. The Mutual Network chose to leave the game and carry Wallace's speech live. Radio station switchboards all across the country were beseeched by angry callers. None was worse than WGN in Chicago, where a sold-out stadium left radio as the only means for thousands to follow the game. Screamed one caller, "He's talking about Roosevelt—we want Washington."[5]

By the time the speech ended and coverage of the game resumed, listeners had missed more than thirty minutes of action. Green Bay added a 34-yard field goal and, after an interception, a touchdown run to its tally. The game ended a 45–28 triumph for the professionals over the collegians, the highest collective points total in the history of the event.

Sportswriters in the press box voted Amby Schindler the All-Stars' player of the game. Nile Kinnick and Washington finished a close second and third, respectively. Green Bay's Buckets Goldenberg was having nothing of it. He called Washington the best player on the All-Star squad. Goldenberg's teammate Carl Mulleneaux echoed the praise and said he did not believe a better back had or would ever play for a team of college all-stars.

Washington's play inspired *New York Daily News* columnist Jimmy Powers to write,

> If I were Tim Mara [New York Giants owner] or Dan Topping [football Brooklyn Dodgers owner] I'd sign Kenny Washington. He played on the same field with boys who are going to be scattered through the league. And he played against the champion Packers. There wasn't a bit of trouble anywhere. Kenny was tackled hard once or twice, especially when he ran a kickoff forty-three yards right through the entire Packer lineup. But that's the routine treatment for all "jack-rabbits." You slam your opposing speed merchants about, hoping to wear them down. Kenny took it all with a big grin.[6]

While Powers's suggestion fell on deaf ears, that of another man did not. Ozzie Simmons turned up at the All-Stars' practice the day before the game and was instantly impressed by Washington. Simmons was the player who integrated the University of Iowa's football program in 1933. In 1935, he led the team in rushing and was named All-America, the first of his race to receive such lofty recognition.

Simmons set about to create opportunity for Washington. A teacher in the Chicago Public School system, Simmons generated a job offer for

Washington. He was offered the chance to teach and coach a high school football team in the city. But another inquiry he made portended something much bigger.

George Halas was considered one of, if not the most, powerful men in the National Football League. As owner and coach of the Chicago Bears, his player signings and offensive philosophy played a significant part in the NFL's growth. Another area Halas received credit for was far more dubious. Men such as Fritz Pollard, the first African American coach in professional football, considered Halas primarily to blame for the exclusion of Black players from the league.

Ozzie Simmons knew Halas in a different light. Simmons told a newspaper columnist that he contacted Halas with Washington in mind. "It would be a great pleasure to see a star like Kenny Washington perform for one of the Chicago teams," Simmons wrote.[7]

Soon, wheels were in motion. Washington was asked to remain in Chicago for a few additional days. He was told that Halas wanted to sign Washington but needed time to try to gain approval from other team owners to break the league's unwritten embargo on Black players. Simmons, in the meantime, offered Washington the chance to earn some extra money. He coaxed him to play in a game for a local all-Black semipro team, the Chicago Panthers. Simmons and his brother Don also played for the team.

While much in the way of possibilities swirled around Washington, he took a step to create his own opportunity. The love-struck football hero made a long-distance call home to his girl. Washington asked June Bradley to board a train and come to Chicago right away. Friends had offered their home for a wedding ceremony. The couple would exchange vows in Chicago.

It was Friday, September 6, when June arrived. The couple hurried from the train station to the Cook County Marriage Bureau, where they filled out the papers and received their notice of intent to marry. A newspaper photographer was tipped off, and a picture of the smiling couple appeared in print two days later.

Washington had a reason for picking September 10 for the wedding. It was the same date that his uncle Rocky and aunt Hazel were wed. On that afternoon in the Chicago home of friends, the beaming couple exchanged vows and became man and wife.

Washington made plans for a Chicago-area honeymoon. It involved sightseeing and enjoying entertainment in the city. Those plans had to wait twenty-four hours, however. The game Washington agreed to play in for the Chicago Panthers was the following evening.

Twenty-four hours after his wedding, Washington took the field in Mills Stadium to enthusiastic applause. The opposition was an all-white semipro team, the Waukegan Collegians. It was quickly apparent, however, that the Panthers' opponent faced trouble. Only twelve players made the forty-mile trip from Waukegan for the game.

When the game kicked off, several people noticed Jimmy Conzelman, coach of the Chicago Cardinals, in the stands and wondered what or who had lured him to the game. The first time Kenny Washington touched the football, he brought everyone in the small stadium to their feet. Washington darted through the line, dodged linebackers, then streaked past defensive backs. In all, he completed an electrifying 60-yard sprint for a touchdown before deliriously cheering fans.

It wasn't long before the unexpected mismatch turned to outright calamity. During the second quarter, two Waukegan players left the game with injuries. By halftime, the Panthers led, 27–0. During the second half, substitutes saw most of the action for the Panthers. When the game ended, the scoreboard read 42–0 in favor of the Panthers, though many agreed the output could have easily been doubled.

The new Mr. and Mrs. Washington spent five more days honeymooning in Chicago. During that time, Kenny broached the idea of staying and settling in the city. Though the response from George Halas had not been favorable, Kenny told June of the teaching and coaching opportunity generated by Ozzie Simmons. June shared that her future ideas and plans were hinged on the couple living in Los Angeles. The thought of a future in Chicago was thus brushed aside, and train tickets were purchased for a return home.

As the couple traveled the plains before their train turned west in Texas, Kenny Washington weighed options. He had likely played his last football game. Baseball was, for all intents, over too. Segregation saw to both. Graduation and law school were more immediate objectives. Washington planned to apply to the law school at Loyola College once he received his diploma from UCLA. He needed to complete just six more units to earn his bachelor of arts degree. One reason the couple ended their honeymoon when they did was the looming start of school. The deadline to register for fall semester classes at UCLA drew near, at the end of the week.

Soon after the Washingtons arrived at Union Station in Los Angeles, career pondering would be halted. For Kenny Washington, unforeseen developments in the professional football arena would send his professional life down an entirely unexpected path.

12

THE DRAWING CARD

In Los Angeles, professional football was barely above an afterthought. Apathetic may have been too strong a description. Indifference was probably closer to the response of sports fans in Los Angeles toward the pro game. While its goals were lofty, the sport repeatedly failed to achieve them and thus faced an untenable future in the city.

Professional football in Los Angeles was the Los Angeles Bulldogs. They were a traveling team owned by the local American Legion Post. Support for the team was minimal. While the Bulldogs were playing before 6,000 on a Saturday afternoon, 20,000 would be cheering dog races in nearby Culver City. Professional baseball, horse racing, and college football held strong public interest. The Bulldogs' and, for that matter, professional football's future in Los Angeles were at the very least uncertain, if not bleak. Until, that is, Paul Schissler entered the picture. Schissler had been coach at Oregon State for nine years before he jumped into the National Football League. He first coached the Chicago Cardinals, then moved to the Brooklyn Dodgers.

After he was fired by Brooklyn following a 3–8–1 season, Schissler moved his family to Pasadena. Schissler invested in property, bought apartment houses, and became a radio sports commentator. All the while he studied the area's professional football landscape. During the summer of 1940, Schissler set about to bring an idea to reality: a new professional football league. By August he had convinced men in San Diego and Oakland to join his plan. Schissler coaxed the new owners of the Los Angeles Bulldogs to abandon their traveling ways and join his effort as well. An ownership group from Phoenix signed on.

On September 15, Schissler brought the men together at the Lankershim Hotel. Investors from Bakersfield joined in the effort. Schissler confirmed he would own and coach the league's sixth entry, a team he would call the Hollywood Bears. When the meeting broke up, the Pacific Coast Football League was born. The first games would be played in one month, on Sunday, October 13, 1940.

Two days after the new league was launched, Kenny Washington and his bride arrived at Union Station from their Midwest honeymoon. Washington was oblivious to the formation of a West Coast professional football league. The only football Washington believed would be part of his future involved an offer he accepted from Babe Horrell to coach UCLA's freshmen running backs. Paul Schissler, however, had a plan to change that.

It was on October 3, ten days before the season was scheduled to kick off, that Paul Schissler achieved his goal. He first signed Woody Strode. Days later, Kenny Washington agreed to Schissler's pitch and joined the new team. When the Pacific Coast Football League formally kicked off its inaugural season on October 20, 1940, it wasn't without its share of stumbles and headaches. The Bakersfield franchise never got off the ground. The Oakland Giants advertised relentlessly on radio and in the newspaper, only to be unsuccessful in securing a place to play.

From the very first time Kenny Washington touched the football in a Hollywood Bears uniform, he was the new league's undeniable star. On the first play of the Bears' first game, a game played in ankle-deep mud in Phoenix, Washington took the snap and dashed 37 yards. Grabbed by tacklers, he lateraled the football to a teammate who ran the rest of the way for a touchdown. In the third quarter of the game, Washington electrified the crowd even more, running 52 yards for another touchdown.

A week later, Washington's combination of passes and runs churned up the bulk of the yardage on scoring drives of 71, 65, and 76 yards in a win over San Diego. Against Oakland he threw a touchdown pass, then thwarted the home team's potential scoring drive with an interception.

Washington's play was the biggest reason the Bears roared through the first half of the season without a defeat. He not only made Hollywood the class of the league, but he also was responsible for the biggest crowds each team would draw at home. Washington, according to Stanley Speer of the *Hollywood Citizen-News*, was the "best one-man drawing card on the coast."[1]

Schissler worked hard to try to establish his team as a Los Angeles mainstay. He livened the atmosphere at Gilmore Stadium and increased the amount of entertainment with pregame performances by singers, quartets, and bands. Drill teams and high school bands entertained during halftimes. A military canine unit put its dogs through drills. Schissler even staged an all-women's 7-versus-7 football game and enlisted the popular actor Mickey Rooney to coach one of the teams. Along with Earl Gilmore, owner of Gilmore Stadium, Schissler put together a knothole gang. Twenty-five hundred children were quickly signed up and received free tickets to games.

Across town, the UCLA football team was in free fall. After coming one play away from a Pacific Coast Conference championship and trip to the Rose Bowl, the 1940 Bruins struggled for any success at all. UCLA failed to win its first 7 games. Attendance plummeted. Rare was the newspaper game story or column that did not trace the Bruins' plight to the graduation of Kenny Washington.

But for Washington, Schissler, and the Hollywood Bears, the euphoria from the team's inaugural-season success came crashing to a halt in the middle of their seventh game. The Bears trailed the Oakland Giants, 3–0, in the third quarter when Washington tried to drive into the line. After a vicious tackle he struggled to get up off the turf. Once off the field, he was taken immediately to Hollywood Hospital for X-rays. After the game, which Hollywood rallied to win, 14–3, Schissler told writers that Washington's injury was minor, just an ankle bruise. In truth Washington had broken a bone in his left foot.

Though the star halfback hobbled about the sideline on a cane, the Bears still managed to whip the San Diego Bombers, 28–7. The injury to Washington threw a wrench in a big promotional effort Schissler had concocted. He paid to bring the American Football League champions, the Columbus Bullies, to Los Angeles. Without Washington, Schissler's hype fizzled. Hollywood offered little challenge and was clobbered, 31–7.

Five days later the Bears squared off against their rivals, the Los Angeles Bulldogs. Washington limped from the locker room in uniform. He tried to warm up before the game but was in too much pain and reduced to a hobble. As he watched from the sideline in driving rain, Hollywood again lost, this time in a 14–13 thriller.

By finishing first and second, respectively, in the Pacific Coast Football League, Hollywood and the Los Angeles Bulldogs earned the right to advance to the league-title game. Hollywood had only one PCFL loss, while the Bulldogs had a loss and a tie to their record. Schissler proclaimed Washington fit and ready for action. "We won five straight with Kenny in the lineup. Then when Washington was hurt, we dropped two in a row. Nobody will deny that Washington is the backbone of our outfit."[2]

A cheer went up from 14,000 fans when Washington trotted onto the field for the championship encounter. It was actually more limp than trot that moved him about. Only the work of the trainer, who tightly wrapped his injured left foot, reduced the pain enough so he could play.

It was the Los Angeles Bulldogs who took command early. Hollywood struggled to mount an effective offensive attack. Minutes into the second half and with the ball at midfield, Washington scampered around left end. As he reached the Bulldogs 25-yard line, a defender caught him and violently flung the Bears' star out of bounds. Penalty flags flew through the air. Washington leaped to his feet. He flipped off his leather helmet. Angered, he screamed at the offender, challenging the man and his teammates to fight. Bulldogs defenders backed away from the scene. A 15-yard penalty for unnecessary roughness was marched off as a heightened zeal surged through the eleven Bears in their huddle.

Washington's powerful right arm brought drama to the fray. Late in the fourth quarter, the hands on the Western Union–sponsored scoreboard clock made opportunity wane. With 3 minutes left to play, Woody Strode blocked a punt. Hollywood recovered the football at the Bulldogs 20-yard line. After three unsuccessful plays, the Bears attempted a field goal for the lead. To loud groans from the stands, the football sailed wide, and with it went the Bears' hopes of winning the inaugural Pacific Coast Football League crown as they lost, 16–14.

Professional football's first season on the West Coast concluded with promising signs. *Oakland Tribune* sports editor Art Cohn wrote, "After being kicked around for several years, professional football is about to take its rightful place in Pacific Coast sports. The West, last to be developed as the National capital of college football, will be the last to see development of the pro game."[3]

Schissler assembled an all-star football game to kick off the 1941 season. The event matched two teams of all-stars. One was a pro all-star team made up of players from the Pacific Coast Football League. The other was a college all-star team with players whose final season had been the previous fall.

Ardent newspaper readers were likely surprised to learn Washington would play. During the summer it was widely reported that Bill Spaulding gave Howard University in Washington, D.C., a strong recommendation to make his former UCLA standout its head football coach. After lengthy deliberation, the school hired a coach with college coaching experience.

Owners of the American Football League's New York Yankees wanted Washington to play for their team. They felt he would lure large numbers of Black fans from Harlem. The offer was generous, but Washington worried it was more talk than substance. He sought proof and asked the team to put its offer in escrow until the end of the season. That's when talks came to an abrupt end.

Summer also brought Washington two movie opportunities. Rather than Harry Popkin films, these offers came from major studios and involved mainstream productions. In May, Washington was cast in a Samuel Goldwyn Studios project, *The Little Foxes*. In June, Washington was hired for a part in *Sundown*, a United Artists project. The story was set in Africa. Washington was cast as the Somali Sergeant Kumakwa in a Nazi-versus-British war plot. The cast, crew, and two special cars with elephants, camels, and zebras were transported by train to Acoma Rock, New Mexico, where shooting took place over eleven days.

In the Gilmore Stadium dressing room, Kenny Washington exhibited nervousness before the game. It had little to do with the opposition and everything to do with the reason close friends and family members were surprised by his decision to play in the game. Kenny Washington was about to become a father.

When the game kicked off, intensity was high, fueled in part by an incentive Paul Schissler negotiated. The NFL's Washington Redskins were holding training camp in San Diego. Their owner agreed to bring his team north to Los Angeles for a game with the winner of the all-star contest.

It was late in the first quarter when Washington raised the decibel level in the nearly packed stadium. He took the snap from center, drove toward left tackle, bounced off a would-be tackler, and churned his way into the end zone for the game's first touchdown. When play resumed following halftime, Washington scored once again, this time dashing around the left end from the 6-yard line.

In the third quarter with his team leading, 20–0, Washington was approached by an assistant coach. What the man whispered into the player's ear made Washington dart for the locker room. He hurriedly changed, then made for Hollywood Hospital. June had gone into labor.

When Washington arrived for practice the next evening, he was beaming from ear to ear. For weeks he had been telling friends and teammates with a wink that the baby would be a girl. In the early morning hours of September 4, June delivered a boy. Mother and father named him Kenneth Stanley Washington Jr.

Washington's All-Stars beat the collegians, 20–14, to earn a date with the 1940 NFL Eastern Division champion Washington Redskins. The NFL team's coach, Ray Flaherty, scouted the all-star game and was full of praise for what he witnessed. "That Kenny Washington is a great back— one of the best in the game. I wish he was going to be on my team next

Friday night instead of on the other team. He could make any team in the National League."[4]

Promotional efforts touting a Kenny Washington–Sammy Baugh duel coaxed a near-capacity turnout for the Friday night game. Unfortunately, the contest of celebrated passers never materialized. In the second quarter, as Washington tried to make an ankle tackle, he was kicked in the face. He remained on the bench and did not return until the fourth quarter.

While he was on the field, Washington was victim to vicious assaults, both verbal and physical. Redskins players kicked the football away to make the referees chase it; then with attentions diverted they slugged or kicked Washington. Play was repeatedly stopped and offenders warned, but it had little effect.

Later in the fourth quarter, Washington was pushed to a breaking point. A Redskins player swung an elbow at Washington's face then trotted to the bench. Flushed with anger, Washington shot to his feet and began to chase after him. The referee grabbed Washington by the jersey. "Kenny! Not here, not now," the official barked. Washington paused. "All right. But that man goes too far."[5]

Despite being on the losing side in a 30–0 game, the postgame accolades were for Kenny Washington. "Say! This is the first time I've had a chance to take a real look at him," said Erny Pinckert, a member of the Redskins' 1937 NFL championship team. "Why, he's the closest thing to Sammy Baugh when it comes to passing that I've ever seen."[6] Paul Zimmerman, the *Los Angeles Times* sports editor, normally conservative in player assessments, suggested Kenny Washington was "better on long throws. As for running ability Washington would be far out in front. And he is far and away the better defensive player of the two."[7]

Washington's play throughout the 1941 season made the claims of Pinckert and Zimmerman difficult to dispute. Week after week, adjectives like "incomparable," "amazing," and "never greater" described his play in print.

Week in and week out, Gilmore Stadium was at or near capacity when the Hollywood Bears played. In one of the rare instances when it was not, 10,000 fans still sat through pouring rain. The Bears drew crowds at least 30 percent larger than those of any other team in the league. When the Los Angeles Bulldogs hosted Hollywood in the Los Angeles Angels' baseball park, Wrigley Field, the crowd count was triple the Bulldogs' usual turnstile count. Among the more than 18,000 were parishioners from People's Independent Church of Christ, whose pastor, Reverend Clayton Russell, dismissed his congregation early so those who wished could be in their seats in time for the kickoff. Those enthusiasts among the faithful included the pastor himself.

In addition to a successful professional football league, Schissler also constructed a powerful football team. He insisted his Hollywood Bears were better than the Chicago Cardinals or Brooklyn Dodgers teams that he coached in the NFL. Optimism for the Pacific Coast Football League and the Hollywood Bears was high heading into the final 3 games of the 1941 season. But as a unique December 7 game approached, a major worldwide event was about to impact the future of the team, league, and star player.

13

DIVERTED BY WAR

A sunny afternoon of Sunday, December 7, 1941, had all the earmarks of another Paul Schissler master promotion. The owner and coach of the Hollywood Bears convinced the Columbus Bulls to come to Los Angeles once again for a game between the champions of the American Football League and Pacific Coast Football League. It was a game Schissler billed the "Little World Championship."

The Ohioans were the class of the Midwest, winners of three successive AFL crowns. Their roster was filled with former NFL players and collegiate standouts from schools in the Big 10 conference.

When 2:00 arrived on Sunday, December 7, 1941, more than 18,000 fans were packed into Gilmore Stadium. The temperature in Los Angeles was on its way to a high of 81 degrees. Weather 45 degrees warmer than in Ohio, where snow covered the ground, was only one obstacle facing the Columbus players. The other was a bad case of station-wagon legs incurred from a long drive to California.

After returning the opening kickoff to its own 33-yard line, Hollywood began the game with a series of run plays, 6 in all. Washington carried the football on 4 of those plays. So enthralling were Washington's runs that the antics of John Sutak, the comedic peanut vendor, were almost a distraction to some fans. On the fourth play, which was from the Columbus 32-yard line, Washington pumped his right arm as if to throw. Seeing the defense react and a gap open, he took off running and wasn't brought down until he reached the 3. Hollywood got into the end zone on its sixth run play and was quickly ahead, 7–0.

It was then that the public-address system kicked on and an ensuing announcement made that sent innumerable emotions rippling through the stands. Japan, the fans were told, had attacked American army and navy bases in Hawaii. The country was at war. Thousands around the oval-shaped stadium leaped to their feet. A loud roar was cast by the throng. As quickly as the sound of jubilation had filled the air, somberness followed. The initial bulletin was followed with calls for servicemen to report to their posts. Next, an announcement summoned all firefighters to their stations or engine houses. For several minutes, the names of individuals were paged. Each was told to answer an emergency phone call. Every time the microphone clicked on, the gravity of an ever-unfolding situation grew.

While Los Angeles became a city awash in frenzy, inside Gilmore Stadium football continued and offered respite. On his team's third offensive possession, Paul Schissler switched strategy. He shifted from run plays to the pass. A series of throws by Washington drove the Bears to the 2-yard line, from where Lefty Goodhue ran it in for Hollywood's second touchdown and a 14–0 lead.

In the second quarter, Hollywood had the ball at its own 5-yard line. Washington broke loose on an electrifying run. With a loud roar emanating from the stadium to the surrounding Fairfax district, Washington galloped 55 yards before he was tackled by Columbus defenders.

As the game wore on, the large crowd slowly thinned out. Among those who stayed, ears were pressed to portable radios. The remaining fans were torn between the game, additional news about the attack in Hawaii, and updates on new actions.

It was the third quarter when Columbus put the scoreboard operator to work. Washington briefly had to come out of the game. He complained of an upset stomach, one of three Hollywood players to claim such. The problem was later traced to oranges eaten by a handful of players in the locker room at halftime. With the Hollywood defense momentarily depleted, the Bulls mounted a drive. They kicked a 39-yard field goal then, in the final minutes of the quarter, drove to the Hollywood 1-yard line. The Bears waged an impressive goal-line stand. They managed to stop the Bulls and gain possession of the football just as the quarter ended. On Hollywood's first play, Washington tried to run the football out of the end zone. He was kicked by a Columbus defender and fumbled. Washington tried to fall on the football to surrender a safety. A Columbus player beat him to it, and the touchdown drew the Bulls to within 5 points of Hollywood, 14–9.

Whether from frustration, embarrassment, or anger at his faux pas, Washington displayed a heightened intensity, and the resulting effort put the game out of reach. On Hollywood's first play after receiving the ensuing kickoff, Washington found Woody Strode with a pass that measured 55 yards and put the football at the Columbus 22-yard line. On the next play Washington found room to run and gained 12 yards. One play later, he connected with Lefty Goodhue for a touchdown to give the Bears breathing room.

For Schissler, Washington, and the rest of the Bears, celebration of their 21–9 victory was muted by the events outside the stadium, in Los Angeles, Hawaii, and Washington, D.C. As fans, coaches, and players exited Gilmore Stadium, they stepped into harsh reality. More police cars than usual patrolled the streets. Journeys home witnessed ack-ack guns and large searchlights being moved into position about the city. The air thundered with the sound of bombers being relocated to area bases. Smaller planes, interceptors, crisscrossed overhead as crew scanned for sight of possible invaders in or above the Pacific Ocean.

As the harsh reality of the morning's attack sunk in, a winning football game became an afterthought. In Hawaii, 2,897 sailors at Pearl Harbor and soldiers and aviators at Hickam Field had been killed. Bombs dropped by Japanese planes had sunk six navy ships. America's Pacific Fleet was crippled by the attack.

Up and down the West Coast fear grew, and unanswerable questions abounded. In Los Angeles, the army wanted to limit the size of gatherings. It shut down horse racing at Santa Anita. Law enforcement no longer had the manpower to handle traffic control; thus, the Rose Bowl was canceled, then after reflection moved away from the West Coast to North Carolina. The NFL's all-star game, the Pro Bowl, planned for Wrigley Field, would not be staged.

Both the Bears and Bulldogs pressed to get their game in. The army mulled whether to cancel all sporting events but instead put a cap on attendance. Finally, four days before Christmas, the teams squared off. A crowd of 10,000 turned up for the matchup. Play was intense. Neither team could cross the goal line save for 1 field goal apiece in the first half. After one particularly forceful clash by the two lines, Kenny Washington turned to the field judge and from his position in the defensive backfield gushed, "Look at them hit! Boy, are they playing football!"[1]

Midway through the third quarter, Hollywood fans feared they were about to witness the Bears' first loss of the season. Los Angeles scored a touchdown to take a 10–3 lead. Coming off the field after the Bulldogs' touchdown, an angry Washington flung his helmet against the back of the bench. Fans in the front few rows heard him holler, "Let's go boys!" to urge his teammates on.

The Hollywood players responded. With 5 minutes remaining in the game, Hollywood received a break. It recovered a fumbled punt on the Bulldogs 40-yard line. Washington entered the Bears' huddle initially minus his helmet but wearing a look of intense determination. On the first play on offense, Washington picked up 12 yards on a run play, then 6 more the very next snap. His pass to Denny Noor placed the football at the Bulldogs 13-yard line. The fourth play of the drive saw Washington thread the needle on a pass to Glen Galvin for a touchdown. The extra point evened the score, 10–10.

With 4 minutes remaining in the game, the Hollywood defense again forced the Bulldogs to punt. This time, Washington was the return man. Once the football fell from the air into his arms, Washington set out on a zigzag path, evading defenders until he was pulled down at the Bulldogs 46-yard line. On first down, Washington gained 11 yards via the run. His next effort averted Hollywood's defeat. Washington spied Woody Strode running downfield. A trio of defenders were in pursuit, but Strode had a step on them. Washington whistled a missile that landed in Strode's palms at the 5-yard line. The muscular receiver managed to squirt through defenders and reach the end zone for a touchdown that, with an extra point, gave the Bears victory, 17–10.

After the game, an exhausted Washington lay quietly atop the trainer's table for several minutes. "I just played by instinct that last quarter," he told a sportswriter.[2] With a nod to L. Frank Baum's novel, Lisle Shoemaker wrote of Washington in the *Daily News*, "He's the wizard of ahs!" The sportswriter added, "He's what ham is to eggs, what scotch is to soda. History's Washington crossed the Delaware, but it couldn't have been any more sensational than the Bears' Washington crossing up the Bulldogs."[3]

Rather than a springboard into the 1942 season, Washington's sensational effort and the Bears' remarkable comeback win would serve only as a memory to fans of professional football in and around Los Angeles. Kenny Washington wanted to serve. Like millions of other men all around the country, he followed instructions and marched into his draft registration center to fill out the required registration card, DSS Form 1. It was from those cards that many would be summoned back for a physical exam, the results of which, along with a review of family and employment status, would place them in a draft classification. Single men in good health were labeled 1-A and became the first conscripted.

For Kenny Washington, life prior to the onset of war was harmonious. He and June had purchased a home at 3114 South St. Andrews Place, less than a mile northwest of the Coliseum in the Jefferson Park section of Los Angeles. Their son, Kenny Jr., barely four months old, weighed 16 pounds and cooed as he crawled across the floor. It was a haven, far from the turmoil of war.

Men like Washington, who were married and with children, received 3-A status under the Selective Service Act of 1940. These men received deferments from the draft because, according to Senator Joshua B. Lee (D-OK), "the family is a fundamental unit of society."[4] Still, Kenny Washington yearned to serve—if not the country, then his community. He pondered options and prospective opportunities while he completed his final few classes at UCLA.

World War II plunged the Los Angeles Police Department into tumult. Within the first ninety days of the war, the department lost 5 percent of its 2,477 officers to either the draft or voluntary enlistment into the armed forces. Chief of Police C. B. Horrall took steps to recruit more officers. The chief was anxious to fill 150 pressing vacancies. It was his hope that more than 900 men would pass the civil service exam. The first wave of recruits brought discouraging results. Of the 2,057 men who applied to join the force, only 442 passed the test.

When the civil service exam was given in early April, Washington was among the men with pencil in hand keen to join the Los Angeles Police Department. On April 13, 1942, he was among the largest class of recruits in fifteen years to begin training. For one month, Washington lived at the police academy in the hills of Elysian Park, just two miles from where he grew up in Lincoln Heights.

After their swearing-in ceremony on May 11, Washington and 144 recruits were assigned to divisions. Washington would work out of Newton Street Station. It was an assignment that put him in a powder keg. The Newton Street Station sat in an area of Los Angeles inhabited by 70 percent of the city's Black population. Mistrust of police permeated the neighborhood. Shootings of unarmed men and racial slurs spewed by white patrol cops were at the core of the animosity. Within the station walls, there were problems too. White officers refused to take orders from Black supervisors. It was a problem so intense it required the intercession of the chief of police to resolve.

Roscoe Washington was one of those supervisors. He was highly regarded within the department and well liked in the neighborhood. In addition to his duties, Roscoe Washington built a program modeled after Boys Town, in Omaha, Nebraska. It offered guidance and support for Black teens and youths. He enlisted his nephew to help. At Thanksgiving, Roscoe Washington's program fed 4,000 youths from the surrounding neighborhood.

In the months before war was declared, the goal of Newton Street Station was to reduce the number of murders committed in the district. After America entered the war, the Newton Street Station became hopelessly stretched thin, especially by new wartime responsibilities: patrolling for dimout violators, dealing with drunken sailors in Central Avenue bars, and searching for soldiers who had gone AWOL.

Kenny Washington was ninety days on the job when the lure of football once again beckoned. His Hollywood Bears coach, Paul Schissler, had designs on a benefit game. Schissler petitioned the police commission for approval to use Washington. It was then that the department newcomer learned about section 270.30 of the police policy manual. It barred officers from holding outside employment. "Here we are shorthanded of police officers and being asked to release one to play football," said Ross R. McDonald, the department's head of personnel.[5] The possibility of injury and losing an officer from an already short-staffed force was at the heart of the rejection.

More than a year later, in November 1943, another appeal was made—this time by the Los Angeles Mustangs. The Mustangs were a team constructed out of the rubble of the Los Angeles Bulldogs who, like the Hollywood Bears, disbanded due to the war. They offered Washington $500 per game and pledged to take out an insurance policy against injury. He took the offer to his superior officer, who advised him not to agree to any contract without the approval of the police commission. A formal request was once again made. Again, it was rejected because Washington "might get injured and incapacitate himself."[6]

Four months into his tenure with the police department, another football season loomed. Friends and passersby frequently asked if football might be in his fall plans. Whether from resignation or dedication, he unequivocally declared, "I'm definitely not going to play pro football this fall. I've played my last game."[7]

14

A MEMORABLE HOME RUN

The voice of the public-address announcer reverberated through the spacious ballpark. Though the World Series was six days past, the game of baseball held center stage in Los Angeles on this mid-October Sunday.

Any time a game took place in Wrigley Field, it was a focal point of Los Angeles sports. The ballpark was not just home to the Los Angeles Angels of the Pacific Coast League, but a baseball mecca in the region. It was the finest minor-league park anywhere in America.

Chewing gum magnate William Wrigley Jr. built the park in 1925. He hired the same architect responsible for the Cubs' ballpark in Chicago. Double decked, with 21,000 seats and ivy on the left-field wall, Wrigley's Los Angeles ballpark was almost an exact replica of the park in which his major-league Cubs played. Two major differences were a Spanish tile exterior and a large twelve-story tower behind the main stands, which featured large clocks on all four sides.

As those large clocks neared 1:30 p.m., names of the batting order were read off. They were a who's who of big-league standouts and included men, such as Babe Herman and Babe Dahlgren, who made up the middle of the batting order of one of the teams. When the announcer reached the third name of the batting order for the opposing team, it was Kenny Washington, the only player on either side who was not a professional baseball player.

The game was a brainchild of one Joe Pirrone. A former minor-league ballplayer, Pirrone plowed earnings from his work in the produce industry into baseball projects. Together with his brother John, he built a 7,000-seat wood ballpark, White Sox Park, at Thirty-Eighth Street and Compton Avenue.

Each fall dating back to 1920, Pirrone staged a professional baseball winter league. Play would commence a week after the World Series and conclude at Christmas. Pirrone recruited players from the big leagues and top Pacific Coast League players. He encouraged owners of Negro League teams to send players as well. Many did. The league brought some of the best from Black baseball to California, such as Cool Papa Bell, Double Duty Ratcliffe, Willie Wells, Satchel Paige, and Chet Brewer.

Always thinking of ways to generate attention for his league, Pirrone hit on an idea—to launch the winter-league season with a heavily promoted exhibition game in Wrigley Field. The game would feature a team of top white players against one made up of players from the Negro Leagues. To add to the appeal, Pirrone would secure a star player to travel to Los Angeles and participate. Dizzy Dean and Pepper Martin of the St. Louis Cardinals joined Pirrone's game in 1932. Cleveland's Bob Feller struck out fourteen in the 1939 game. Joe DiMaggio drew 5,000 fans when the game was played in the Hollywood Stars park, Gilmore Field, in 1940. One year later, both Ted Williams and Jimmie Foxx featured in Pirrone's showcase event.

Pirrone had a commitment from Satchel Paige to headline his 1942 game. However, after pitching in 4 of the Kansas City Monarchs' 5 games in the Negro World Series, Paige wired Pirrone that his arm was sore. He needed a rest and wasn't coming to the West Coast. It was then that Pirrone turned to another prospective drawing card, and Kenny Washington agreed to play in the game.

When Washington's name was announced as playing second base and batting third for the Royal Colored Giants, cheers of 6,000 fans filled the air. It had been two months since the civil service board rejected Washington's latest request to play football. Baseball, however, was another story. Upon joining the Los Angeles Police Department, Washington was recruited to join the department's baseball team. His first game in June ended a hiatus from the game of more than four years. Not since the spring of his sophomore year at UCLA in 1938 had Washington played the sport competitively. Now he was on the same field with some of the best players in the game.

It was in the bottom of the first inning when Washington took his first turn at bat. The Joe Pirrone All-Stars had scored 4 runs in their half of the inning. The tally seemed an ample lead for their pitcher, Larry French. The left-hander was fresh from his fourteenth season in the big leagues. With an excellent curveball, a screwball, and a newly mastered knuckleball, French won 15 and lost just 4 games for the Brooklyn Dodgers during the summer of '42, success that earned an invitation to pitch in the All-Star Game.

As he readied for his at-bat, Washington heard the applause as French retired first George Harris of the Louisville Black Caps and then Chet Williams of the Homestead Grays. When it came Washington's turn to step into the batter's box, few could have expected what was about to take place.

It happened when French delivered a fastball. His arm swept across his body from a three-quarter angle as the baseball shot from his hand toward the outer third of home plate. A loud thwack of hard bat-on-ball contact sent the baseball high into the air and both Peanuts Lowrey and Babe Herman hustling toward the fence in right-center field. The All-Stars' center and right fielder paused when they drew within 6 feet of the wall. It was clear any further pursuit was futile. Each could only listen as the ball rattled off the farthest corner of the bleachers for a home run, and a cheer rose up from the stands.

As Washington trotted around the base paths, awestruck onlookers threw out estimates of how far the home run traveled. Their guesses ranged from between 390 and 470 feet. Whatever the distance, the mere feat of hitting a home run off of a big-league All-Star was something Washington called "thrill enough to last a lifetime."[1]

Later in the game Washington hit a screaming drive to the outfield wall. By the time the ball was retrieved and returned to the infield, Washington was on third base with a triple. In his third time at bat, Washington singled, then stole second base. Though his team lost, 6–1, Washington was clearly the star of the game, outshining both his teammates who played professionally in the Negro Leagues and the opposition, which had six big-league players in their lineup.

With permission from his employer, Washington continued to play in Pirrone's winter league while off duty. A week after his stellar performance in Wrigley Field, he had 3 hits in a game, 2 of which were doubles. Teammates noticed pitchers walk off the mound and shake their head when Washington forcefully drove balls into the outfield. One newspaper was quick to hail Washington as the best hitter in the winter league. Buoyed by the experience, Washington said, "I would like the chance to play organized baseball. I hope the day will come soon. If I'm given that chance, I'll do my level best to succeed."[2]

As winter moved closer to spring of 1943, Kenny Washington found himself an unwitting part of controversy. The war and, more specifically, the military's need for manpower wreaked havoc with the rosters of professional baseball teams. The pursuit of players by ballclubs was never-ending. In Los Angeles, the Hollywood Stars lost sixteen players to military service and had just seventeen under contract as spring training loomed. "We are signing all the talent in sight," said Oscar Reichow, who ran the Stars.[3] In truth, Reichow had not managed to sign any. While he confessed to wanting players from Southern California, Reichow actually cast an eye south to Mexico, which was not involved in the war and held the potential for replacement ballplayers.

A pair of reporters, Halley Harding of the *Los Angeles Sentinel* and Herman Hill of the *Pittsburgh Courier*, seized on the need. They suggested the void could be readily filled with Black players. The men pressed the two local teams, the Hollywood Stars and Los Angeles Angels, to give Kenny Washington a tryout. Oscar Reichow deferred the matter to the Stars' manager, Charley Root. The former Chicago Cubs pitcher rejected the idea out of hand. The response was different, though, when Harding and Hill met with the man who ran the Angels, Clarence Rowland.

Rowland told the newspapermen he was amenable to the idea. "We want ballplayers who can deliver," he said and added that his manager "will give everyone a fair trial. We hope to make this new move without undue fanfare or publicity."[4] Days later, Rowland backpedaled. He said he did not want to cause friction within the ballclub. Bill Sweeney, the Angels' manager, claimed the team had too many players already under contract.

In response, the Los Angeles County Board of Supervisors issued a sharp rebuke of the two teams. A resolution was placed on record opposing discrimination against Black ballplayers. It singled out Kenny Washington as a player who deserved opportunity.

When Opening Day of the 1943 Pacific Coast League season arrived, Art Cohn, a columnist for the *Oakland Tribune*, did not ring the new season in on a celebratory note. Cohn called for Congress to include baseball in its ongoing investigation of discrimination toward Blacks in the military. Cohn cited, as a prime example, the case of the Stars and Angels denying Kenny Washington a tryout:

> Every day, we read in the papers that Coast League managers are crying over the lack of players, yet they will not consider many greater players who would strengthen their club, like Kenny Washington. Kenny would be a tremendous asset to any Coast League club, both on the field and at the box office, but he was not even given a tryout.[5]

Labor unions added their voice to the fight. United Automobile Workers Local 887 and CIO Union of the North American Aviation company passed resolutions urging the Stars and Angels to reconsider and give tryouts to Washington, Chet Brewer, and others. The unions called for members to picket outside Wrigley Field when the Stars and Angels met Memorial Day weekend.

Despite the efforts, none of the Pacific Coast League clubs would budge from their stance. Regardless of the need for ballplayers, no club in either the major or minor leagues would integrate its roster. That left Washington confined to police department baseball in the spring and summer, then Joe Pirrone's games during the winter.

In the spring of 1943, the police department culled the best players from its various station houses into one departmental team. Several of the men had professional or college baseball experience. A small handful had played in the Pacific Coast League. The newly constructed team took on all comers. They faced teams in the region's highly competitive semipro leagues, college teams, even teams from military bases.

No matter the competition, Kenny Washington excelled. His grand slam was the highlight of a win over UCLA. He had 4 hits in a game against Loyola College. When the police played a team from El Segundo, Washington clouted a 400-foot home run. He had 2 doubles and hit a line drive back up the middle so hard that one observer hyperbolized it nearly tore a pitcher's hand off in a game with a navy team.

When the LAPD team traveled to an Army Air Corps base in Santa Ana, the game offered an enticing matchup. The army's star player was none other than New York Yankees great Joe DiMaggio. Only a year earlier DiMaggio had captivated the nation as he amassed a record 56-game hitting streak. Even playing service ball, DiMaggio's exploits were followed closely by the press, especially when he hit in 12 straight games.

In 3 turns at bat against the LAPD, DiMaggio singled once. It extended his hitting streak in service games to 13. However, the highlight of the game came from the bat of the LAPD center fielder, Kenny Washington, who ripped a home run. Onlookers estimated the ball traveled more than 450 feet.

Spring of 1944 brought acclaim to the Los Angeles Police Department baseball team. The morale-boosting activity earned financial support from the Police Relief Association. It brought enough to the coffers to expand the team's schedule. The LAPD team continued to play area colleges and military teams. Now it was also able to accept invitations to travel for games and tournaments out of the Southern California area. Such was the interest in the team that even the chief of police occasionally traveled to out-of-town games with the players.

Central to the team's success was Washington. Through the first 14 games, he clouted 5 home runs and belted 3 triples. It was decided he would play center field rather than shortstop. The move paid dividends when his strong throwing arm cut down a number of runners who dared try and score on hits and fly-ball outs.

Twice LAPD beat UCLA's future league champions. In one of the wins, Washington raced home to score the winning run in the tenth inning after a teammate singled. He sent a home-run ball far beyond the left-field fence in a game at USC while another was the highlight of a romp past the Occidental College team. Scouts for big-league teams discreetly conceded to sportswriters that Washington's baseball skills were every bit as good as his talent at football.

Washington's uncle Rocky rarely missed one of Kenny's games, whether in the Los Angeles area or 380 miles away in San Francisco or Oakland. His pride swelled when fans and sportswriters would stop to praise, "You've got a good boy in Kenny, on and off the field." Roscoe Washington would grin and reply, "Yeah, he's a good boy. When he sticks his head up too high, we bat it down."[6]

Summer brought World War II toward the start of a fourth year. The numbers serving in the military continued to increase from less than 2 million before the Pearl Harbor bombing to 11 million in 1944. Each time military leaders made a request of Congress for more men, conscription requirements were changed. Age eligibility was lowered. Disqualifying physical problems were given less consideration and were, in some cases, ignored altogether.

Kenny Washington received notification from his draft board that his status was changed. His deferment as a married man with child was now brushed aside. Washington's new classification was 1-A, which put him at the top of the eligibility list for induction into the armed forces. The draft was about to change the path of Kenny Washington's life, only it would not be the draft he expected.

15

I GOTTA HAVE THAT WASHINGTON

When Bill Freelove entered a room, something big was likely to happen. He was a big man, who stretched a tape measure at least seventy-six inches. His favored double-breasted suits covered 300 pounds of girth. Freelove ran a company that produced parts for airplanes. In the summer of 1943, that company's productivity was taxed to meet the demands of an escalating war effort, and Freelove had a bank account that proved it.

Bill Freelove was not just a big man with a big company but also a man with big ideas. His creative side was sated by promoting events. In 1943 he set out to assemble his biggest idea yet: a professional football league. He knew just the person who could make it successful—Kenny Washington.

In his teens, Freelove became enamored with football. He played it in school, served as a water boy for the Los Angeles Bulldogs and for the NFL's Washington Redskins when they trained on the West Coast. When Paul Schissler put his Hollywood Bears on hiatus in 1942, Freelove stepped in. He appealed to the Pacific Coast Football League to fill the vacancy with one he would own, the Los Angeles Mustangs. His request was rejected. Then and there, Bill Freelove vowed that he would crush the PCFL. He would start a league of his own.

During the spring of 1943, Freelove traveled the West Coast, meeting with business associates, acquaintances, and well-heeled individuals who his research said might make good prospective team owners. He urged the Los Angeles Bulldogs to leave the PCFL behind and join his league. When they refused, he recruited two well-known restauranteurs and sportsmen, who launched the Los Angeles Wildcats, and hired Detroit Lions coach "Gloomy" Gus Henderson to lead the team.

As if two teams weren't competition enough for the Bulldogs, Free-love gave millionaire construction magnate Andy Smith a third area team, the Hollywood Rangers. Golfer "Babe" Didrikson Zaharias and her husband, George, signed on to own a San Diego entry.

On June 26, 1944, amid fanfare at the Lakeside Golf Club, Freelove announced the creation of his eight-team professional football league. In addition to the four Southern California teams, the American Professional Football League would play in Oakland, San Francisco, Portland, and Seattle. Each ownership group made a $5,000 deposit into the league's account. A constitution and bylaws were agreed to. Orders were placed for uniforms.

Then there was the matter of players. With three Los Angeles teams vying for area talent, Freelove proposed a way to solve any potential fighting—a draft among the three with a unique format. Draft order would be determined by a coin toss. Players would be chosen by position. For example, once all the prospective centers were selected, guards would be picked, then tackles, and so on.

Regardless of format, one player was on every team's mind. "I gotta have that Washington on my club. He's just what the doctor ordered for my system," said Henderson of Kenny Washington.[1] The Wildcats' coach vowed to meet any trade demand if it would bring him the rights to Washington. Because of this intense interest, all three teams agreed to select backs by a blind draw out of a hat. Whoever pulled Washington's name had to give up two players, one to each of the rivals.

Washington may have been every coach's target, but there was no guarantee he could or would play football. In the summer of 1944, Washington was deeply involved in a juvenile program as part of his responsibilities with the police department. Still, Freelove loudly boasted to reporters that Washington would play for his Mustangs. The team owner pointed out that the Los Angeles Police Department ranks grew with large numbers of officers and community service volunteers since the start of the war. Freelove vowed to meet with higher-ups in order to secure the availability of Washington.

On July 29, owners of the three Los Angeles clubs and the new AFPL commissioner, Jerry Giesler, gathered at the toney Jonathan Club in downtown Los Angeles. Over a couple of hours, names of 148 players were pulled from a bowl by the three teams. The final position to be picked were backs. When Bill Freelove drew a slip of paper, his eyes lit up. His very own team, the Los Angeles Mustangs, had drawn the slip of paper with the coveted name of Kenny Washington.

As excited as Freelove and his coach were as they left the private club, their mood would quickly change. They found the police department inflexible, and Kenny Washington disinterested in their salary offer.

It wasn't that Washington was reluctant to resume playing football. He wasn't. In fact, he confided to family members that he lacked the disposition for police work. Together with his uncle Rocky, who handled negotiations, Washington made it known that playing for the new league's standard pay of $100 a game was entirely out of the question.

Washington was unyielding in his stance, especially since the negotiator on the other side of the table was a businessman with deep pockets and a man who counted on Washington to pull big crowds to his team's home games.

While the draft assigned players to the three Los Angeles teams, only those teams and none other in the league were bound by the agreement to fill their squads in that manner. The other five teams in the league were free to recruit and sign any player they wanted. A month after the draft, one team exploited that loophole and in doing so wreaked controversy in an explosive manner.

On Monday, August 28, Kenny Washington abruptly resigned from the Los Angeles Police Department. The next morning, the owner of the San Francisco Clippers announced he had signed Washington to a three-year contract worth $22,000. His pay, $750 per game, was one of the richest agreements in all of professional football.

Bill Freelove was furious. He charged the Clippers with violating league rules and protested loudly to the man hired as commissioner of his league. "At no time did I agree to play with the Mustangs or sign a contract," Washington said on arriving in San Francisco. "I think Freelove is being a little unkind in causing me trouble now."[2] The commissioner, Jerry Giesler, sided with San Francisco "to not disappoint the public and in the interest of fair play."[3]

The first time Washington suited up for the San Francisco Clippers, just under 10,000 fans braved wet conditions to witness his debut game at Kezar Stadium. Fans cheered as Washington broke two long runs and connected on a pass and run that covered 80 yards. His heroics were not enough, however, to avert a 20–9 loss to the Hollywood Rangers.

Anyone who thought two years away from football would dull Washington's skills was sadly mistaken. He blitzed through opponents with aplomb. In the Clippers' second game, 14,000 came to Gilmore Stadium and saw Washington throw 2 touchdown passes to former Fresno State All-America Jack Mulkey in a 20–13 win over the Los Angeles Wildcats.

In Seattle, Washington averaged almost 11 yards every time he ran with the football. He tallied 210 yards rushing in a 35–10 triumph over the Bombers. When Bill Freelove's Mustangs came to San Francisco, Washington got a measure of revenge on the third play of the game. He shot through left tackle, straight-armed several defenders, then won a 68-yard sprint to the end zone. It helped the Clippers achieve a 27–7 victory.

Washington took a kickoff 95 yards for a touchdown to beat the Los Angeles Wildcats, 35–23. But in a big first-place battle with the Hollywood Rangers, Washington limped from a muddy field with a torn leg tendon. Minus its star player for the second half, San Francisco lost, 27–6.

The injury did not hold him out of play the following week when, in Los Angeles, he threw a touchdown pass to help the Clippers down the Los Angeles Mustangs, 21–6. A 54-yard touchdown run and catch of a 28-yard scoring pass were highlights of a 20–7 win over the Portland Rockets.

Back-to-back wins sent the Clippers into their final game of the season and one last chance to topple the first-place Hollywood Rangers. The pairing pulled the biggest crowd of the season—15,000—into Kezar Stadium. While the turnstile count and a $19,000 gate pleased Virgil Dardi, who owned the Clippers, the afternoon brought little in the way of excitement to the fans. The game was a defensive duel. Washington failed to complete a single pass. Not until the final 9 seconds of the game, when Hollywood kicked a field goal, did anyone put points on the scoreboard. The 3–0 final score saw Hollywood complete an undefeated season, while San Francisco finished, 7–3.

Kenny Washington's drawing power produced optimism for pro football's future in San Francisco. "Professional football is beginning to be a big thing in our town," wrote *San Francisco Examiner* sports columnist Prescott Sullivan.[4] Around the league things were not quite as rosy. When the American Professional Football League kicked off in September, Freelove boasted that it would rival the National Football League. By November, trouble had cropped up in several cities. Rumors made it into print that the Los Angeles Wildcats were about to cease operations. Owners of the team vehemently denied the claim. The Oakland Hornets canceled two games. It was reported they could not field a team. In truth, they did not have the money to pay their players. A wealthy shipbuilder came to the rescue, and the team resumed play. In San Diego, an angry George Zaharias challenged Bill Freelove to fight when the league shut his team down. "When I went into this thing, they told me I couldn't lose. So, what happens? I lose $20,000 and then they say I ain't in the league no more," Zaharias lamented.[5]

Despite owning the biggest drawing card in the league, the San Francisco Clippers found themselves with money trouble. Their payroll, $4,000 per game, was highest in the league. Each home team was obligated to pay the visiting team $3,000. The Opening Day crowd of just over 9,000 at Kezar Stadium generated a paid gate of $10,000. In the weeks that followed, bad weather made crowd counts fall by half. The team tried to boost revenue by playing 2 games in Fresno, 190 miles to the south, with mixed results.

Fans who stayed away, however, missed good football. Washington and Clippers end Jack Mulkey were hailed the best passing combination in all of professional football. Opponents up and down the league lauded Washington as the best player in the APFL. "We don't waste his talents," said the Clippers' coach, Mike Pecarovich. "So far we have achieved excellent results."[6]

No sooner was the season done when Washington was called to serve his country. The United Service Organization, USO, was under criticism for not providing entertainment for Black servicemen. Wendell Smith of the *Pittsburgh Courier* had for months urged the secretary of war to send Black athletes to entertain Black troops. "Negro morale is usually so far down you can't touch it with an oil well drill. That, of course is due to conditions under which the Negro soldier lives and fights," Smith wrote.[7] He singled out baseball stars Satchel Paige and Josh Gibson, Olympic hero Jesse Owens, and Kenny Washington as sports heroes who could improve morale of Black soldiers, sailors, and airmen.

In February 1945, the USO and the government agreed to stage a series of camp shows at bases where Black soldiers and airmen were stationed. Dan Burley, managing editor of the *Amsterdam News*, offered to coordinate the tour. It would cover three months and encompass the European and Asian theaters. Burley phoned Kenny Washington, who quickly signed on. On March 5, with boxing champ Henry Armstrong, Washington boarded a train for New York City. There, they were to meet up with Owens and Joe Lillard, the former Chicago Cardinals standout who was now a New York City police officer. The foursome would make up the entertainment for this special USO tour.

Under strict secrecy and shrouded by cover of darkness, a large Douglas C-54 rumbled down the runway at New York's LaGuardia Field. On board were Washington, Burley, Armstrong, and Lillard. Owens was pulled from the tour when the draft board denied him permission to leave the country. He was replaced by Bill Yancey, who was once heralded as the fastest man in basketball with the traveling New York Renaissance team and a shortstop of big-league caliber during several seasons with the Homestead Grays, Philadelphia Stars, and New York Black Yankees. Yancey was now a respected baseball scout. As the large four-engine, prop-driven plane headed north toward Newfoundland, the calm within the main cabin was in stark contrast to where they were headed.

At Ramitelli Airfield near Campomarino, Italy, Washington put on football passing demonstrations. He joined with enlisted men and civilians in games of baseball to which Yancey, the scout, marveled that he was "a natural ball player."[8] When Washington climbed into the boxing ring and sparred with Henry Armstrong, it brought loud cheers of delight from the pilots and ground crew of the 332nd Fighter Group.

While the group was in Italy, news came through that Germany had surrendered. The end to hostilities in the European theater shifted the group's attention to men still fighting the war in the Pacific. It was then the sports stars were sent to traverse the thousand-mile Ledo-Stilwell Road, from Assam, India, to Chungking, China. Washington, Armstrong, Lillard, Yancey, and Burley visited bases where they put on boxing and football-passing demonstrations, joined in base baseball games, spent time with wounded soldiers in hospitals, and talked sports with jeep and truck units they encountered along the road.

In Calcutta, India, Washington and his tour cohorts were greeted enthusiastically by Black soldiers who were kept isolated out of fear over how they might be treated by locals. Smiles welcomed the men when they met up with the all-Black Forty-Fifth Engineering Battalion, which was building a vital supply highway to China. In Burma, men of the 3651st Quartermaster Truck Unit cheered Washington's football passing exhibition and Armstrong's boxing prowess.

Conditions were like nothing Washington, Armstrong, Lillard, Yancey, or Burley had ever encountered before. The timing of the trip brought them into the region just as monsoon season began. Heat was searing, humidity stifling.

During talks to servicemen and in question-and-answer sessions, both Burley and Yancey stressed that as renowned a football standout as Washington was, he was equally talented in baseball. The sportswriter and the scout prodded Washington about his baseball aspirations. He refused to be drawn into the talk. He knew it was futile to try to pursue playing professional baseball and told the men his focus was solely on football.

On July 7, the loud screech of wheels to pavement at LaGuardia Field in New York brought Washington and his compatriots back home. For eleven weeks their Sports Unit 500 had traversed more than 25,000 miles.

Once in New York City, the men made a beeline for the Hotel Theresa. Outside, they encountered a large throng who hoped to meet members of a traveling orchestra. When Washington and Armstrong were recognized, the men were mobbed. They happily complied with handshakes and autographs but once inside hurriedly retreated to rooms and the first hot shower they had enjoyed in nearly three months.

While Washington was away, the professional football landscape on the West Coast changed. The Pacific Coast Football League and the American Professional Football League merged. Bill Freelove was angry that his fellow owners broke from the agreed-upon business plan. As a result, his brainchild succumbed to financial failure. Owners of PCFL clubs were angry too. They remained intensely bitter toward Freelove—so bitter they barred the man and his Los Angeles Mustangs from the remade league.

Upon his discharge from the army, Paul Schissler revived the Hollywood Bears. That news was all it took for Washington to inform the San Francisco Clippers that he wanted out of his contract so he could play at home. With flashbulbs popping and the subject dapper in a light brown suit and bow tie, Washington signed a contract for $400 per game, twice what anyone else in the league would earn. "He's the greatest football player in the nation, major leagues included," Schissler said proudly.[9]

With Woody Strode still serving in the Army Air Corps, Schissler knew Washington would need receiving targets to throw to. He achieved that goal by signing a heretofore unspectacular player by the name of Ezzrett Anderson. A standout lineman at all-Black Kentucky State, Anderson moved with his family from Arkansas when his father gained work in a Los Angeles–area munitions factory. He was 6 feet 4 inches tall, had size 15 feet and equally large hands, and, in the words of one sportswriter, "carries himself as loose and limber as a sack of grain with rubber arms and legs attached."[10] After a game in which he shone, players complimented Anderson's "sweet feet." From the kudos evolved "Sugarfoot," a nickname that would stay with him for the rest of his life.

Washington returned to the Hollywood Bears with spectacular form. At City Field in San Diego in the first game of the 1945 season, 10,000 fans were sent into shock when they witnessed Washington fling a ball 65 yards in the air to his new receiving target. "Sugarfoot" Anderson made a spectacular one-handed catch. Two plays later, Washington followed a crushing block leveled by his center and dashed 15 yards into the end zone for a touchdown. Though Hollywood came up short, the 21–13 outcome would be its last loss for a long while.

The following week, Washington spun, cut, and darted his way 37 yards to find the end zone and help Hollywood beat the Los Angeles Bulldogs, 9–7. Against San Francisco, Washington took an interception back 42 yards for a touchdown during a 36–0 romp past his old team. The Bears had to wait for the fifth game of the season to exact revenge on San Diego, but they got it, 21–14, on the back of 2 touchdowns by Washington. In San Jose, 22 of Hollywood's 38 points came on a Washington field goal, a touchdown pass he threw, another score that he ran in, and 5 extra points off his left toe.

Through five weeks of the season Washington led the league in scoring and rushing. His 5 touchdowns, a field goal, and 7 extra points were more than twice what his teammate Johnny Petrovich had tallied, 40–18. In yards rushing, Washington's 481 were 170 more than Petrovich, who was second.

As impressive as his statistics were, it was before games that Washington truly aroused wonderment. During team warm-ups he and Anderson would put on a passing exhibition that made fans and opponents marvel. It would begin as a game of catch near midfield. After a few throws each player would take a few steps back until they were on opposite 40-yard line stripes. More tosses and another move would place each man on opposite 30-yard lines. Finally, Washington would be on one 20-yard line and Anderson the other as they flung a football back and forth, 60 yards in the air.

When Paul Schissler realized Anderson had arm strength comparable to Washington's, he created several new plays. Each called for Anderson to line up at end, then on the snap drift into the backfield, be pitched the football and throw downfield, sometimes to Washington, who would have slipped from the backfield and run a pass route.

When Thanksgiving arrived on November 22, 1945, millions of Americans had a great deal to be thankful for. What the government called Operation Magic Carpet brought almost 700,000 troops home from the Pacific. Already more than one and a half million soldiers, sailors, and marines were back from Europe. Among the men who returned from service in the Pacific was Woody Strode, who was promptly signed by Schissler and rejoined the Hollywood Bears in time for their big game with the rival Bulldogs.

Two weeks before the post-Thanksgiving meeting with Hollywood, the Bulldogs pounced on the opportunity to acquire a star of their own, a quarterback just released from the navy. Frankie Albert, a heralded Southern California high school player, gained renown when he quarterbacked

Stanford to an undefeated season in 1940, then capped it with a Rose Bowl win over Nebraska. He was an All-America and considered one of the greatest passers ever to play on the West Coast.

Sportswriters had a field day promoting the meeting of Frankie Albert and Kenny Washington. Forecasts of a memorable matchup came true, but nobody could have guessed just how memorable the afternoon would be.

On Sunday, November 25, Wrigley Field was filled to its 22,000-seat capacity for the Hollywood Bears game against the Los Angeles Bulldogs. Whether inspired by the duel with Albert or merely capitalizing on opportunity, Washington produced a performance that eclipsed his marvels at UCLA. The stuff of immortality struck on the first play of the second quarter. Sixty-one yards from the end zone, Washington heaved a pass that Woody Strode caught for a touchdown.

Fans had barely finished their gleeful celebration of the pass when the cannon-armed flinger struck again. From his own 35-yard line, Washington unleashed a long pass toward the end zone. In the end zone Sugarfoot Anderson, along with three Bulldogs defenders, leaped and reached for the high throw. When Anderson pulled down the football for a touchdown, bedlam broke out.

An astounded observer, Maxwell Stiles, assistant sports editor of the *Los Angeles Mirror*, raced from the press box to the field. Having made note of where Washington stood when he released the pass, Stiles marched off the distance the ball traveled in the air. It was 71 yards.

While Washington shone, Albert struggled. He completed just 2 of his 16 passes and left the game in the third quarter, injured, after being gang-tackled while trying to scoop up the football at his own 5-yard line.

Once the game ended, fans rushed onto the field and mobbed Washington. He fought to break away and celebrate his team's 24–7 win. Paul Schissler, the Hollywood coach, was a geyser of superlatives. "You can have Sammy Baugh, Harry Gilmer, Cecil Isbell, Sid Luckman, or any other passer you care to name but just give me Kenny Washington. I've watched Kenny for about 10 years as a fan and coach and I'll repeat what I've said before—he's the best!"[11]

Hollywood surged into first place a week later. Washington brought a near-capacity Gilmore Stadium crowd to its feet in the third quarter, when he followed a host of blockers into the end zone for a touchdown that brought Hollywood a 14–6 victory.

Barely three weeks after their first meeting, the schedule maker brought Hollywood and the Los Angeles Bulldogs, Kenny Washington and Frankie Albert, together again. Determined to rejoin the title pursuit, the

Bulldogs coaxed several players whose NFL seasons had ended to join their club. It only took 8 plays for the Bulldogs to score first. In the second quarter, they threatened to score again. With the Bulldogs at the Hollywood 6-yard line, a hard hit by Washington forced Albert to fumble. Washington recovered the football to stop the drive.

Washington was responsible for 2 Hollywood touchdowns. One was a 33-yard pass to Anderson. The other came on a 4-yard run. The 14 points from Washington's 2 touchdowns, however, were not enough. The Bulldogs celebrated revenge with a 17–14 triumph.

After a resounding 48–0 win over Oakland, Hollywood and their rivals, the Bulldogs, met one final time. For the Bears, the Pacific Coast Football League title was on the line. In the early minutes of the game, Hollywood's title hopes went from confident to questionable. On a pass attempt, Kenny Washington was smothered by several Bulldogs linemen. When the Bears' star player rose to his feet, he limped from the field with an injured left knee.

Minus Washington, Hollywood struggled to mount much of an attack. With just 5 seconds to play and the game tied, 10–10, Schissler resorted to desperate measures. He sent Washington back into the game with orders not to run, but to heave a long pass for the end zone. Washington complied. From the Hollywood 40-yard line, Washington fired the football 60 yards into the end zone, but the pass fell incomplete.

All was not lost, however. Mathematically the tie worked in Hollywood's favor. They finished the season with 1 win more than Oakland and thus earned the 1945 Pacific Coast Football League title.

Washington finished as the league's leading scorer with 65 points accrued from touchdowns, field goals, and points after touchdown. He was second in the league in rushing and third in passing yardage.

As rewarding as the statistical success and accompanying platitudes were, the knee injury he suffered was disconcerting. All-star game opportunities and, with it, the chance to make some extra money were now unlikely. There were concerns on the horizon for the future of the Pacific Coast Football League as well.

A new league was being formed out of Chicago. Its plans were to be nationwide in scope. Already a well-heeled investor was involved in negotiations to own a team in Los Angeles. Its presence could pull interest and damage the Bears and Bulldogs at the box office. Another team was planned for San Francisco.

Questions swirled over whether the proposed new league would provide the opportunity afforded Black players by the Pacific Coast Football

League. Rumors abounded that integration was very much a part of the proposed league's plan. In fact, to establish the league and put itself on solid footing, both of the California teams were said to have designs on landing one player in particular. A player who would generate attention and fan interest. Both of the new California teams wanted Kenny Washington.

16

THE JOIN JACKIE DILEMMA

Few could have guessed as they watched four men enter the office at 2101 Ontario Street East in the Canadian city of Montreal that their actions were about to cause the sort of change that would reverberate throughout baseball. A chill was in the air, not unusual for an October day in eastern Canada. On this Tuesday, October 23, 1945, actions of the four men would bring a chill to some who toiled in professional baseball and warm the hearts of many others.

Within the brick office at Delorimier Downs Stadium, Hector Racine, a bespectacled man of fifty-eight with thinning hair, impeccably dressed in a dark three-piece suit, sat beside a ballplayer. Contract papers were spread on the desktop before them. Leaning over the two as a photographer captured the moment were Branch Rickey Jr., head of the Brooklyn Dodgers' minor-league operations, and Lieutenant Colonel J. Romeo Gauvreau.

Only the day before, a Montreal newspaper with information of an important meeting at the stadium office guessed in print that the city may be gaining a major-league baseball team. When told the next day what the meeting was actually about, the reporter said with a sigh, "What's so big about that?"[1]

To many, the signing was, in fact, very big. The player whom Racine, the president of the Montreal Royals, and Gauvreau, his vice president, were signing was a Black man, Jack Roosevelt Robinson. The signing ceremony was orchestrated by Branch Rickey, president of the Brooklyn Dodgers. For three years at a cost of $25,000, Rickey had three of his scouts scour the American Negro Leagues as well as games in Mexico and Cuba in a search for the right player to break baseball's so-called color line. The scouts gave Rickey twenty-five names. From that effort, one player emerged in Rickey's eyes as the clear choice: Jackie Robinson.

It was actually almost two months earlier that a surprised Jackie Rob-inson accepted Rickey's summons and traveled to Brooklyn, New York. There in the Dodgers' Ebbets Field office, Robinson was taken aback to learn that Rickey was keen to sign him. The Dodgers' executive proposed Robinson spend the 1946 season in the minor leagues with Montreal, his club's top farm team. A bonus and salary were discussed, as was a deadline. If Robinson agreed to the momentous calling, he must sign a contract before November 1.

In Los Angeles, 2,500 miles away, news of Robinson's signing brought both elation and surprise. While Robinson's hometown paper, the *Pasa-dena Star-News*, and the *Los Angeles Times* trumpeted the news with large headlines, friends of the former UCLA standout were somewhat perplexed. "We would have thought a guy like Kenny would be more ideal because of his temperament. He was more self-contained. Jackie was so volatile," said Tom Bradley, a UCLA track and field teammate and friend of both men.[2]

Within baseball, reaction was mixed. For almost everyone agreeable to the move was another who was incensed by it. Noting that major-league All-Stars such as Bob Feller had played with and against Negro League players during fall and winter barnstorming tours, International League president Frank Shaughnessy said, "If it's all right for them to play with Negroes after the season is over then it's equally all right during the season."[3]

Former St. Louis Cardinal and Hall of Famer Rogers Hornsby, a Texan, said flatly the integration of baseball would not work. Charles Gra-ham, president of the minor-league San Francisco Seals, said, "Baseball is ready if the public is."[4] Scouts boasted with glee that top prospects from the Deep South would reject the Dodgers to avoid having to play on an integrated ballclub. Rival players criticized the Dodgers' president. "Rickey doesn't know how the 'southern boys' will take it," said Philadelphia pitcher Bobo Newsom.[5]

Fury erupted from at least one of the owners of Robinson's Negro League team, the Kansas City Monarchs. "We won't take it lying down," said T. Y. Baird, who added, "Robinson signed a contract with us last year and I feel he is our property."[6] It was a charge Rickey, a lawyer by trade, brushed aside. "They were not leagues at all," he said. "I failed to find a constitution, by-laws or a uniformed players contract, and I learned that players of all teams became free agents at the end of each season."[7]

Wendell Smith, sports editor of the *Pittsburgh Courier*, offered salve to Baird's wound. "Side tip to the Kansas City Monarchs: Kenny Washington, who was Jackie Robinson's teammate at UCLA is as good a ballplayer and maybe better than Robinson."[8] Unbeknownst to Washington, two very strong advocates were pushing on his behalf as well. The first man was Wendell Smith. The other was Jackie Robinson himself.

Weeks before Robinson signed with Montreal, Rickey confided the impending move to Smith. He had come to trust and respect the sportswriter. In fact, Rickey often sought Smith's insights about Negro League players. During their conversation, the Dodgers' president shared his plan to follow the Robinson signing with that of a second Black player, who would serve as teammate, roommate, and confidant at Montreal.

In the days after Robinson's signing was announced, Rickey received a letter from Smith. "I am suggesting that you consider very seriously the possibility of Kenny Washington, who was Jackie's team-mate at UCLA," Smith wrote, then added, "He is a much better ball player than Robinson."[9]

News of his historic signing made Jackie Robinson's world frenetic. His seventy-two hours after leaving the Montreal Royals' office were especially hectic. Radio stations and newspapermen sought interviews. There was packing to do. Robinson had to catch a flight to Miami. From there, he would travel to Venezuela to participate with a group of Negro League All-Stars in a two-month barnstorming tour. Afterward, Robinson would return home to Pasadena and marry his fiancée, Rachel Isum. Sunday, February 10, was circled on the calendar for their nuptials.

Somewhere in all of that, Robinson and Washington connected. The men hadn't spent much time together in the five years since UCLA. While Washington remained a fixture in Los Angeles, Robinson moved around the country. Pressed to financially support his mother, he left UCLA before graduating, first to take a government job, and then to play semipro football in Hawaii. When World War II broke out, he joined the army and for three years was posted at bases in Kansas, Texas, and Kentucky. Upon being discharged in 1944, Robinson accepted a job offer from his former pastor in Pasadena. The man had been made president of Samuel Huston College in Austin, Texas. He wanted Robinson to coach the basketball team and teach physical education. It was a role Robinson might have held on to for many years if only a chance encounter with a scout for the Kansas City Monarchs had not occurred. The Monarchs were training not far from the Huston College campus. Robinson was encouraged to try out for the team.

When the two spoke following Robinson's momentous signing, the subject of baseball was broached. Washington was told the Dodgers were going to sign a second Black player. The door was open, opportunity was there to pursue a long-held dream. Results of their conversation were bared when a reporter pressed Robinson about a subject he considered sensitive.

A small number of vocal Black critics of Robinson's defection from the Negro Leagues charged it would begin the league's demise. More big-league clubs, it was predicted, would follow suit and sign Negro League stars. In fact, just one day after the Dodgers announced Robinson's signing, the owner of the New York Giants, Horace Stoneham, declared his club would also sign Black players. Within the Negro Leagues, worry broke out at the prospect of losing popular players and what it would do to both the quality of play and fan interest.

Robinson was angered by the charge. "If I make good it will stimulate millions of colored boys to concentrate on baseball. I've made one convert already," he said. Robinson then confided who the convert was—Kenny Washington. "He is going to take his first serious crack at baseball next year."[10]

Washington never shied away from professing baseball to be his sport of choice. "I would like to have the opportunity to play organized base-ball," he shared in a conversation with *Pittsburgh Courier* writer Herman Hill. When asked about Robinson's claim that Washington would give up football for baseball and whether he might also sign with Montreal, Washington replied that his former UCLA teammate had been vague. "I don't know whether it was Jackie's idea, or somebody had instructed him to ask me."[11]

As calendar pages turned to reflect the arrival of 1946, Branch Rickey remained keen to find a second Black player who would play with Robinson in Montreal. Washington told friends that baseball scouts had contacted him. But for Washington, the timing was all wrong. Their inquiries came after Washington had received another offer, one that he had verbally agreed to accept. He said he could not in good conscience back out of the commitment. Asked about the interest of the baseball scouts, Washington told a reporter, "I answered no, because I had other plans."[12]

What Washington could not reveal was that he had agreed to sign a contract for the 1946 season. It was an agreement that left him unable to pursue professional baseball. He was about to become a pioneer as well.

17

CUTTING INTO HIS SKILLS

As reporters and photographers entered the room, they were about to witness professional football's entry into a new realm. For five months the game had been subject of a series of epic events, each one connected.

The first took place on the afternoon of September 1, 1945, when it was announced that several deep-pocketed businessmen—oil barons, lumber moguls, and industrialists—had formed a new football league, the All-America Football Conference.

In Cleveland, where the new AAFC team pried Paul Brown away from Ohio State, signings of Midwest college standouts by the new coach, obtaining a deal to play home games in the large Municipal Stadium, and the resulting enthusiasm from the public shot distress into the city's NFL team, the Cleveland Rams. On January 12, 1946, the Rams' owner, Dan Reeves, stood up at a meeting of the National Football League team owners and declared, "Gentlemen, I'm moving my club to Los Angeles."[1]

Barely seventy-two hours after the Rams' stunning announcement, the planned agenda for the Los Angeles Coliseum Commission's January 15, 1946, meeting underwent major revision. The nine commissioners had expected to discuss the price for new lights and review revenues and expenditures from a December high school football game. Instead, the agenda, and one man's agenda, would thrust Kenny Washington to the forefront and set the stage for change in the NFL.

When the clock struck 2:45, the Coliseum commission meeting was called to order. Never before had the nine commissioners and their attorney looked out at such a large gathering. The meeting room was packed beyond capacity. Reporters from seven Southern California newspapers sat alongside or close to Charles "Chile" Walsh, the general manager of the Rams.

Once the minutes of a previous meeting were put into the record, the subject of professional football became the topic. The first two who rose spoke of the benefits a National Football League team meant for Los Angeles. Chile Walsh stood next. A check for $5,000, a down payment on a portion of the stadium lease, was in the man's breast pocket. The Rams' general manager, a native of the area, formally expressed his team's wish to make the Coliseum its home field.

Opposition soon came in incendiary fashion and from an entirely unexpected source. Halley Harding made a request to speak. He introduced himself as editor of the *Los Angeles Tribune*, a weekly newspaper that served the African American community. Harding explained that editors of two other Black newspapers, the *Courier* and *Sentinel*, authorized him to speak on their behalf as well.

Harding began with the salutations of a polished public speaker. His compliments to the Hollywood Bears and Los Angeles Bulldogs, "who have players of all races and creeds on those teams," tipped everyone off to his objective.[2] Harding excoriated the NFL for its unwritten ban on Black players. He pointed out that the Coliseum was built with taxpayer money, and that Blacks were among those who paid taxes. Following his almost four-minute speech, Harding stated he was flatly against granting a lease to the Rams as long as they refused to integrate.

A clearly shaken Chile Walsh shot to his feet. "We have no rule prohibiting Negroes from playing in our league."[3] Walsh then declared, "Kenny Washington is welcome to try out for our team anytime he likes."[4] The discussion continued for several minutes before the commission tabled the agenda item with the promise to take the matter under advisement.

Walsh accepted an invitation to join Harding for cocktails at the Last Word Club on South Central Avenue. When the Rams' general manager arrived, he realized he had stepped into an ambush. Harding was in the company of a group of sportswriters, columnists, and editors, ten in all. The men represented newspapers and news services that served the Black community. They pressed Walsh to sign Kenny Washington. The men also touted two additional members of the Hollywood Bears for consideration, Woody Strode and Chuck Anderson. Walsh professed a sincere interest in Washington. He was adamant, however, that he would not sign Washington should he still be under contract to the Hollywood Bears.

The next morning Chile Walsh boarded the Super Chief at Union Station. His destination was his home in Cleveland. Reporters sought out the Hollywood Bears' business manager, Bill Schroeder, for clarification about Washington's contract. Schroeder said the Bears "very definitely" would not stand in Washington's way but would expect financial compensation for Washington's contract.[5]

In late February, with Chile Walsh still in Cleveland, questions about the sincerity of his promise soon appeared in newspapers. What no one knew, however, was that Walsh had directed the Rams' new publicist, Maxwell Stiles, to handle the matter clandestinely. First, Stiles secured an agreement with Paul Schissler to buy Washington's contract from the Hollywood Bears for $10,000. Next, Stiles met with Washington and his uncle Rocky. Talks were far from smooth. Washington was concerned he would be the only Black player the Rams signed. He threatened to play in the AAFC unless Woody Strode was given consideration. It was agreed the Rams would sign Strode.

Washington and the Rams then agreed to a salary of $12,500, second highest in the club to the $20,000 paid to the team's star quarterback, Bob Waterfield. With terms agreed, Stiles drove to Washington's home. As they gathered around the kitchen table, the player signed what was a historic contract. As Stiles prepared to leave the house, he requested one final agreement, that the two sides keep the deal quiet. The Rams wanted to break the news with a splash once Walsh returned from Cleveland.

On Thursday, March 21, 1946, reporters gathered at the ornate Hotel Alexandria in downtown Los Angeles. Little did most realize that this latest pro football announcement would be even more momentous than those that announced formation of the AAFC and the move of the first major-league team to play on the West Coast. As the men of the press entered the appointed room, there stood Kenny Washington, smartly dressed in a double-breasted suit and an unceasing smile. The National Football League was becoming the first major sports league to integrate.

Chile Walsh was effusive with praise. "In [Bob] Waterfield and Washington, the Rams will present two of the most valuable players in football today," he said. "I have heard many fine things about Washington, both as a player and as a man and I feel certain he will be a credit to our football club and to his race."[6]

News traveled quickly into newspaper newsrooms and radio station studios. When it reached Jackie Robinson in Florida, where he was training with the Montreal Royals, he gushed, "That's great! He's a great football player and Los Angeles will make a lot of money with him in the lineup. People will come from far and near to see him play."[7]

Newspaper columns carried a variety of perspectives. "Buster" Miller in the *New York Age* urged readers not to laud the Rams' altruism. Miller opined that the move to sign Kenny Washington "goes to show that box-office is a more potent opponent for Jim Crow than any other, and it really is remarkable how quickly team owners can shed their prejudices when it becomes financially advantageous to do so."[8] George T. Davis, sports editor of the *Los Angeles Herald Express*, wrote, "Kenny Washington's acceptance into the ranks of the National Football League is something that should have happened years ago just after this great player graduated with All-America honors from UCLA."[9] Claude Newman in the *Valley Times* noted that Washington "has more at stake in this than just a job to play professional football. He has the people of his race behind him, goading him on to prove to everyone that the Negro has his place in pro football just as he should have in organized baseball."[10]

Amid the celebration was a very portentous matter, one that loomed silently—Washington's fitness. The knee injury suffered in his final game with the Hollywood Bears was both significant and potentially debilitating. Dick Hyland of the *Los Angeles Times* wrote, "Washington's 'break' is coming five or six years too late. Washington has become a beaten-up ballplayer who is neither so strong nor so quick in his reactions as he was before the war. Kenny Washington will work his head off to prove this prediction wrong, and I hope he does."[11]

On April 11, less than four weeks after the celebrated announcement, Washington lay on a gurney being wheeled into the operating room at Cedars of Lebanon Hospital in Los Angeles. An examination revealed alarming severity to his injured knee. Surgery was urged and not just to one knee but to both.

Dr. Daniel Levinthal, a Beverly Hills surgeon with vast experience treating professional athletes, performed the procedures. The most severely damaged was Washington's left knee. It required removal of torn cartilage, a substantial procedure. Levinthal's work on Washington's right knee was far less invasive and involved removing a loose fragment. After the procedure concluded, Levinthal announced that things went well. "Derangement of the left knee was corrected," he said.[12] The surgeon pronounced Washington's condition "excellent." Recovery, he cautioned, would be extensive, involve a great deal of therapy, and take close to two months.

When Maxwell Stiles dropped by the hospital to visit Washington, the Rams' publicist was surprised by what he found. The newest member of the Rams had papers strewn about, each with diagrams of offensive plays. On his overbed table were eleven saltshakers. Washington would study the Xs and Os on a sheet of paper, then slide the saltshakers around the tabletop to replicate the plays. If Washington could not be out on the field learning the Rams' offense, then he would spend his recovery week in the hospital improvising in his hospital bed.

In May, Woody Strode secured his final discharge papers from the Army Air Corps. As promised, the Rams purchased Strode's contract from the Hollywood Bears and signed Washington's former UCLA and Hollywood teammate.

Six weeks before training camp was to begin, Washington embarked upon an arduous rehabilitation plan. One of the most strenuous facets involved a three-to-four-mile hike every other day in Baldwin Hills in south Los Angeles. There, Washington traversed trails that zigzagged past sagebrush and toyon bushes. He walked up the mountain and down into canyons. The first half of the hike gained 315 feet in elevation, and from the peak he could look out over Los Angeles. Washington's frequent one-hour hikes of the 500-foot-high mountain range helped rebuild the strength in his legs and expanded his stamina.

On the eve of training camp, Washington was confident. At a send-off party he encountered Stiles. "Max," he said, "if this operation is successful, I'll show them some football the National Football League has never seen before."[13]

Cameras clicked to capture the moment as Washington walked onto the campus of Compton College on Monday, July 29. He was one of thirty new players on a team of fifty-nine who would stroll onto the school grounds, be assigned a dormitory room, then meet with the Rams' equipment manager and be fitted for his helmet, pads, jersey, and pants. Compton College would be home for Washington and the Rams for a month as the team went through drills to prepare for its first exhibition game.

Adam Walsh had filled many of his summer months pondering. The Rams' head coach and brother of the general manager wondered how he would use Kenny Washington in his offense. He decided Washington would play quarterback, a position that would take advantage of his remarkable throwing arm and put less stress on recovering knees. The position decision did not eliminate Walsh's unease. At the root of his dilemma was the offense he ran, the T formation. It was less creative and more straightforward than the single wing that Washington operated from at UCLA and with the Hollywood Bears.

Unlike the single wing, in which the ball was snapped from center to a back 5 to 7 yards behind the line of scrimmage, the T formation was created to cut down on the fumbles that came from such a long snap. In the T formation, the quarterback crouched directly behind the center. He took a direct snap, then backpedaled to either hand off or pitch the football with an underhand toss to a back, or pivot and pass to a receiver.

The full-fledged start to training camp put Washington under intense scrutiny. It was noticeable to everyone that Washington favored his left leg. The right knee was sufficiently healed. Surgery on the left, however, had been more arduous. Washington moved about practice with a brace on his left knee. His running style was different to those who had watched him at UCLA or with the Hollywood Bears. He lacked his normal speed. The fluidity of his gait was replaced with jerkiness and trepidation.

For Kenny Washington, training camp was a plunge into one of the biggest challenges he had ever faced in the sport of football. Yes, there was the pressure of being a pioneer. But far more intensity involved mastering the transition to the quarterback position in the T-formation offense. No offense in the game could have been more diametrically different from what Washington was familiar with than the Rams' T formation. At UCLA and with the Hollywood Bears, the single wing showcased Washington's skills. The scheme had a creative aspect to it, one that gave a player like Washington many play options from which to choose, depending upon how the defense reacted.

Conversely, the T formation was technical. It required precision, strict adherence to sets, angles, and prescribed responsibilities. Where Washington previously enjoyed the ability to study a defense from a position 7 yards behind the line of scrimmage, now he had to make quick judgments from a crouched position directly behind the center. As a halfback, Washington moved in accordance with the reaction of the line, either straight forward, diagonally, or laterally. The quarterback, upon taking the snap from center, either backpedaled to prepare to pass or turned at a 45-degree angle, oblivious to the line play, as he made a handoff to a back.

Coaches at both the professional and collegiate level who implemented the T formation would quickly find that quarterback play was essential to the system's success. For a quarterback who had never operated in the T formation, there were coaches who suggested it could take as long as an entire year to master the offense.

For Washington, daily drills were arduous. It brought footwork and body positioning requirements that were entirely new. There were also nuances, sleight of hand tricks to master. While seemingly minuscule in nature, they were big in feature. Repetition was essential to instill timing, important to prevent collisions between quarterback and halfback in the backfield. Still, it was not uncommon for the quarterback and halfbacks to painfully knock knees should one or both take a wrong angle on a particular play.

Three days into camp, a drill was stopped. Washington was taken aside, and an intensive tutoring session broke out. Bob Snyder, the backfield coach, and Bob Waterfield gave Washington their sole attention to help him master faking handoffs, fooling defenders by palming the football, and the proper technique for flipping the ball to a back.

Washington couldn't have asked for better tutors. Snyder was widely regarded as both an excellent teacher of quarterbacks as well as for his expertise with the T-formation offense. During his playing days, Snyder was the backup to Sid Luckman on the Chicago Bears' 1940 championship team. He worked with the Bears' coach, George Halas, to develop the T formation. As a college assistant coach at Notre Dame, Snyder mentored Angelo Bertelli and Johnny Lujack, both of whom won the Heisman Trophy. On joining the Rams for the 1945 season, he was instrumental in Waterfield's development.

Washington saw the pluses and minuses to both offenses. "In the single wing you can get to going so much faster," he explained, "you get more room to run. In the 'T' the hole is there, then it isn't." But he appreciated that there was a smaller risk of injury in the T formation. "The defense doesn't get such a wide-open shot at the ball carrier because of the quick opening plays."[14]

It was ten days into training camp when Adam Walsh paired his team up for an intrasquad scrimmage. Waterfield was designated quarterback for the Blue unit, the first teamers, while Washington was assigned to quarterback the second unit, the Gold team. By the end of the session, it was Washington who stole the show. He rifled a pass 40 yards. Another covered 50. "Well, about three of those a game and we'll stay right where we are now, champions," said Adam Walsh.[15] The highlight of the day was a naked reverse, in which Washington completely fooled the defense and would have had 60 yards of open running room in front of him had it been a real game rather than a controlled scrimmage.

Over the next two days Washington basked in platitudes. Adam Walsh praised his rookie quarterback. The coach declared that Washington's knee was recovering better than expected. That, however, is when trouble struck. It happened during a drill. Washington took a snap from center and began to pivot when the long cleats on his black high-top football shoe caught in the grass. Pain shot through his left knee.

At first it was assumed Washington had aggravated the old injury. There was also the thought pain could be from scar tissue. Washington resumed training. Forty-eight hours later, he was checked by his surgeon, who was alarmed by what he discovered. Washington's left knee was badly swollen. Dr. Levinthal ordered Washington back to the hospital. An infection was diagnosed. Fluid was drained, two ounces in all. Total bed rest for forty-eight hours was prescribed. As for a return to practice, Levinthal declared, "Until the scar tissue heals sufficiently, he must have no contact work."[16]

Looming was the Rams' first exhibition game, a ballyhooed meeting in Chicago with the College All-Stars. Washington had been prominent in local promotion of the game. The day before the Rams were to board a train for Chicago, Dr. Levinthal told Washington, as well as Chile and Adam Walsh, that he considered the knee healed and ready for game conditions.

Like the arrival of longer days and warmer weather in the spring and colorful leaves in fall, the College All-Star Game was a symbol. For football fans, the annual meeting of top college stars and the NFL champions marked the beginning of football season. On this night, however, the game was different and meant far more than its previous twelve editions. To many, the 1946 game represented a return to normalcy following four years of war. Among the 13 million African Americans thoughout the country, the game signified something else entirely—change and opportunity. A Black man was about to play, at long last, for a team in the NFL.

In all, 97,380 fans would pack the stadium. Among the throng were fathers and sons, coaches and players, and such heads of industry as Frank McCaffery of International Harvester and Sewell Avery of Montgomery Ward. The commissioner of baseball, "Happy" Chandler, ushered in his two sons. George Halas treated his Chicago Bears players to tickets. More than 4,000 wounded soldiers and sailors received seats from a charity. Those without tickets as kickoff approached were left to the dilemma of whether to listen to the game on radio or pay a price five times face value from scalpers who hawked extra tickets outside the stadium.

City leaders boasted that one-third of the fans traveled from out of town, arriving by train, car, or air. One, Carl Nordblom, hitchhiked 460 miles from Pittsburgh just to see the game.

Two days earlier when the Rams stepped off a train from Los Angeles, photographers were on the platform at Dearborn Station to snap pictures when the players disembarked. As luggage and equipment were gathered, Rams coach Adam Walsh surprised Washington and Strode when he handed each $100 with instructions to go and find their own accommodations. The inference was that the grandiose Stevens Hotel on Michigan Avenue, where the Rams would headquarter, would not accept Black guests.

The players made off to the Pershing Hotel on Chicago's South Side. There, Washington and Strode stepped into a slice of nirvana. The sting of being unable to stay with their teammates was eased somewhat by a building that housed Chicago's biggest diner and its largest beauty parlor and magnet for the women of the neighborhood. In the basement of the hotel was Budland, one of Chicago's hottest jazz clubs. It just so happened that on that night, none other than the incomparable Count Basie and his band were on the bill.

When nightfall turned Chicago's South Side from sunlit to neon illuminated, Washington and Strode made their way to Budland. It was while the two men listened to music and nursed Tom Collinses that they were surprised to see Bob Waterfield and five Rams teammates enter the club. Waterfield eagerly announced that Washington and Strode could stay at the team's hotel across town. Strode waved an arm, pointed out an array of beautiful women, along with Count Basie and his band. Washington laughed that being separate from the rest of the team meant the coach's 10:30 p.m. curfew couldn't be enforced. "You sons of bitches," Waterfield said with a laugh. "You're living good."[17]

Once the clock struck 8:30 on game night, the much-anticipated event kicked off. The largest radio audience outside of a presidential address listened to Harry Wismer describe the action on a network of 325 stations throughout America and via shortwave hookup to military bases in Europe and Asia. It did not take long for those listeners or the fans in the stands to realize the Rams were but a shell of their 1945 championship team. The defections of offensive linemen to the AAFC corroded the strength of the team's attack. Waterfield was put under relentless pressure. The running game could not get into gear. Midway through the first quarter, Elroy "Crazy Legs" Hirsch of the College All-Stars took the ball around left end and broke loose on an electrifying 68-yard touchdown run. Each failed offensive possession by the Rams brought cries of Washington's name from the stands.

Throughout the first half the Rams' defense kept them in the game. The All-Stars were unable to add to their tally once halftime arrived. In the third quarter, however, the collegians struck again. This time it came through the air in spectacular fashion. The All-Stars had the ball at their own 38-yard line. As Hirsch sprinted down the sideline, the All-Stars' quarterback, Otto Graham, looked to his left and lofted a high-arcing pass. The crowd erupted with a mighty roar as Hirsch caught the pass over his right shoulder at full gallop. He won the footrace with a Rams defender over the final 18 yards to score the game's second touchdown and boost the All-Stars' lead to 14–0.

For the Rams, a night that quickly stepped into a realm of frustration sank into an abyss of embarrassment. Incomplete passes, interceptions, stuffed run plays, and fumbles were hardly the kind of play associated with professional football champions, particularly against an opposition of recent college players. Adam Walsh began to unload his bench.

Cries from the stands for Kenny Washington continued. They were finally answered in the fourth quarter. With 5 minutes left in the game, Walsh sent an offensive unit onto the field that included Washington and Strode. The ovation grew loud when fans recognized that Washington was in for Waterfield at quarterback. On his first play from scrimmage, a pass play was called. Washington scanned the field but found no receiver open. He saw a gap between his left tackle and guard. Alertly tucking the football, Washington darted through the hole. By the time defenders captured him, he had gained 10 yards and put the ball at the 30-yard line. Evidence, however, of Washington's physical condition was clear for all to see. As he rose after being tackled, the new Ram limped back to the team's huddle.

Desperate to score, the Rams were in need of a big play, the kind their offense had failed to produce all night. Time was not on their side. On his second play, Washington found Strode in the clear downfield. He lofted a long looping pass, the kind that had produced so much excitement with the Bulldogs and Bruins. As fast as Strode churned, he was unable to reach the throw, which fell incomplete. On third down, again Washington put the football in the air. He rifled a bullet down the middle of the field, but either by a play-calling mix-up or missed assignment, nobody was near the football as it whistled past and fell to the turf untouched.

Washington's second series came with just over a minute to play in the game. The Rams inherited the ball in a precarious spot, at their own 13-yard line. A pass play was called, but the worst possible thing happened—a bad snap from center. Washington flubbed the football. As he struggled to get a firm grasp on the ball, a defender shoved him backward into the end zone. Washington lost his balance and fell toward the turf. As he did, the football shot from his hand. A frantic race for the ball ensued. Washington quickly spun to his right and crawled on his belly in pursuit of the loose ball. A defender dove to try and beat Washington to it. The tweet of the referee's whistle awarded 2 more points to the College All-Stars. The safety was the final points of the game, which the college standouts won, 16–0.

Once the game had ended, more than 500 sportswriters pecked and pounded typewriters in the press box. None in the large reporting pool typed words more poignant than Wendell Smith:

Football history was made when Washington and Strode came into the game with five minutes to play. It marked the first time that Negro players have played in the All-Star game with the professional team against the collegians.[18]

As he entered his first season in the National Football League, Washington was carrying more than just a football each time he ran. As one writer noted, he was carrying the banner for his entire race. How Washington performed and the way he went about it would dictate the receptiveness that team owners, general managers, and coaches would have toward giving opportunities to more Black players in seasons to come.

18

DAWN OF A NEW DAY

It was 2:30 on the afternoon of September 29, 1946. At that moment, the referee looked up from his wristwatch and blew hard into his whistle. Following the shrill sound, a brown leather football hurtled end over end toward the east end zone of the Los Angeles Memorial Coliseum. The crowd of just over 30,000 fans let out a cheer. High above the playing surface, in a broadcast booth in the press box, the baritone voice of Bob Kelley described the kickoff return to listeners on KMPC radio.

The moment was significant. It represented both a historic beginning and, before the game was done, an important end. Kickoff did not just begin the 1946 National Football League season; it marked the official arrival of major-league sports on the West Coast. Geographic relocation brought change to the game. For the transplanted Rams and their opponent, the Philadelphia Eagles, playing in sweltering 96-degree weather in late September was also something completely foreign.

It was 38 minutes into the game when the ending occurred, an end to a dubious practice within the National Football League. It was brought about by a play that changed the Rams' fortunes in the game. Throughout the first half of play, Bob Waterfield was masterful. The Rams' quarterback deftly carved up the Eagles' defense. He drove the Rams 75 yards in the first quarter, almost all of it amassed on his passing. By halftime he had completed 6 of 9 passes thrown, and the Rams sat on a 14–6 lead.

In the early moments of the third quarter, Waterfield dropped back to pass. To his left and unrecognized, the Eagles' 250-pound lineman "Bucko" Kilroy charged past his blocker. With no one to slow his path, Kilroy smashed Waterfield to the turf. The Rams' star was slow to get up and groggy once he did. The grimace on his face told coaches on the sideline all they needed to know. Adam Walsh summoned Waterfield's backup.

Figure 18.1   Washington brought an end to segregation in the NFL when he joined the Los Angeles Rams for the 1946 season. *Photo courtesy of Vic Stein,* Herald-Examiner *collection, Los Angeles Public Library*

From the press box, Bob Kelley chattered into the microphone that Bob Waterfield was injured and leaving the field. Kenny Washington was going into the game.

Once Washington reached the huddle, an abhorrent practice was officially abolished. Not since November 30, 1933, when Joe Lillard left the field at Wrigley Field following the Chicago Cardinals game with the Chicago Bears, had a man of Washington's race appeared in an official National Football League game. Twelve seasons of exclusion, a policy long denied but in plain view for all to see, criticized yet rebuffed, was now disposed of. Football had done what no other big-league sport yet dared to do. Integrate. Neither baseball, nor basketball, nor even ice hockey had yet put a Black man on its playing surface.

Washington repeatedly brought his teammates to the line of scrimmage. He barked signals with confidence. Walsh didn't want Washington running lest he reinjure his knee. It brought a cheer from the crowd when Washington hit Jim Benton with a pass that gained 19 yards. But for the most part, Washington's throws sailed high, whether rushed by oncoming defenders, anxiousness, or a passing technique put awry by pain from his injured left knee.

The Rams' offense soon bogged down. Philadelphia's caught fire. Two scoring tosses gave the Eagles a lead. With his team trailing, 23–14, in the final minute of play, Washington dropped back in his own end zone to throw a long desperation pass. As he stepped back, his right foot crossed over the back line. It gave Philadelphia 2 more points via a safety and made the final score 25–14.

Consternation coursed through the team in the days that followed. The Rams once again were beset by injuries. The shortage of players made Walsh tinker. His tinkering was done with Kenny Washington in mind, specifically moving him to fullback. It was two weeks, and only after beating the Green Bay Packers in their second game, then tying the Chicago Bears, when Washington debuted at the new position against the Detroit Lions. When he trotted onto the field no introduction was needed. A loud roar from the crowed drowned out sound that burst from the stadium's speakers.

In the second quarter, Washington caught a pass from Jim Hardy, then eluded Detroit defenders for a 36-yard gain. In the stands, Chile Walsh hollered, "Look at that boy run, and he's only got one leg!"[1] In the final minutes of the third quarter, the Rams recovered a fumble on the Detroit 14-yard line. Bob Waterfield returned to the field and called Washington's number on 3 successive plays. The first gained 10 yards. The second put the football at the 3-yard line. That's when Washington took a handoff from Waterfield, then followed his center into the end zone for his first touchdown in the National Football League.

In the aftermath of the Rams' 35–14 victory, statistics showed Washington was the team's leading rusher, with 49 yards on 8 carries. Moreover, local newspapers were awash with superlatives. Bob Hoenig wrote in the *Hollywood Citizen-News*, "He is the rave of the town—and in L.A. that's quite a trick."[2] The *Los Angeles Daily News* praised, "Kenny gave every indication he is regaining his old pigskin prowess."[3] Bigger yet was the praise from his head coach. "I believe he can become one of the greatest fullbacks in National Football League history if his knees hold out," Walsh said.[4]

A week later in Chicago against the Cardinals, Washington was even better. The Rams used him as a receiver out of the backfield. He repeatedly caught short passes, then used his speed and elusiveness to add on more yardage. His first catch produced an 11-yard gain; then another went for 13. Washington extended the drive with a catch, then picked up 8 more via the run. It was after he caught still another short pass, then turned it into another 13-yard gain, that 38,180 Comiskey Park fans rose to give him a standing ovation. It was a lone bright light in a 34–10 Rams defeat.

As quickly as excitement at Washington's successes swelled, it burst. On a run in the second half, Washington had just managed to evade a defender, then pushed another aside with a stiff arm when suddenly a tackler from his blind side blasted him. Not only did Washington have pain in his bad knee, but the force from the hit left the metal knee brace he wore mangled. As a result, Washington never got into the game a week later in Detroit and only sparingly against the Chicago Bears in the Coliseum.

When the Rams landed in Boston for their game with the Boston Yanks, reporters staked out their arrival. A few were keen to ask Bob Waterfield about rumors that he and his wife, the actress Jane Russell, were separating. "There's absolutely no truth in it," the quarterback snapped.[5] Roger Birtwell of the *Boston Globe* sought out Kenny Washington, but not to talk about football. Birtwell was anxious for Washington's response to a story that had broken in Los Angeles, spawned by the manager of the Brooklyn Dodgers, Leo Durocher.

Earlier in the week, Durocher was in Los Angeles to appear on a radio program hosted by the comedian Jack Benny. His arrival sparked interest among reporters, who were out to confirm the real reason for his trip to Los Angeles. Reports of a romance with the married actress Laraine Day had been fodder for gossip columnists and reporters. When Day met Durocher at the Burbank airport, salacious headlines followed in many of the city's newspapers the next morning.

Romance and celebrity were the last things John B. Old wanted to speak with Durocher about. The *Los Angeles Herald-Express* sportswriter wanted to talk baseball, specifically Jackie Robinson. He learned that

Durocher would be at the Brown Derby for a party hosted by Benny. Old dropped by the celebrity mecca on the off chance he could score an interview with the Dodgers' manager.

When Benny's get-together broke up, Old approached Durocher. The sportswriter asked about the Dodgers' plans for Robinson in 1947. "My guess is that he'll make the grade," Durocher replied.[6] He further regaled Old with insights about the upcoming season, told of the Yankees' pursuit of him as manager, and plans for his coaching staff. Then, Durocher dropped a bombshell. He revealed that the Brooklyn Dodgers were going to sign Kenny Washington.

By the time Old's story broke, Kenny Washington was on an airplane. The Los Angeles Rams were on a twenty-hour journey through New York City on their way to Boston. Once inside the terminal at LaGuardia Field, Washington was recognized by newspaper columnist Lou Swarz. The woman approached both him and Woody Strode. When the Rams' publicist, Maxwell Stiles, saw the conversation taking place, he moved to intercede. As Stiles got within earshot, he soon realized Swarz, who merely dabbled as a columnist for the *New York Age* when not performing her one-person show around the country, was simply engaged in idle chitchat with the two.

By the time the Rams arrived in Boston, the *Los Angeles Times*, *Sentinel*, and *California Eagle* had run with their own versions of Durocher's comments. Roger Birtwell caught up with Washington and asked if he had the opportunity to play professional baseball. The Rams' fullback replied that yes, he had talked with Jackie Robinson recently. Baseball was indeed part of their discussion but, Washington said, no offer was discussed, suggested, or even hinted at.

The conversation between Washington and Robinson that was referred to happened ten days earlier. Washington was one of a trio of keynote speakers to heap platitudes at a testimonial banquet. No sooner had Robinson returned to Pasadena after winning the International League batting title with a .349 average and helping Montreal win the Little World Series when the Men's Club of the Scott Methodist Church announced plans for the event.

The Thursday night affair brought several hundred friends, family members, and enthusiastic Pasadenans. City leaders lavished praise on Robinson. He in turn credited his mother's letters for giving him strength and praised his wife, Rachel, for giving him courage. Robinson told of his first road trip to Baltimore, a city south of the Mason–Dixon Line, the demarcation line that separated free states from slave states and in 1946 the states with and without segregation laws. "The fans were hostile, and I got a good going over," Robinson said. "My wife was along on the trip, and that night in our room she cried. She wanted me to quit. I will say I never heard anything worse thrown at me on that first trip than I did in college football."[7]

For Washington, the talk about playing professional baseball was in no way indicative of dissatisfaction with his football employer. "I like playing with the Rams," he said. "It's pretty tough in this league. When those linemen hit you, they aren't fooling. They play for keeps."[8]

Yet, as it had since his youth, baseball continued to gnaw at Washington. He yearned to play professionally. Throughout the winter of 1946–1947, rumors of Washington joining the Dodgers continued to persist. John B. Old's story was carried nationally by *Sporting News*. In December, *Pittsburgh Courier* sports editor Wendell Smith, who had a direct pipeline to Branch Rickey, reported an imminent signing:

> You can expect an announcement any day now that Kenny Washington of the Los Angeles Rams football team has been signed by the Brooklyn Dodgers and will probably be assigned to Montreal for the 1947 season.[9]

Sam Lacy, the sports editor for the *Baltimore Afro-American*, reported virtually the same thing less than a month later.

In Boston, Washington played sparingly in a 40–21 loss to the Boston Yanks in Fenway Park. He carried the football 3 times and gained 30 yards. A week later he spent the afternoon on the bench as the Rams walloped the New York Giants, 31–21, at the Polo Grounds. Washington also sat out the season finale, a 38–17 win over Green Bay.

Four months after the football season, the question of whether the Rams would have Kenny Washington for 1947 or lose him to baseball was answered. Leo Durocher was in the Dominican Republic. Laraine Day, who had received a Mexican divorce and married Durocher in Mexico, was sunning with another actress and baseball fan, Gail Patrick. Patrick was a part owner of the minor-league Hollywood Stars. The subject of Kenny Washington playing baseball was raised. "I know all about Kenny," Patrick said. "I've seen him on various sets from time to time. They tell me he was as good a baseball player as Jackie [Robinson]. Too bad his knees are shot."[10] Durocher was more succinct. "His knee was on the bum."[11] The Dodgers would not be signing him.

19

LIKE OLD TIMES

The man paced the playing field. A widow's peak and receding hairline belied his age, thirty-three, young for one of his position. Stern of features, the tenor of a voice that barked commands confirmed a passion for the game of football. When he addressed people, be they players or sportswriters, the word "brother" became a title. "Don't try to do too much today," the man barked. "The most stupid thing you could do would be to pull a muscle."[1]

Bob Snyder represented change to the Los Angeles Rams. Training camp opened eight months after the disappointing 1946 season ended. The Rams' failings spawned turmoil at the top. A 6–4–1 record was considered to be a huge letdown following a championship campaign. It spun change. Adam Walsh resigned as the team's head coach.

It was six weeks later that Bob Snyder was elevated from his role as backfield coach to head coach. A day later, Chile Walsh resigned as general manager. His relationship with the Rams' owner, Dan Reeves, was hopelessly mired in acrimony, fractured by disagreement over who had the final say on player decisions and the hiring and firing of a coach.

As Snyder navigated the fifty-six players on the practice field of Loyola University, he carried with him optimism. It came from what he saw on this first day of preseason drills. As the players completed wind sprints, the coach couldn't help but smile when he saw who crossed the finish line ahead of his teammates. He saw a player who cavorted about on a football field like his old self again. He saw the Kenny Washington he had heard so much about when he arrived with the Rams from Cleveland.

During the spring and summer months that followed the 1946 season, Kenny Washington embarked upon an arduous quest to rebuild himself. He played countless games of handball at the police academy with Bob

Waterfield, convinced the quick starts and stops of the game would help him regain his ability to accelerate swiftly and change direction quickly on a football field. Almost every day for seven months, Washington pedaled myriad miles on an exercise bike. He took up golf. Low scores satiated a competitive ego. The miles Washington walked on the course proved far more important, for they served to further strengthen his legs. In the spring, Washington rejoined the police department baseball team. In a game against his alma mater, he clubbed a 420-foot home run off UCLA's best pitcher. In the evening he would meet up with Waterfield at a local park. Occasionally, teammates would join to run pass routes and sharpen their execution of run plays.

Through it all, Washington was keen to test his knee under intense football competition. He was anxious to learn the results of his hard work. With the Rams' approval, Washington suited up with the UCLA football team for its spring practice. He played in the Bruins' spring game. He insisted there was no pain. He was also able to accelerate and cut in ways that encouraged him.

Preparing for the season was not all that consumed Kenny Washington's time. A return to motion pictures also became part of his spring. In early April, Washington received an invitation to test for a part in a 20th Century Fox motion picture. The project was *Foxes of Harrow*, an adaptation of a novel set in pre–Civil War New Orleans. The director, John Stahl, liked Washington's screen test and hired him for the role of Achille, a plantation slave owned by a New Orleans gambler, the film's star, Rex Harrison. Filming took place in May and June.

Throughout the summer, Washington's grueling exercise routine carried with it an ominous partner—impendance. Three months after the 1946 season concluded, Washington and the Rams sat down to talk contract. Dan Reeves made it clear that while he wanted Washington back, he did not want the battered, minimally productive player of 1946. Washington had to be healthy and had to play better, or there was no place for him on the roster. The Rams' owner issued a proposal—a raise. It was a bonus actually, payable only if Washington was fit and able to play in the season opener, September 29, in Pittsburgh. In the event Washington was injured and unable to contribute to the team, he would agree to step away from football and retire. The two sides shook hands in agreement.

That contract stipulation made Washington the talk of camp once preseason drills began. Writers who considered Washington's 1946 play to be proof he was washed up questioned whether he would make the team. To Bob Snyder there was no question. The new Rams' coach was a Kenny

Washington fan, sold on the fullback by the flashes he had seen a year before. "He was only of use to us for about five minutes all season long. But in those five minutes he showed enough as a ballcarrier to convince me that all that had been said about him was pretty much the truth."[2]

It was during Washington's physical that he first raised training camp eyebrows. As the doctor slid the weight from side to side and balanced the bar, he called out Washington's weight, 203 pounds. It was clear to teammates and coaches just with the naked eye that Washington's summer workouts had made him not only heavier but stronger too.

Once noncontact drills faded, intense hitting began. Then players were put through controlled scrimmages. Washington proved his mettle. He ran like in the heralded Kingfish days at UCLA and with the Hollywood Bears and not in the tentative style of his rookie season with the Rams. A week prior to the Rams' first exhibition game, a public intrasquad game was planned for Gilmore Stadium. Fans were encouraged to select the backfield starters for the Gold and Blue teams. Washington finished a narrow second to Jim Hardy in voting for the Gold team quarterback.

Before more than 10,000 fans, the two Rams squads generated a high-scoring, wide-open offensive thriller. In the final quarter, it was Kenny Washington who produced the play of the night. With the Gold team trailing by a touchdown, Jim Hardy sent Washington on a pass route toward the end zone. The quarterback led his intended receiver. Washington went into a full dive and caught the football in the end zone. While fans cheered and teammates celebrated, Washington lay unconscious. After snaring the football, he had slid across the grass and slammed his head against the hard metal barricade from the auto racetrack that encircled the field.

From his seat in the stands, Washington's uncle Rocky realized what had happened. He ran onto the field and applied ice to his nephew's head. Amid the concern and confusion, Washington's teammates missed the extra point and lost the game, 35–34.

A crowd of almost 81,000 roared its delight when, in their first exhibition game, Washington bulled over several linemen to score a touchdown in the Rams' 20–7 win over the Washington Redskins. Snyder used Washington through almost the entirety of the game, both on defense and offense. The next day, however, Washington returned to the hospital. It was determined surgery was needed to remove a bone spur from his knee. Recovery would keep him out of the team's three remaining exhibition games.

While Washington recovered, his best friend Woody Strode was released by the Rams. The move meant Washington would be the lone Black player with the Rams and in the National Football League in 1947.

The Rams, minus Washington, traveled to the Midwest, where they trounced the Boston Yankees, 24–0, in a driving rainstorm in Des Moines, Iowa. Then three nights later they clobbered the Detroit Lions in Indianapolis, Indiana, 31–0. After a physically drained team took a 30–13 beating at the hands of the New York Giants, Bob Snyder stood before his players and apologized for scheduling three games in eight days.

Washington boarded an American Airlines flight and joined his teammates in Pittsburgh for their season opener. On a Monday night, September 29, he displayed the skills that Snyder and his coaching staff had heard so much about. In the second quarter, Washington took a lateral from Bob Waterfield, darted around right end, and dashed 9 yards into the end zone for a touchdown. In the fourth quarter he took a handoff and followed his left guard for 6 yards into the end zone to cap a 48–7 Rams win.

The following Sunday in Green Bay, Washington received his first NFL start. He was the top Rams rusher, amassing 54 yards on 9 carries. But late in the game as he tried to fight his way into the end zone, a Packer defender punched the football from Washington's arm. Green Bay recovered the fumble and after the final gun celebrated a 16–14 win as Washington wept in the Rams' locker room and blamed himself for the loss.

While Washington drew praise for his return to form, few knew that it came at a price. In both games his body was battered. A malicious hit in the Pittsburgh game left Washington with a sprained finger, which gave him trouble securing the football. During the week that followed the Green Bay loss, the Rams readied for their game with Detroit in Ann Arbor, Michigan. But while the players practiced daily, Washington was, instead, in a hospital.

During the Green Bay game, he was kicked in the face and briefly knocked cold. In the days that followed, his eyesight was askew and he suffered from a persistent headache. Doctors traced the trouble to nerve damage. Washington first incurred the problem when he slammed into the metal guardrail in Gilmore Stadium and was knocked unconscious during the Rams' intrasquad game. The kick to the face in Green Bay exacerbated the problem.

When the Rams took the field for their 1947 home opener, a crowd that numbered 69,631 cheered from the stands. The turnstile count was an NFL single-game attendance record. Across the field from the Rams' sideline, the Chicago Cardinals were being hailed as the best in team history.

It was in the second quarter that a vaunted Cardinals defense was sheared by Washington. The Rams had recovered a fumble on the Cardinals 31-yard line. On the first play of their offensive possession, Waterfield turned to his right and shoveled the football toward Washington. Before he could reach the line of scrimmage, a Cardinals defender had a clear shot at him. Washington lowered his left shoulder and knocked the pursuer away. The blow made Washington stumble. He steadied himself with a hand to the back of a blocker. As he reached the 25, another Cardinal came across the field. But as he reached out and attempted to wrap his arms around Washington, the Rams' runner used a hip fake to free himself. At the 10 another Cardinal began his reach when Washington angled to his left and escaped harm. To the howls of the fans, Washington again angled to his left and crossed the goal line for the game's first touchdown.

The Rams' second touchdown was set up by a punishing block by Washington. The team built on the 2-touchdown advantage and won, 27–7. The Rams were lauded about town for a successful start to the season. The record of 3 wins against 1 loss put the team in first place in the Western Conference. Accompanying praise for the team were accolades for Washington. Through 4 games he had 4 touchdowns and averaged 7.47 yards every time he carried the football.

Critics who painted Washington negatively in 1946 were chastised. Bob Hoenig of the *Hollywood Citizen-News* took a particularly hard shot. "Critics lined up on opposite sides of a verbal battle, a number of them proclaiming loud and long that 'Kenny Washington is through!' They were right! Kenny Washington is through—through with permitting anyone to doubt his greatness."[3]

A journey to Philadelphia created a matchup of the two leading rushers in the National Football League, Washington and the Eagles' Steve Van Buren. The pairing helped to lure an overflow crowd of 38,903, the biggest in Eagles history, into Shibe Park. While the throng came to cheer star rushers, defense hogged the limelight.

Philadelphia carried a 14–0 lead into the fourth quarter when the Rams got the football on a turnover in Eagles territory. A 20-yard run by Washington put the football at the 4-yard line. Washington took in a short pass from Waterfield but was stopped at the 1. It took 2 tries, but Wayne Hoffman punched the football across the goal line to cut the gap to 14–7.

A later Rams drive was stopped inside the 5-yard line, and the 14–7 score became the final. A small consolation was Washington's rushing duel with Van Buren. Washington and the Rams gained almost three times the yards that Van Buren and the Eagles gained.

Headlines trumpeting Washington's resurgence greeted the Rams' arrival in Chicago. Words like "dangerous" and "nightmare" were bandied about to describe his play through the first half of the season. There was no mistaking the mood during the week. Everyone felt it. This was a grudge game. The Cardinals were out for revenge, keen to reverse the defeat they were handed by the Rams in Los Angeles two weeks before.

The animosity, if not the talent on the field, put fans in almost every one of Comiskey Park's 47,000 seats. Once 1:30 in the afternoon and kick-off arrived on November 2, cool, crisp, ideal football weather painted the double-decked stadium. Through the first 10 minutes of the game, neither team was able to score. It was the Cardinals who were first to make the home crowd stir. They put together a drive that punched inside the Rams 10-yard line and threatened to score. Just as quickly as anxiousness rose, calamity struck the Cardinals. A handoff was fumbled. The football was recovered by the Rams, who took over possession at their own 8-yard line.

The Rams were in a perilous position, and their first play call seemed inauspicious. On first down, Waterfield pivoted to his left and shoveled the football to Washington. With a quick jab step, the Rams' back cut through a seemingly invisible hole between his left tackle and guard. Just beyond the line of scrimmage, two Cardinal defenders lunged. Both appeared to wrap arms around Washington's hips, only for the back to find a higher gear and leave the defenders flailing at air. Once in the open field, Washington veered to his left, toward the east sideline. By now every one of the 40,575 fans realized something extraordinary was unfolding. As Washington neared the Cardinals 22-yard line, three pursuers closed. He paused, turned his body 45 degrees to the right, and by running sideways, parallel to the sideline, made two of the defenders run by him and miss. The last pursuer was the Cardinals' fastest defensive back. As he closed, Washington thrust out his right arm and with a powerful stiff arm knocked the defender to the turf.

All about Comiskey Park astonishment mixed with awe as Washington crossed the goal line, 92 yards from where the play began. Ed Champagne, the Rams' rookie defensive tackle and a southerner from Louisiana, leaped from the bench with glee. When he landed, he came down awkwardly and injured his knee. George Trafton, the Rams' line coach, was dumbfounded by what he witnessed. He called the hole Washington ran through "no bigger than my car key," then added, "He's the greatest football runner I've ever seen."[4] The play was historic, the longest touchdown run from scrimmage in Rams history. It was a record that would stand for decades.

In the game's final minutes, the Rams' pursuit of a comeback was spitefully foiled. It happened on an innocent play. Washington carried the football and picked up a small gain. After he was brought down, a trio of

Cardinals piled on after the referee's whistle had blown. A penalty flag was thrown. But in the heap, one or more of the Cardinal defenders maliciously wrenched Washington's left leg and sent him limping off the field in pain.

In the locker room after the game, the injury and a 17–10 loss dampened exuberance over Washington's record run. That he had run for 146 yards and was the leading rusher in the Western Division, second to Steve Van Buren in the entire NFL, was not celebrated. Concern for Washington's injury was ominous. The team doctor feared the back might miss the team's next 3 games. "It's terrible. Things couldn't be worse," said the Ram's owner, Dan Reeves.[5]

With his team fighting to remain in the championship chase, Washington pleaded to play the following week. He begged for an injection of Novocain, but Snyder would hear none of it. "He has more guts than most players I can recall having seen or known," the Rams' coach said.[6] With Washington sidelined, the Boston Yanks sent the Rams to their third consecutive defeat, 27–16.

All of the strong play that fueled the Rams to 3 wins in their first 4 games and a spot atop the conference had long since crumbled amid a hail of injuries and inconsistent play. When the team exited the dugout at Wrigley Field in Chicago for its eleventh game of the season, 3 losses in their previous 6 games had dropped them toward the bottom of the division standings. Their opponents, the Bears, now occupied the penthouse in those standings, and the odds in the game did not favor the Rams.

Rain and a muddy field curtailed any offensive outbursts. By the fourth quarter, it was still anybody's game. With the Rams trailing, 14–10, Snyder sent Washington on. In 5 plays they charged 75 yards upfield. Washington's 11-yard scamper gave the Rams a first down at the Bears 20-yard line. One play later, Bob Waterfield fired a touchdown pass, and the Rams pulled out a 17–14 victory.

It was a sparse crowd that filed into the Coliseum for the Rams' final game of the 1947 season. Rather than the playoffs, the Rams sought a win to give them an equal number of wins and losses. Big plays, a 66-yard punt runback by Fred Gehrke, and a 60-yard touchdown pass from Jim Hardy to Gehrke put the Rams on top, 24–10, at halftime. In the second half, a special play drawn up by Snyder was called. It was straight out of the single-wing playbook, a direct snap to Washington at left halfback. He shot past the right guard, then scampered 23 yards into the end zone to cap a 34–10 Rams win.

Though his playing time was depleted by injuries, Washington finished fourth in the league in yards rushing. He carried the football 60 times

Figure 19.1   Washington was in demand to speak at banquets, appear at boxing matches, and even judge beauty pageants. *Photo courtesy of Ted Merriman, Shades of LA collection, Los Angeles Public Library*

during the season and gained 444 yards. Every time he touched the football, Washington averaged 7.4 yards, best in the league.

Once the season ended, Washington was a man in demand. Requests to speak at banquets poured in. He received film offers and accepted a role in a World War II story, *Rogues Regiment*. Washington was recruited, along with Jackie Robinson, to play in a charity basketball game with actors such as Burt Lancaster, Jackie Coogan, Mickey Rooney, and Robert Mitchum. The celebrities were greeted by a sellout crowd of close to 7,000 at the Shrine Auditorium who cheered and howled as Red Skelton's "Mean Widdle Kids" and Ronald Reagan's "Ruffians" played to a 16–16 tie and raised $17,000 for the Pacific Lodge Boys Home fund.

In the spring, the Rams extended a new contract offer. They wanted Washington back for the 1948 season. But along with the events and opportunities, pondering took up a big part of Kenny Washington's off-season. He was now thirty, old for a football player. When he got out of bed in the morning, his body broadcast the results of the pummeling and the pounding through aches and pains. Every offer to act coupled with every ache and body pain served to raise the specter of a career change. Retirement was mulled more than ever before. As the summer of 1948 arrived and the start of training camp drew near, one burning question was on Kenny Washington's mind: Would the 1948 season be his last in professional football?

20

CALLING IT A CAREER

White lines on the black chalkboard diagrammed a purpose. Eyes of the two dozen defensive players gazed from their chairs as the coach forcefully drew Xs and Os, then barked out the role of each player. Containment was the name of the game, as it was for many of the Los Angeles Rams' defensive schemes. It was hoped that the white lines on the board, along with teaching on the field and a bit of luck during the game, would send the ends on a proper rush angle, the tackles through the right lane, and defensive backs into the correct coverage to contain the opposing offense.

As Kenny Washington sat among his teammates, his own containment was fading, the personal containment long exhibited in such an admirable way. An anger simmered within. That anger was headed for a point of fury.

For fifteen years Washington had been a model of control. Whether in high school games or at UCLA, with the Hollywood Bears and now in the National Football League, he had endured taunts, verbal slurs, threats, and physical assaults. Through it all Washington exhibited extraordinary strength of character. Now, however, the Los Angeles Rams had pushed him to the brink. Kenny Washington was mad, fighting mad.

During their first two seasons in Los Angeles, the Rams had become, if not successful, at least envied around the league. Players who endured harsh winter conditions playing in Green Bay, Detroit, and Chicago could be excused for their jealousy toward Rams players, who played in winter warmth and sunshine. The Rams made envy swell in the summer of 1948, when preseason training involved participation in a motion picture and training camp on a private island in Hawaii.

During the summer of 1948, Kenny Washington was cast in a movie for Howard Hughes's RKO Pictures. Given the working title *Interference*, the film carried a football story. It featured Victor Mature as a quarterback with a heart ailment and Lucille Ball as the team secretary. When filming began on July 7, the project was quickly mired in chaos. The director, Jacques Tourneur, was from France and had never in his life seen a football game.

To bring a greater sense of realism to the football scenes, Washington recruited twenty-two of his Rams teammates. Eddie Kotal, a Rams scout, was brought in as technical advisor. Shooting left the RKO lot and moved to Wrigley Field, where Kotal replicated practice drills.

As filming wrapped up, Washington became part of a publicity stunt. Knowing Washington's history, publicists hailed the ploy as the longest pass ever thrown. It began with Victor Mature throwing a pass during a scene shot at Wrigley Field. It was six days later when Washington was brought onto the RKO lot, nine miles away, and filmed catching Mature's pass. The facetious claim by the studio publicity department of a record nine-mile pass that encompassed six days to complete generated plenty of ink for the film in many of the local newspapers.

Participation in the movie left some of Washington's teammates bitten by the acting bug. Others vowed that once shooting was complete, they were done with the bright lights for good. "Too monotonous," said Rams tackle Gil Bouley. "We do the same thing over and over."[1]

Once training camp began in earnest, Washington's focus was solely on football. He shone in drills and had 3 long runs in the Blue-Gold scrimmage. In the annual charity game against the Washington Redskins, he scored the Rams' lone touchdown. On that run, Washington shook loose from a tackle. He was then hit head-on at the 2-yard line by the opponents' 228-pound Clyde Erhardt. Washington, his powerful legs churning, ran right over the man and into the end zone.

Hours after the exhibition game, the Rams' preparation for the 1948 season was turned upside down. Bob Snyder resigned as head coach. It came as a shock to many and was entirely unexpected to all but, perhaps, Snyder's doctor, who had been treating the coach for severe stomach ulcers and urged him to step down. Clark Shaughnessy was quickly made head coach. He was a coaching legend, the innovator of the T-formation offense. The first time Rams players met the wiry fifty-six-year-old was the day of his hiring, at the airport as they departed for an atypical training camp destination, Hawaii.

Hawaii represented the antithesis of the usual image of preseason training camp. Whereas camp was normally nondescript, full of tension, and a time of abject seriousness, Hawaii conjured glamour, shimmering waters, picturesque beaches, the epitome of relaxation. For the sixty Los Angeles

Rams players, their visit would be anything but. Glamour, yes, but rest and relaxation on picturesque beaches was out of the question.

After flying twelve hours on a Pan American Airways DC-4, the Rams were taken to Coconut Island, a luxurious retreat in Kaneohe Bay eighty miles from Waikiki Beach. The reason for the exotic training camp location had to do with ownership of the hideaway. Ed and Harold Pauley, Los Angeles oilmen and part owners of the Rams along with Dan Reeves, had recently bought Coconut Island. The slice of paradise was a twenty-acre island of coral 1,600 feet in length, with an average width of 500 feet. One could only set foot on Coconut Island by invitation. The Pauleys proposed to build a private resort. Bringing the Rams would generate publicity for their idea.

Plans called for a week of training in Hawaii with 2 exhibition games against local semipro teams. Each day was planned down to the second. Players were awakened at 7:00 a.m. They were expected at breakfast thirty minutes later. By 9:00 a.m., they were to board boats for the ten-minute ride across the bay to Kaneohe Navy Air Station. Players would change into football gear in the locker room, then hit the field in Dewey Stadium, the base stadium where they would practice for two hours. Lunch was at noon back on Coconut Island before a return boat ride to the base and another two-hour practice. Dinner was followed by evening meetings. Players were ordered in bed by 10:00 p.m., with lights out by 11:00.

Just two days after the Rams arrived in Hawaii, the team played the first of its 2 scheduled exhibition games. Their opposition was a local semi-pro team, the Hawaiian Warriors. A bus strike held down the expected crowd. Still, 21,000 flocked to the rare visit by a National Football League team. The Labor Day duel was never close. In the 41–20 Rams' romp, Shaughnessy used all of his players and played Washington and Bob Water-field little, much to the displeasure of the local ticket buyers.

At the end of the week, on Friday night, the teams met again. It took the Rams only 4 minutes to drive for their first touchdown. From there, a route took shape. Stung by criticism for not using his best players earlier in the week, Shaughnessy pulled out all the stops. The result was a 42–7 pasting.

The morning after the game, the Rams left their practice paradise for home. An arduous forty-eight hours lay ahead. The team would get less than a day at home before traveling once again, this time to Dallas, Texas. It was then that Kenny Washington could no longer contain himself. He told the Rams he would not go.

Washington's beef was not with the travel. As grueling as another five-and-a-half-hour flight would be, it was not such a short turnaround that perturbed him. What Washington balked at was going to Texas, being made to play in a Jim Crow state. He refused to do it. It was a protest that caught Dan Reeves, the Rams' owner, completely off guard.

During the previous April, Reeves entered into a five-year agreement with the Salesmanship Club of Dallas to bring his team to their city for an annual exhibition game. The club, made up of influential business and civic leaders, planned to use the yearly game as a fundraiser to send underprivileged boys to summer camp.

When the Rams gathered at Municipal Airport, Washington's absence was conspicuous. It was explained that he had a commitment to reshoot a scene for a movie. In truth, Washington had vowed not to set foot in Texas, where Blacks and whites were not permitted to compete on the same athletic field and where lynchings of Blacks had recently been in the news.

The abolition of lynching was a hot topic nationally during the summer and fall of 1948. President Harry S. Truman asked Congress to make lynching a federal crime. Southern Democrats fought the request. Strom Thurmond, governor of South Carolina, assailed the president. "Is there anyone left who does not know that the South has almost wiped-out lynching without outside assistance? Lynching is murder. We all know that. And murder is a violation of state laws," he said.[2]

While southern politicians pointed to law enforcement statistics that showed a decline in lynchings, there were many who said the killings of southern Blacks were still happening, only by other means. Any decline, they believed, was because bodies were disposed of, never to be found.

Historically, Texas sports promoters made agreements with out-of-state teams to leave their Black players at home. It was only eight months earlier, in January 1948, when the matter of integrating a Texas football field reached a zenith. Penn State accepted an invitation to play SMU in the annual Cotton Bowl game on New Year's Day. Since the game's inception in 1937, organizers had made it clear that Black players could not play in the game.

As they prepared for the 1948 Cotton Bowl, Penn State's players were firmly against the notion that two of their talented teammates, Wallace Triplett and Dennie Hoggard, could not participate in the game. The players refused to vote on the matter or even discuss it. Their stand was firm, and it sent game organizers into a panic. Hotels in the city would not accommodate both Blacks and whites. A solution was found. Penn State was instead housed on a navy air base nine miles out of town.

Triplett and Hoggard not only played in the game but were significant contributors. Triplett scored the game-tying touchdown. Hoggard dropped a desperation pass in the end zone on the final play of the game. The 13–13 tie became historic as the first integrated college game in the state of Texas.

On learning of Washington's complaint, Dan Reeves did not sit idly by. He went to work on the game organizers. Finally, two days before the game, Reeves was able to assure Washington that he would not face repercussions. The next day, twenty-four hours before the game, Washington boarded a United Airlines flight for Love Field in Dallas.

When Washington ran onto the field at Dal-Hi Stadium, he received a loud ovation. Especially vociferous among the crowd of 15,000 were the more than 500 fans who sat in a fenced-in segregated seating area.

It was during the first quarter when Washington initially handled the football. He took a handoff from Bob Waterfield, sliced past his right tackle, and gained 8 yards. After Jack Banta earned a first down, Washington's number was called again. He took the football from his quarterback, found a seam among the mass of linemen, and shot through. A loud cheer rose from the stands, the loudest of the night, as Washington dashed and darted past the Eagles' linebackers. It was only after he gained 25 yards that Eagles defenders managed to bring him down. As Washington walked back to the huddle, his ears were filled with the sounds of a standing ovation from appreciative fans.

The Rams only scored once, in the fourth quarter, and lost the game, 21–7. Washington's rushing tally totaled 60 yards. More significant, Kenny Washington had become the first of his race to play in a professional football game in the state of Texas.

When the 1948 season kicked off, Kenny Washington was an opening game starter for the first time since joining the Rams. His play in training camp and in preseason games both impressed the Rams' new head coach, Clark Shaughnessy, and had sportswriters frothing that the Kingfish of old was back. But against the Philadelphia Eagles in the team's second game, Washington suffered yet another injury. This one put him on the bench for the second half of the game and kept him out entirely against the Chicago Bears a week later.

Injuries became a recurring theme for Washington during the first half of the 1948 season. One week it was a knee, the next a hip, during still another game he suffered an ankle sprain. It was in the Rams' seventh game of the season that Washington entered at the start of the second quarter. The first time he carried the football, he shot through a gap in the line and gained 12 yards. From that point on, Washington never came off the field. As much as Clark Shaughnessy was enamored with Washington's rushing, he had become an even greater admirer of his blocking and pass route running.

On November 14, 1948, the air of a professional football Sunday afternoon was all about the New York City borough of Manhattan. Cool weather and dark skies enveloped the Polo Grounds. Though dreary, it was vastly better than the icy rain of two weeks before. Enthusiastic fans exited the El at 155th Street. Cars brought more across the Harlem River from the Bronx via the metal-truss Macombs Dam Bridge.

Ticket takers noted that among the 22,766 fans, there were greater numbers of Blacks for this particular game than usual. While not usual for a Giants football game, it was a sight the box office workers and ushers at the Polo Grounds had seen before, particularly when Joe Louis fought Billy Conn in the stadium in 1941.

In the locker rooms below the stands, the New York Giants and Los Angeles Rams readied for their afternoon contest. The Rams arrived in New York a struggling football team, losers of 4 of their previous 5 games. Injuries were an overwhelming reason. Key performers such as Bob Waterfield, Fred Gehrke, and Dick Hoerner had missed games. So too had the player many came to see, Kenny Washington.

It was in the first quarter that Washington first electrified the New York crowd. The Rams surrendered 2 points when Waterfield was tackled in the end zone for a safety. On the ensuing kickoff, Washington fielded the ball and managed to dash 33 yards before he was brought down. On third down, he took a handoff from Waterfield. One yard past the line of scrimmage, Washington was seemingly stopped. With a twist of his upper body, he shirked free of the Giants' tackler and began a sprint toward the end zone, 31 yards away. At the 1-yard line, Washington was hit by two defenders. He fought to stay upright and with two mighty steps crossed the goal line for a touchdown that sparked loud applause and gave the Rams a 14–9 advantage.

When the game ended, the Rams had their most resounding win of the season, 52–37. Washington played almost the entire game and finished as his team's leading ground gainer with 76 yards. As he sat in front of his locker and peeled off his sweat-soaked, dirt- and grass-stained uniform, Washington was approached by Frank Finch. The *Los Angeles Times* sportswriter sought to ask about the game but never expected what he was about to be told. "I just don't have the desire to play anymore," Washington said.[3] Incredulity hit the sportswriter as Washington continued, "I'm tired of football now and I've made up my mind to retire."

Once the news reached Los Angeles, it sparked a flurry of action. Sports columnists phoned civic leaders; politicians contacted business executives. Letters to the editor arrived at newspaper offices. Each had the same idea—to see a day set aside to honor Kenny Washington.

As work went on to construct an appropriate tribute, Washington fought to help the Rams salvage a disappointing season. He shone in a 24–10 win over the Green Bay Packers. His play in the third quarter initiated a critical scoring drive. On 3 successive plays he burst through the line with impressive runs. On the fifth play of the drive, with the Rams 7 yards from the end zone, Washington was again given the football and scored to cap the victorious afternoon.

In the middle of the first week of December, the Rams flew to Washington, D.C., for their final away game of the 1948 season. Kenny Washington was almost immediately inundated with interview requests. When the Rams arrived at Griffith Stadium the morning of their game, Washington tried to enter the stadium. A security guard refused him entry. Despite the player's protests, the man would not relent. It was only after a member of the Rams' staff was summoned and confirmed that Washington was a member of the team that he was allowed to enter.

Whatever ire Washington harbored from the incident was released on the football field several hours later. In the second quarter, as the Rams held a 14–0 lead, Washington took a handoff, cut up the middle through the mass of grappling linemen, then darted 19 yards before he was tackled. Two plays later, Washington completely fooled defenders to create the Rams' third touchdown of the game. He ran what looked to be a short pass route. Once the defenders were lulled into believing it was, Washington pivoted and streaked 30 yards upfield toward the end zone. Jim Hardy hit him with a beautifully thrown pass, and the Rams had their third touchdown of the afternoon.

The Rams were in a jovial mood, a day removed from their 41–13 win in Washington, when they landed at Municipal Airport in Los Angeles. By beating Washington, the Rams had won 3 of their last 4 games to even their record for the season at 5–5. A now healthy Kenny Washington tallied a touchdown in each of the wins.

No sooner were the propellors brought to a stop and the cabin door pushed open than men separated Washington from his teammates. They hustled the puzzled Rams fullback to a waiting car. As they whisked him toward downtown Los Angeles, he was told only that the mayor wanted to speak to him. Whether feigned or real, the men insisted they had no idea of the subject matter. It was only after Washington set foot inside city hall that the sound of applause suggested the reason for the secrecy.

While being escorted toward the mayor, Fletcher Bowron, Washington caught sight of his wife and seven-year-old son, adding to his surprise. Applause waned as the Rams' standout reached the mayor.

Bowron wore a broad smile. A roundish man of sixty-one with a receding hairline and round, wire-rimmed glasses, the third-term mayor chuckled at the four-inch height disparity between himself and Washington. Bowron read from a proclamation that declared the upcoming Sunday, December 12, 1948, would be Kenny Washington Day in the city of Los Angeles.[4]

Unbeknownst to Washington, a committee had been formed and engaged in a drive to produce a fitting halftime tribute at the Rams' Sunday game with the Pittsburgh Steelers. While Washington and the Rams were out of town, several newspapers ran ads and columnists urged readers to make contributions so a fitting gift could be purchased.

In the forty-eight hours before the Rams' final game, tributes filled newspaper columns. Braven Dyer in the *Times* quoted Paul Schissler: "Smart? Listen Doctor, he called signals all those years he played pro ball for me. Yes sir, Kenny Washington was quite a football player . . . just about the best that ever came along."[5]

Chicago Defender columnist Libby Clark shone a light on Washington's place in football history. "Kenny's grid performances both at UCLA and in pro ball set the pace throughout the country for other Negro gridsters who have since basked in as much 'football glory' as the 'Kingfish' himself."[6]

The *Times* sports editor, Paul Zimmerman, lauded Washington's character. "We not only will be saluting one of the greatest athletes of all time, but also one of the finest gentlemen. Not in the memory of any spectator has Washington been guilty of unsportsmanlike conduct on the gridiron, although his coaches and fellow players down the avenue of years can remember cases where the Kingfish might have been justified in aggressive action."[7]

Ned Cronin, sports editor of the *Los Angeles Daily News*, suggested, "I have been wrong in my life three or four times—well three times easy—but on one score where I figure I'm dead right is if somebody had thought to remind owners in the National Football League that the Emancipation Proclamation actually was on the books, Kenny Washington would have earned a starting berth on any all-time, all-pro backfield ever to be offered for public consumption."[8]

A gray sky carrying with it the threat of rain likely contributed to a less-than-hoped-for crowd count. At kickoff, 27,967 fans were in Coliseum seats. Throughout the week, the Rams' publicity staff touted the likelihood of 40,000 ticket buyers. Another contributor to the crowd count were parties held around the city at which the television broadcast of the game was a focal point.

Through much of the first half, the Rams' offense struggled to move the football. They failed to cross midfield through the entire first quarter. Pittsburgh, on the other hand, was driving toward possible points when Washington intercepted a pass at the Rams 22-yard line. In the second quarter, Shaughnessy shook up the attack. He replaced Waterfield with Hardy. The new quarterback recognized that the Steelers expected the Rams to showcase Washington in his final game. Hardy alertly switched strategy and used Washington as a decoy. He faked a handoff and sent him into the line. Several Pittsburgh defenders bought the fake and moved to stop Washington. Hardy instead threw a pass to a wide-open "Red" Hickey for the first touchdown of the game.

The Rams scored again in the final 45 seconds of the first half to lead, 14–0, at the intermission. As the Steelers retreated to their locker room, many of the Rams and their coaches mingled about near midfield as a ceremony to honor their teammate began.

For more than fifteen minutes, a parade of well-wishers praised the retiring Ram. Washington's high school coach, Jim Tunney; his coaches at UCLA, Bill Spaulding and Babe Horrell; and Paul Schissler offered words of praise. Clark Shaughnessy stepped to the microphone and hailed Washington as "one of the greatest backs of all time," then added, "not only was he a great player, but he contributed morale to the Rams."[9]

Washington was showered with gifts. Rams captain Fred Naumetz stepped forward to present Washington a gold watch, a gift from his teammates. Washington received a large gleaming trophy from Bill Schroeder of the Helms Athletic Foundation, then announced it would be donated to Lincoln High School to present annually to its most valuable football player.

From the donations received, Washington was gifted a television set. A college fund was established for his son. Then, gasps followed by applause filled the air as the final gift was driven onto the field—a brand new 1948 Ford sedan. Camera shutters clicked and newsreels whirred as Washington stepped to the microphone. "The cheers you fans have given me," he said, "went to my heart, not to my head."[10]

When the game ended and the scoreboard read 31–14 in the Rams' favor, Fred Naumetz handed Washington the game ball. Several players on both sides stopped to shake his hand. In the stands, a woman sat silently. For more than two hours she had done so with her hands neatly folded in her lap. Yellow roses tied with blue ribbon were pinned on her shoulder. Throughout the afternoon, she had sat with her daughter-in-law and brother-in-law. It was the first time in the woman's forty-six years she had

Figure 20.1   Washington reads prepared remarks at halftime of his final game. The trophy was donated to his alma mater, Lincoln High School, where it annually recognizes the most valuable player of the football team. *Photo courtesy of* Los Angeles Daily News *Negatives, Library Special Collections, Charles E. Young Research Library, UCLA*

witnessed a football game. At times she would applaud. Other times she would shake her head. "All those men piling on top of each other . . . they must weigh a lot," she said with a sigh.[11]

The woman swelled with pride at the ovation and the halftime recognition for the player who was the focal point of the afternoon attention. It was not lost on her that everyone in the stadium, both whites and Blacks, stood to give the player a standing ovation at the end of the game.

Through it all the woman maintained her composure. That is, until she was approached by a child, a blue-eyed boy with wavy blond hair, who asked, "Are you Kenny Washington's mother?" When the woman silently nodded the boy said, "Gee, what a swell thing to be."[12] It was then that Marion Washington's eyes filled with tears.

21

BACK TO THE BIG SCREEN

The calls began almost immediately on the announcement of retirement. With each call to Parkway 4750, the realization grew that retirement from football would not be accompanied by any lack of direction, projects, or new career opportunities. For a stretch of days, it seemed as though many, if not all, of the calls brought Kenny Washington a plethora of job offers. The proposals ranged from serious to conceptual, sublime to ridiculous. Dauk's, a large appliance store on Crenshaw Boulevard, offered a sales position. Its owner felt people would flock just to meet the gridiron legend. There was a proposed business investment with boxers Joe Louis and "Sugar" Ray Robinson. Management at KMPC floated the idea of a radio show.

When a 3-win 7-loss season cost Bert LaBrucherie his job as UCLA football coach, supporters pushed for Washington to be his replacement. "Don't snort at that," wrote Maxwell Stiles in the *Los Angeles Mirror*. "Presumably one doesn't have to be Caucasian to get a job."[1] Gordon Macker of the *Daily News* was tipped that Washington would get the job. When he called Washington for confirmation, the retired Ram said he'd never been contacted by anyone at UCLA.

Rumor spread from Canada that Washington would resume his professional football career north of the border. Les Lear, a teammate on the '46 Rams, was made head coach of the Calgary Stampeders of the Canadian Football League for the 1948 season. Lear convinced Woody Strode to join the team, and the Stampeders won the Grey Cup. In his quest to improve the team, Lear signed "Sugarfoot" Anderson for 1949. On the heels of Anderson's signing, rumors flew that Washington would also join the Stampeders. There was, it turned out, no truth to the talk at all.

What was fact was a call from the minor-league baseball San Diego Padres of the Pacific Coast League. The Padres extended Washington the offer of a tryout. As much as the desire to play professional baseball gnawed at Washington, he had to decline. It was a matter of timing. He had just accepted an offer, and it was from a man who would not take no for an answer.

Darryl F. Zanuck was one of the most powerful men in the motion picture industry. Driven by incessant work habits. He was deft at generating scripts; such was his knack for understanding what the public wanted, a reporter said he had a psychologist's intuition. Zanuck rose from gag writer for slapstick comedy producer Max Sennett to head of production at Warner Brothers Pictures at the age of twenty-seven. By the time he was thirty-one, he was vice president of 20th Century Films and three years later orchestrated their purchase of the bankrupt Fox Film Company, from which he emerged with 30 percent ownership of the newly combined companies.

Zanuck's fingerprints were seen in many facets of just about every film the studio produced. He involved himself in writing and editing. He was often first at the end of the day to review the dailies, the unedited film shot that day. Once concluded, memos flew from his office filled with critiques, criticisms, and directions for change. Nine of his films received Best Picture nominations. Two, *How Green Was My Valley* and *Gentleman's Agreement*, earned Academy Awards.

Each year Zanuck took on one special project, often a film that carried a social message. "It must have the punch and smash that would entitle it to be a headline on the front page of any successful metropolitan daily," he said.[2] His pet project for 1949 was *Pinky*.

For months Zanuck cloaked the project in complete secrecy. He put two veteran screenwriters to work adapting a screenplay from the novel *Quality* by Mississippi author Cid Ricketts Sumner. Once completed, the script numbered an unheard-of 163 pages with a whopping 242 scenes. Zanuck gave the film his studio's biggest budget of the year, $2 million.

The film, like the novel, involved the story of a young Black woman, Pinky, who leaves her home in rural Mississippi to attend nursing school in Boston. The woman is of such light complexion that everyone assumes her to be white. Pinky does nothing to correct their belief. She falls in love with and becomes engaged to a doctor who is white. Throughout their relationship, Pinky continues to conceal her true ethnicity. Zanuck's project would be the industry's first major film with an interracial love story.

Figure 21.1   Kenny Washington and Jeanne Crain with a child actor from the controversial 1949 film *Pinky*. *Photo courtesy of the author*

Zanuck involved himself in the casting process. He pondered Olivia de Havilland for the role of Pinky. Gene Tierney and Linda Darnell wanted the part, but Zanuck did not consider either what he was looking for. When he tested Jeanne Crain, he felt he had found his lead. Ethel Waters, who had transitioned from successful jazz singer to star on Broadway, was cast as Pinky's grandmother. Zanuck negotiated the release of Ethel Barrymore from her contract with MGM and gave her a significant role.

One of the film's subplots involved Pinky's return to her hometown. A local doctor hears that she has come home and attempts to convince her to stay. He proposes she help young women in the community. Zanuck had a man in mind for that part. He offered it to Kenny Washington.

When Washington received the call, he had just finished shooting for another film, *Rope of Sand*. In it he played the part of John, trusted confidant of the film's star, Burt Lancaster. The story line entailed the pursuit of hidden diamonds in Africa. To achieve authenticity, filming was done near Yuma, Arizona.

Pinky would be shot entirely on the 20th Century Fox lot in Los Angeles. Once John Ford was hired to direct, filming began in early March of 1949. The makeup and wardrobe specialists outfitted Washington in a way few football fans would recognize their hero, with glasses for a professorial look and a three-piece suit.

Production got off to a bad start. Zanuck was unhappy with daily results. There was tension on the set. Twice in one day Ford berated Waters, which flustered the Broadway veteran so much she flubbed subsequent lines. At the end of the day the director told her his outburst was calculated. The scene called for her to be angry; she wasn't. Ford hoped the dressing-down would evoke the attitude needed. It did.

A week into filming, production came to an abrupt halt. Reporters were told Ford was injured in a fall at his home. Days later the story was amended to say a case of shingles drove the director to bed. In actuality, Zanuck was unhappy with Ford and fired him. He told the press Ford would need two to three months to recover, and Elia Kazan would complete the film.

When Zanuck reached Kazan, the veteran director was in New York preparing to travel to London. He asked for a few days to organize his affairs. The cast and crew waited while Kazan traveled across country by train. Once he arrived in Los Angeles, filming resumed after a seventeen-day pause.

With Zanuck at the helm, production went smoothly. Filming was completed in forty days. Washington had speaking parts and appeared in the early scenes and again in the latter segments of the film. The film culminates with his character's idea being realized.

Pinky premiered in theaters in September 1949. In New York City it broke the one-week box office record. The *New York Daily News* heralded it the best of the September releases. Jeanne Crain was applauded as courageous for tackling the role. Her popularity drew 6,000 pieces of fan mail per week, second only to Betty Grable at the studio. Reviewers in general circulation newspapers offered favorable assessments. The *Los Angeles Times* called the film "such an engrossing experience that its full impact can hardly be denied."[3] It was called "a brave movie" by the *Los Angeles Daily News*.[4] Marjory Adams wrote in the *Boston Globe*, "Pinky is more than an ordinary drama. It strives to deal a blow against misunderstanding and hatred."[5]

Papers that served a Black readership felt otherwise. Complaints raged about the casting. "You want to tell a story of a light-skinned Negro girl in love with a white doctor: okay—then show it on screen," opined Robert Ellis.[6] Several critics argued that a Black actress—Lena Horne, in particular—deserved the title role. Reviewers felt the story unrealistic. "Well, my opinion of 'Pinky' can be summed up in two words, 'IT STINKS,'" wrote Gertrude Gibson in the *California Eagle*. An underlying theme of the criticism was a lack of realism. "How can a studio, how can an industry that doesn't employ Negroes as writers, associate producers, directors, cameramen, technicians—how can they write, direct, or produce a sincere and sensitive picture relating to Negro life?"[7]

Still another reviewer felt the film's problem was a disconnect between advertising promotion and actual story. "The film makes no attempt to solve the race problem which would be folly at most. Instead, it tells an honest story about one girl, and there is never any doubt that she portrays only an individual and not an entire race."[8]

In December, *Pinky* opened in theaters in the South. It played without incident in Memphis and Atlanta. In February 1950 when the film was to open in Birmingham, Alabama, a furor erupted. The manager of the Martin Theatres group was ordered to turn the film over to the chief of police, who assembled a panel to review *Pinky*. After conferring with members of the panel, Chief of Police Floyd Eddins ordered the film banned from all Birmingham theaters.

In Marshall, Texas, the local Kiwanis Club deemed *Pinky* immoral and voted to demand East Texas Theatres not show the film. Their action moved the city commission to reactivate a long-dormant censorship board specifically to consider the matter. The Texas banishment of *Pinky* became a matter for courts to decide. More than two years later, in June 1952, the question would reach the United States Supreme Court. In a unanimous ruling, the court declared the city of Marshall had been wrong to bar showing of the film.

Pinky reaped a bountiful harvest when awards were announced in February 1950 in Hollywood. Film critics named it one of the ten best pictures made in 1949. The announcement of finalists for Academy Awards included Jeanne Crain for Best Actress. Ethel Waters and Ethel Barrymore were two of five finalists for Best Actress in a Supporting Role. For Waters, her nomination marked just the second time a member of her race had received an Oscar nomination.

In addition to awards, *Pinky* proved a hit at the box office. The film grossed more than $4 million, sixth best among 1949 releases. It was the second-most successful film released by 20th Century Fox Studios during the year.

While Hollywood was celebrating its award winners for 1949 film projects, Kenny Washington was already at work on his next picture. The film involved his friend and former UCLA football teammate, Jackie

Robinson. Washington was cast as the manager of Robinson's semipro baseball team in *The Jackie Robinson Story*.

Robinson was to play himself in the film. In an interview with an Associated Press reporter, he said, "I'm a ballplayer not an actor," then joked, "If Kenny can do it, so can I."[9]

Fans gathered trying for a glimpse of the stars whenever and wherever scenes were filmed, be it Gilmore Stadium, neighboring Gilmore Field, or La Palma Park in Anaheim. Even fans of the acting persuasion, like Van Heflin, were spotted among the gawkers.

As filming approached March, an angst grew to complete the baseball scenes. Robinson was pressed to wrap up work and travel to Florida for spring training. He wasn't alone. For four years, Washington and Robinson had been inexorably linked to rumors of baseball opportunity. As the spring of 1950 approached and such talk emerged once again, this time it was with substance. A fresh start with a new sport awaited.

22

A BASEBALL SHOT AT LAST

The clattering of metal spikes on the concrete floor signaled the sports-writers to attention. Their intended target was coming. A hard rain three days earlier had soaked the field inside Phoenix Municipal Stadium. So instead of taking batting practice, the New York Giants agreed to let sportswriters, photographers, and newsreel cameramen have an hour to get interviews and pictures of the manager, coaches, and players.

When Leo Durocher stepped into the dugout on this first day of spring training, he was keen to talk about his new double-play combination. The acquisition of Eddie Stanky and Alvin Dark in a blockbuster winter trade with Boston had been big news. Instead, he was surprised to find the writers had another subject in mind—the attempt by Kenny Washington to play big-league baseball.

Durocher was peppered with questions about the former Los Angeles Rams halfback. "Well, I've never seen him, but I'm ready to give him a good look," the manager said. One reporter blurted that Washington could throw as well as the strong-armed former Giant Willard Marshall. "Okay," Durocher said with a smile. "He's got a great arm." Another, a writer from Los Angeles, said Washington could outrun anyone on Durocher's ballclub. "Now he can run too," the manager replied. Yet a third sportswriter told the manager that Washington seldom missed with the bat and could send baseballs a country mile. Durocher smiled, "I do know he's a very nice guy—I've talked to him."[1]

Washington's arrival in the Giants' camp had been facilitated weeks earlier. During a gathering at Durocher's lavish home not far from the Pacific Ocean in Santa Monica, California, the Giants' manager was cor-ralled by Tom Harmon. The two men distanced themselves from the other guests and settled at Durocher's bar. As they sat on bar stools constructed of four baseball bats and a catcher's mitt, the former Los Angeles Ram turned sportscaster regaled Durocher with tales of his friend's baseball talents. Kenny Washington, Harmon told the manager, had a powerful throwing arm, ran well, and best of all, could hit for tremendous power. Durocher was intrigued.

Baseball had been on Kenny Washington's mind for more than a year. Not long after he retired from the Los Angeles Rams, Bing Crosby came calling once again. Rather than boxing, Crosby this time had a baseball proposition in mind. He was part owner of the Pittsburgh Pirates and had watched Washington play in amateur ball games. Crosby extended the offer of a tryout with the Pirates. Washington's role would be that of a pinch-hitter. It was at almost the same time Washington heard from the San Diego Padres. Only a year earlier the Padres integrated the Pacific Coast League by signing John Ritchey, a Negro Leagues catcher. Now, they wanted to add Washington for the 1949 season.

Both offers were appealing. The timing, however, was once again wrong. Washington had accepted movie offers. The shooting schedules would conflict with spring training; thus, he turned both Crosby and the Padres down. He did so, however, with a pledge: that once he finished his motion picture commitments his focus would shift to baseball.

In February 1950, the Giants' offer was announced. Newspapers all across the country, even *Sporting News*, carried reports of the arrangement. By the time Washington left for the Giants' camp in Phoenix, he was optimistic. He had been hitting, running, and fielding five days a week for two months. During that time, his workouts had shed twenty-two pounds. He weighed 212. Yet there were undeniable obstacles before him. Washington had not played high-level competitive baseball in six years. His knees were scarred from surgeries that had dulled his running speed and driven him out of professional football. Bigger yet, Kenny Washington was thirty-one. He was the oldest rookie in any big-league spring training camp. His was an age when most men wrap up a professional career, not begin one anew. "If it were anyone else, I would discount his chances," said radio broadcaster Sam Balter. "But Kenny Washington is no ordinary athlete."[2]

Five days into camp, Durocher split his squad into two teams and pitted them in a game. The Eddie Stankys beat the Bill Rigneys, 5–4. But the highlight of the game for the 3,600 fans came in the eighth inning. That's when Kenny Washington drove a pitch by Dave Koslo, the 1949 National League earned-run-average champ, clear out of Phoenix Municipal Stadium for a home run. Nearby, a sportswriter for the *Arizona Republic* scribbled one word in his notebook: "prodigious."

Figure 22.1   Washington spent months training for his long-sought shot to play big-league baseball. *Photo courtesy of Larry Rubin*

Two days later Washington again shone with the bat in another intra-squad battle. This time he did it with 2 hits. Many observers felt he should have been credited with a third, that an out call on a close play at first base was questionable at best. "He has looked great at bat," Durocher said. "I hope he can make the team."[3]

It was once the Giants began to square off against other teams that Washington's quest began in earnest. A shortstop at UCLA, Washington's preference was the infield, but Hank Thompson was entrenched at third base. Alvin Dark and Eddie Stanky were locks to play shortstop and second base. In fact, much of the starting eight was set. If there was one open job with the slightest possibility for a challenger, it was right field, where the 1949 starter Willard Marshall had been traded away. In all, Washington was one of seven players in camp to compete for the position.

It was in Tucson against Cleveland that the Giants played their first exhibition game. Washington was Durocher's choice to play right field and hit third in the batting order. He went hitless in 2 at bats. The next afternoon Washington again was Durocher's choice to play right field. Before he was substituted, Washington failed to reach base in 2 turns at bat. It would be the last time Washington would play with the Giants' first nine.

Following the series of games in Tucson, Durocher announced he would guide the Giants' "B" team, and he wanted Washington with him. Most of the B team's games were against Pacific Coast League clubs, teams at the top tier of the minor leagues. Washington held his own. But for every game in which he had a hit or two against minor-league clubs, Don Mueller would rap out 3 in games against big-league clubs and stake a claim for the right-field job.

Each night after training sessions and exhibition games, players were on their own. Some ventured to the dog track to take in greyhound races. Others headed for the Buckhorn Spa east of nearby Mesa to soothe sore muscles in the mineral baths. Washington, on one night, decided to take in a movie. There were several cinemas just across the street from the team's hotel. When Washington attempted to buy a ticket, however, he was refused.

Once back at the hotel, Washington sought out his teammate, Monte Irvin. He was incredulous. "Damn, am I going to have to go through this again . . . fight the civil war all over again?" Washington said. Irvin, who had played in the South, shrugged, and told Washington it was the way it was. "Maybe I can't beat it, but I'll fight it," Washington vowed.[4]

Each night for a week, Washington returned to the same cinema. He approached the box office and asked to buy a ticket but each time was refused. His campaign only ended when the Giants left Phoenix in the final weeks of March.

Washington's quest to stick with the Giants came down to a series of exhibition games over the final two weeks of March. Durocher broke up his team into two squads for a pair of tours in California. The Giants' "A" team would play the Pittsburgh Pirates in Fresno, Stockton, Sacramento, and Oakland. The "B" team would head to Southern California and play the University of Southern California in Los Angeles, the United States Marine Corps at Camp Pendleton in Oceanside, the Seattle Rainiers of the Pacific Coast League in Palm Springs, and the St. Louis Browns in Burbank.

Durocher felt it important to accompany the B team. He wanted a final firsthand look at both Washington and Monte Irvin. The manager wasn't alone. The Giants' powers that be—Horace Stoneham, who owned the ballclub; Chub Feeney, the general manager; and Carl Hubbell, who oversaw the minor-league operations—made the trip as well.

Washington was in familiar surroundings in the Giants' first game in Southern California, Bovard Field at USC. It was a place where he had played while at UCLA and with the police department team. His return to the USC campus would produce Washington's biggest game in a gray New York Giants flannel uniform and display the baseball talent that evoked awe so many years before at UCLA. Durocher wrote Washington's name on the fifth line of the Giants' batting order. In the top of the first inning, he came up with Monte Irvin and Roy Zimmerman on base and smashed a fastball down the third-base line to the outfield wall. Both Irvin and Zimmerman scored while Washington streaked around the basepaths until he was held by Durocher at third base with a triple.

When Washington came to bat in the eighth inning, the bases were loaded. He seized upon a hittable pitch, a fastball over the outer third of the plate. Washington extended his strong forearms, made solid contact, then jogged toward first base while the ball sailed over the wall in right-center field for a grand slam. His 6 runs batted in headlined the Giants' 14–6 triumph.

Against Seattle in Palm Springs, Washington faced a veteran pitcher with big-league experience, Rugger Ardizoia. The baseball commissioner, "Happy" Chandler, turned up for the game. He applauded as Washington shone. The Giants entered the ninth inning trailing, 7–4. Washington came to bat and smashed his second hit of the game, a single, which put 2 more runs on the scoreboard. The Giants were unable to add to their rally, however, and lost, 8–7.

As the Giants' B team prepared for their final game of the exhibition trip, it was abundantly clear to many who followed the team that Kenny Washington's chances of making the club waned. "Kenny can hit a fastball as far as the greatest sluggers," a veteran scout confided to a *Los Angeles Times* sportswriter. "But all those years of football took too much out of him."[5]

The Browns threw their best pitcher at the Giants that afternoon. Ned Garver was a right-hander whose success came from throwing sinkers

Figure 22.2   Washington belts a grand slam during an exhibition game with the New York Giants. *Photo courtesy of Larry Rubin*

and sliders, changing speeds on his fastball, and keeping hitters off balance. He frustrated Washington throughout the afternoon. In the Giant hopeful's first time at bat, he grounded out meekly to the third baseman. His next turn produced a roller that went through the shortstop's legs for an error. In the sixth inning, Washington flied out to left field. He faced a left-handed pitcher, Stubby Overmire, in the eighth inning and reached base on a fielder's choice. In the outfield, Washington's day was equally futile. In the first inning he lost sight of a towering fly ball in the sun and heard groans from the stands as it dropped to the grass uncaught. Later in the inning he made an ill-advised stab at a hard-hit line drive. The ball got by him, and the hitter wound up with a triple. After the game, Durocher pulled Washington aside and delivered bad news. He would not make the team. "Nobody in our camp has worked harder than Washington," the manager told reporters.[6] "Washington has tremendous power, but I was disappointed in his throwing. Football must have tightened up his arm and shoulder muscles."[7]

Team executives pondered placing Washington with their farm club at Jersey City, New Jersey. "Make no mistake, Kenny can really rap the ball. I think Washington would stand a fine chance in Triple A," Durocher said. When the idea was broached, Washington declined. He told the Giants he preferred to play for a club on the West Coast. Durocher offered Washington a glowing endorsement. "Some coast league club is missing a bet if it doesn't give him a trial."[8]

Within forty-eight hours some club did. The very day Washington was cut loose by the Giants, Los Angeles Angels manager Bill Kelly complained in the newspapers, "We need more right-handed hitting power."[9] Behind the scenes, Kelly's boss, Don Stewart, was at work to fill the void. One of his first calls was with Kenny Washington. The men agreed to meet two days later, on Tuesday, April 4. When that meeting concluded, Washington signed a contract and Stewart called him "a welcome addition to our club."[10]

Ink on the contract was barely dry when Washington stepped onto the green grass of Wrigley Field in an Angels uniform. The night was the Angels' home opener. An especially boisterous crowd of 7,688 cheered the sight of the former football star.

The next night while losing to San Diego in the bottom of the ninth inning, Kelly hollered Washington's name in the Angels' dugout. On cue, the powerfully built star grabbed a bat and strode to home plate. Washington's introduction sent cheers echoing about the double-decked ballpark. From the mound, Roy Welmaker sized up the Angels' pinch-hitter. A seasoned veteran, Welmaker had joined the Padres after stellar seasons in the Negro Southern League and Venezuela. The tall left-hander delivered a fastball, and in an instant the crowd was thunderstruck. With a mighty swing Washington sent the baseball hurtling through the air toward the left-field wall, 340 feet away. A roar went up from the crowd, loud at first but one that faded as the path of the baseball hooked, and the ball landed beyond the wall but foul. Once Washington reassumed his stance in the batter's box, Welmaker fired yet another fastball, and again Washington drove the baseball out of the park. Again, though, it hooked foul. The duel came to an end when the pitcher snapped off a curveball that Washington swung at unsuccessfully to the umpire's cry of "strike three."

By the middle of April, the Angels were struggling. The team wallowed in sixth place in the eight-team Pacific Coast League. Kelly was a frustrated man. Among the team's problems was the play of its third basemen. Lloyd Lowe, Jeep Handley, and John Lucadello had experience only in the lower levels of the minor leagues. Clearly all three players were overmatched in Class AAA ball. Efforts to sign Ken Keltner, whom Cleveland let go, failed to reach fruition. Desperation swelled. Out of frustration came opportunity. In the late innings of a 6–1 loss to Sacramento, the Angels' manager gave Kenny Washington a shot at the position, inserting him into the game as a defensive replacement.

When the Angels arrived in San Diego on April 19 for a series with the Padres, Washington's name was on the manager's lineup card, the starter at third base and the seventh hitter in the batting order. Washington's play in the 11–9 Angels' win prompted Kelly to start him again. But the next night's game involved a play that would impact Kenny Washington's future in baseball. It occurred in the bottom of the seventh inning. The Angels were trailing San Diego, 4–0. Like his teammates, Washington's 2 turns at bat against the Padres' "Red" Embree had been futile. In the bottom of the seventh, San Diego's Jack Graham was hit by a pitch. The former New York Giants and St. Louis Browns outfielder was advanced to second. Sensing an opportunity, Graham broke for third in an attempt at a stolen base. Washington scurried to the bag and knelt to take a throw from the Angels' catcher, Nelson Burbrink. Graham slid feetfirst. His metal spikes tore through Washington's pant leg and flesh. The resulting injury was both bloody and painful. Kelly was left with no choice but to remove Washington from the game.

The injury couldn't have come at a worse time. The Angels were six days from a deadline to cut a handful of players from the club. The Pacific Coast League permitted its teams to keep more than twenty-five players through the first month of the season. From May 1 on, each team could carry no more than twenty-five players. The Angels were five players over the limit. Kelly and Steward met several times to discuss options. One choice seemed obvious. Washington had played in just 6 games and still was without a hit. In his 8 official at bats, he was a strikeout victim 4 times. Thus, on April 28, when the Angels sent to the league names of four players they had released, Kenny Washington's was among them.

After breaking the news, Al Wolf of the *Los Angeles Times* expressed what many longtime followers were no doubt thinking. "Too bad Kenny Washington made such a belated diamond debut. All hands are agreed that in his college days the Kingfish was miles ahead of Jackie Robinson. But Kenny couldn't cut it at this late date."[11]

23

THERE WILL NEVER BE ANOTHER

The warm sun beat down on the man as he walked across the airport tarmac. Higher temperatures meant it would only be a matter of weeks before the airport and the city, Rome, Italy, would be teeming in frivolity. Tourists would arrive on cue from all corners of the world.

Acting, quality roles, and big pay convinced Woody Strode to move here and leave Hollywood behind. On this day, however, merriment was the furthest thing from Strode's mind. Normally friendly if not outright personable, the former athlete was a picture of consternation. It was a phone call that sent Strode hurrying to the airport. The call brought particularly bad news. His best friend was in a Los Angeles hospital. He was unlikely ever to leave. Kenny Washington was dying.

In the twenty-one years since Kenny Washington's last competitive game, he was seldom out of the spotlight. Rare was the sports banquet at which Washington wasn't either feted or asked to speak or emcee. He was a fixture at UCLA football games, where he sat alongside a former baseball teammate, Jim Devere, politely shook hands with fans, and differed with those who insisted his records would never be broken. "They'll all be broken," he would say.[1]

Washington's postfootball competitive endeavor became golf. It surprised few when he was soon shooting in the mid-to-low 70s and contesting for high finishes in community and regional tournaments. "Long, hard, and right on the button," said George Heaney, the pro at Brookside Golf Club of Washington's game.[2] When Charlie Sifford, the first Black golfer on the PGA Tour, agreed to design clubs for the Burke Golf Company, he gifted one of the first sets to Washington.

Professional baseball beckoned again but in a different way. When the Dodgers moved west from Brooklyn in the fall of 1957, their owner,

189

Walter O'Malley, sought Washington out. O'Malley asked Washington to consider being a part-time scout. Washington accepted the request and soon was funneling leads about potential prospects to the team's area scouts: Kenny Meyers, Tom Lasorda, and a former high school opponent, "Lefty" Phillips. During spring of 1963, the relationship and trust Washington built with a high school sensation, Willie Crawford, helped persuade the highly coveted outfielder to sign with the Dodgers. In time, Washington was asked to aid the Dodgers' sales effort to help generate interest in the team among the Southern California African American community.

Washington's influence never waned. He joined the largest liquor distributor in Southern California, Young's Market. After twelve years Washington was recruited by J. V. Elliott and became its national sales representative, handling Cutty Sark Scotch. It was five years later that Buckingham Corporation, the national importer of Cutty Sark, persuaded Washington to become their vice president and lead sales and marketing efforts toward African American consumers.

Washington's influence also benefited his former team. Following the 1948 season, the Rams signed Tank Younger, a sensational fullback from Grambling College in Louisiana. "I saw Washington play some games for the Rams and I figured I'd like to play on the same team," Younger said.[3] It marked the first time a player from an all-Black college was signed by an NFL team and would open the door for many more to follow. Younger became a star and the first of his race to play in the NFL All-Star Game.

The winter of 1956 brought to Kenny Washington the pinnacle of sporting acclaim, induction into the National Football Foundation Hall of Fame. A poll of sportswriters generated 1,600 names that were submitted to the foundation's honors court for consideration. Eleven were chosen. Washington, Frankie Albert, and Otto Graham were along the class of inductees. The class of 1956 was feted at a gala held at the Statler Hilton in Los Angeles prior to the start of the NCAA Convention.

In August 1957, Washington and his wife, June, expanded their family. They adopted a toddler, sixteen-month-old Karin Lynn. It was at this time that the Washingtons' son reached his teenaged years and began to generate acclaim of his own as a football and baseball standout. Father-son games of catch in the yard and pointers from Dad helped Kenny Washington Jr. achieve All-City status as a T-formation quarterback at Dorsey High School. But the younger Washington chose to forge his own path in life. He objected every time a coach gave him a uniform with his father's number, 13. When time came to select a college, the younger Kenny chose USC, the archrival of his father's alma mater. He also opted to make baseball his primary sport rather than that which his father was acclaimed for, football.

A nervous dad sat in the stands whenever Kenny Washington Jr. played. The senior Washington would anxiously fold foil chewing gum wrappers and fidget in his seat as his son excelled on the field below. In the spring of 1963, Kenny Washington Jr. tore through the collegiate season with a .361 batting average. His play helped USC win the College World Series, where he was selected to the All-Tournament team as the left fielder.

The junior Washington's collegiate success brought a professional baseball contract. He spent six seasons in the Los Angeles Dodgers' minor-league system and ascended to their top farm club. In 1970 Kenny Washington Jr. crossed the Pacific and played part of one season in Japan before he was cut.

In the spring of 1969, consternation grew among Washington's family and friends. The man who achieved Herculean feats on a football field faced a health crisis. Fatigue and shortness of breath plagued Washington. He saw specialists across the country. Between May and November, Washington spent 140 of 195 days in hospitals in New York City, Baltimore, Washington, D.C., and for the final two months, at UCLA Medical Center in Los Angeles.

The doctors' diagnosis was concerning. Washington had contracted polyarteritis, a rare heart and lung disease that caused fluid to build up around the heart. The disease brought on extreme fatigue and caused muscle and joint aches as well as abdominal pain. Worse was the prognosis. There was no cure. It could, however, be managed, and Washington's doctors tried to shower him with optimism.

During Washington's lengthy stay in UCLA Medical Center, he became overwrought with despair. Doctors around the country had tried several forms of treatment with no success. Another approach was suggested, to insert a device in Washington's heart. On the day of the procedure, eight doctors stood over him while he lay prone on an operating table. As he was being prepared, Washington became convinced the optimism of the doctors was just talk, patronizing. Convinced that this, like all the treatments before, would do nothing, Kenny Washington gave up hope.

After the procedure, Washington confided to family members that while under anesthesia, he had a vision. He told of seeing a longtime friend and former teammate who died a year before. The man's voice implored Washington, "Don't come here and try to get my job. We have an all-star show every night."[4] Washington emerged from the operation with renewed fight. Doubts about his doctors, the staunchest of supporters, were erased. On November 10, 1969, Washington was able to go home. He was unsteady on his feet, but hopeful physical therapy could remedy that.

Frequent callers and visitors heard a new Kenny Washington. "I'm so glad to be here," he would say. To a reporter he implored, "Don't worry about money or any of the other materialistic things in life. Be thankful you've got your health."[5]

For almost three months Washington saw improvement. Then complications set in, and he returned to UCLA Medical Center. Worry grew among his close friends. Two, Mike Frankovich and Jim Tunney Jr., decided to take action. Frankovich had coached Washington on the freshman football team at UCLA. He was now a successful producer in the motion picture industry. Tunney, principal at Fairfax High School, was the son of Washington's high school coach and an acclaimed NFL official.

The men launched plans to stage a banquet in tribute to Washington. The lavish Palladium on Sunset Boulevard was secured. A-list entertainers were arranged to appear. When Washington found out, he balked. Frankovich and Tunney coaxed and cajoled. They promised the proceeds would be split, with a portion to defray Washington's medical expenses and the rest used to start a college fund for his daughter.

On Tuesday, September 29, more than 1,000 people—entertainers, sports stars, city leaders, and even NFL Commissioner Pete Rozelle—filled the venue. His longtime friends were buoyed by the sight of Washington, voice once again strong and gait steady. The evening featured a plethora of tributes. When it came Washington's turn at the microphone, he thanked the gathered. "I get tired pretty easily." Then sternly added, "I think I'll whip it."[6] The crowd rose to its feet. Their applause filled the room. Washington expressed gratitude to Dan Reeves. He thanked Walter O'Malley. He closed with an emotional thank-you to the group. "This tribute to Kenny Washington should be a tribute from Kenny Washington to you."[7]

By the summer of 1971, Washington's condition had grown worse. Doctors were forced to take action. It was on June 11 that Washington was once again admitted to UCLA Medical Center. He was placed in a private room. This time, optimism was gone. Doctors somberly offered a dire prognosis.

It was thirteen days after his admittance, on a Friday morning, June 25, 1971, that Angelenos at their breakfast tables, while commuting on buses, or sipping coffee in diners opened up their morning newspaper. Shocking news of sixteen deaths from an explosion in a water district tunnel in the neighborhood of Sylmar consumed much of the front page. Alongside were stories about a grand jury hearing into the leaking of Vietnam War papers.

For many, the most startling news was in bold type across the very top of page one of the *Los Angeles Times*. It read: "Kenny Washington Dies." For some, the headline induced a grimace or the slow shake of the head. To a great many others, news of Kenny Washington's passing brought sadness and grief.

It was at 6:15 the previous evening when Kenny Washington took his final breath. He had urged his children and grandchildren to promise they would take care of his mother. The days that followed brought reflection, both painful and joyous. It evoked longing and reminiscence. Among some, the loss severed emotional links to the innocence of their childhood. "Kenny Washington was the first real sports hero of my youth," wrote *Los Angeles Times* columnist John Hall.[8] Still more were made to pause and reflect on the joy Kenny Washington brought to their life. "I fell in love with football the first time I saw Kenny Washington play for the old Hollywood Bears," typed Brad Pye Jr. in the *Sentinel*.[9]

When the Los Angeles City Council assembled just fifteen hours after the football star's passing, Tom Bradley made a motion that the meeting be adjourned in Washington's honor. "He was a great friend of mine," Bradley said. "In my judgement he was the greatest football player who ever played the game."[10]

County supervisors ordered the Olympic flame in the cauldron high atop the east end of the Los Angeles Memorial Coliseum be lit in Washington's honor and remain lit until after his funeral. Supervisor Kenneth Hahn hailed Washington as "an all–America in character, civic responsibility, and good sportsmanship," then added, "every citizen of Los Angeles County can be proud of his achievements."[11]

Holman United Methodist Church was stretched almost beyond capacity by Washington's funeral. The crowd of mourners, among them Woody Strode, Olympic gold medal winner Rafer Johnson, Dodgers pitching star Don Newcombe, Tank Younger, and many current and former Los Angeles Rams, was estimated at over 1,400. Sadness and grief mixed with an air of lament throughout the sanctuary hall. Dr. L. L. White, the church pastor, delivered a eulogy filled with praise and inspiration. "The painful thing is that his color kept Kenny from proving his greatness for many years," said the pastor, who hailed Washington as a Black pioneer and a man who found goodwill in others.

Noting the apostle Paul's words to the church of Philippi, White said, "Kenny lived in a world of crooked and mean people where he was able to shine among them like stars lighting up the sky."[12]

EPILOGUE

Greatness is defined in many ways. For those who rely on the authority of a dictionary, *Merriam-Webster* defines "greatness" in a simplistic manner, "the quality or state of being great." The Bible offers a written definition of greater specificity. "Whoever wants to become great among you must be your servant," or greatness is measured through service.[1] In his play *Twelfth Night,* produced in 1602, William Shakespeare writes, "Some are born great, some achieve greatness, and some have greatness thrust upon them."[2]

In the realm of sports, greatness is often tied to productivity. Statistics provide a definitive measurement. Emotional response to remarkable physical feats often causes the word "greatness" to be affixed. D. Wayne Lucas, the legendary trainer of winning Thoroughbred racehorses, explained greatness as an equation. "Greatness comes from a test of time and doing it over and over. That's what made the Celtics, that's what makes the Yankees. That's what makes it in sports."[3] In other words, excellence over time equals greatness.

Few of his era would deny that regardless of the definition, Kenny Washington and greatness are synonymous. During the three decades that immediately followed his passing, there was little shortage of teammates, coaches, and opponents able to give firsthand accounts of his remarkable talent. "Kenny Washington was the best football player I ever saw in my life and that includes everybody I ever knew," said the Hall of Fame quarterback Bob Waterfield.[4] For Hall of Fame player Bronko Nagurski, Washington was "one of the greatest football players I have ever viewed in action."[5] Fellow National Football Foundation Hall of Fame member Frankie Albert called Washington the greatest player he ever played against. As time has passed, however, so too have many who were able to give witness to Washington's remarkable talent. Their void leaves the current day to employ other means by which to quantify Washington's legend.

For decades, coaches and scouts have practiced comparative evaluating, a measuring-stick approach comparing one player's skills with those of another. In the 1950s and '60s, players in other parts of the country used this to explain Washington to those who never saw him play. Leslie Horvath, the 1944 Heisman Trophy winner from Ohio State and teammate of Washington's with the Rams, would explain Washington to friends in his home state through comparison to the preeminent back of the day. "He was not as strong as Jim Brown, but he could do more things," Horvath said.[6]

During the 1970s, when O. J. Simpson rose to prominence in pro football, there were those who cautioned against calling him better than Kenny Washington. "O.J. is a great college runner but please don't call him the greatest," Johnny Lucero wrote to the *Los Angeles Times*. "Never did one man do so much for a team as did Washington for UCLA."[7]

To measure Kenny Washington's greatness statistically is to appreciate not only the records he established both at UCLA and with the Los Angeles Rams, but also their longevity. During the 1939 UCLA game with the University of Montana, Washington rushed for 164 yards on 11 carries. His average of 14.9 yards per carry has remained a UCLA single-game record for eighty-two years. Washington concluded his three varsity seasons at UCLA with 1,915 yards rushing. That career rushing record stood for thirty-four years before Kermit Johnson eclipsed the mark in 1973. Washington established his record during a time when teams played 10-game seasons. Johnson, a brilliant player, performed in an era when the college football season ran 11 games. Johnson was also a standout during a time when UCLA's then coach Pepper Rodgers implemented a run-based offense, the wishbone. The average number of plays per game during Johnson's era was between 70 and 85. In Washington's day it was 50 to 70. Washington's record remained a target for thirty-four years. Johnson's career record of 2,495 yards was broken three years later by Wendell Tyler and has since been broken three more times in the subsequent forty-five years.

Perhaps the most staggering of Washington's UCLA records is his 1939 mark for durability. In the Bruins' ten 60-minute games that season, Washington played on both offense and defense, returned kicks and punts, and occasionally kicked extra points. He played a total of 580 of 600 minutes. Twenty-first-century football has become a specialized game. It is extremely rare for a player to play both offense and defense. Suffice it to say, Washington's mark will likely never be broken.

The 2022 season marks the seventy-fifth anniversary of Washington's record touchdown run from scrimmage for the Rams. His 92-yard touchdown run against the Cardinals on November 2, 1947, remains the longest touchdown run from scrimmage by a member of the Rams. Moreover, it is also the eighteenth-longest touchdown run in NFL history.

Like the ancient Greeks, who lionized their gods with statues and works of art, civic leaders in Los Angeles have immortalized inspiring symbols of community greatness. In 1972 Washington was added to the Court of Honor in the Los Angeles Memorial Coliseum. Within the peristyle arches at the east end of the stadium, a large plaque that featured Washington's bust was embedded into one of the pillars. On the plaque it was inscribed, "An All-American for All America." A year later the City of Los Angeles designated the intersection of North Broadway and Lincoln Park Avenue in Lincoln Heights as Kenny Washington Square.

For all his athletic feats and remarkable talent, there are those who believe Washington's greatest impact is in the trail he blazed for others. During a time of deep segregation in college sports, Washington not only excelled but did so with dignity and a manner of comportment that helped to enlighten oppressors and bring opportunity to others. He was, said his teammate Jim Devere, "a humanistic, sensitive man."[8]

Among the administrators and coaches at UCLA in the latter half of the 1930s, there is little question about the significance of Kenny Washington's impact on the university's football program. "There is no question he put UCLA on the map. No one heard of UCLA until he came here," said Devere.[9] There are others who believe that impact was far greater. "UCLA forced other schools to join the party," said J. D. Morgan, a tennis player at the time who later became athletic director. "If anything, we led the way," he said of the 1937, 1938, and 1939 Bruins football teams, which fielded four Black starters.[10]

Washington not only took UCLA football to new heights, but he also took the school to new places. In addition to being the first Black player on the Bruins' baseball team, he was the first of his race to serve on the UCLA Student Council. When Washington was hired to coach the backs on the 1940 freshman football team, he became the first Black coach at UCLA.

Washington's influence was appreciated far beyond the UCLA campus. He "set the pace throughout the country for other Negro gridsters," noted *Chicago Defender* columnist Libby Clark.[11] It was two years after Washington was signed by the Rams before any other NFL team integrated. In 1949, a year after Washington retired from football, George Taliaferro became the first Black player chosen in the NFL draft. "I always

Figure 24.1   Washington is memorialized in the Memorial Court of Honor at Los Angeles Memorial Coliseum. *Photo courtesy of Los Angeles Memorial Coliseum*

said if I can ever get into an organized football arrangement, I'm going to be like Kenny Washington," Taliaferro said.[12] Still, by 1950 only four of the ten NFL teams had signed Black players. Two years later only one team, the Washington Redskins, had yet to integrate. Their owner, George Preston Marshall, would hold out until 1962, when he was threatened with eviction from his stadium unless he integrated his team. "The limitations have been lifted and, now the sky's the limit," wrote Lem Graves Jr. in the *Pittsburgh Courier*. "Come to think of it, that's all a plain Negro citizen in this country needs—a chance to get to the top."[13] By the end of the twentieth century, 67 percent of NFL players were African American.

In addition to the confirmation and quantification of Washington's legacy, we are also left to ponder just how great Kenny Washington truly may have been were he not denied opportunity because of the color of his skin. "Kenny would have been the greatest of all time and that includes Thorpe, Nagurski, and Nevers and the rest, if he had played in the NL as soon as he got out of college in 1939," said his coach with the Rams, Bob Snyder.[14] Hall of Fame quarterback Bob Waterfield concurred. "If he had come into the National Football League directly from UCLA, he would have been, in my opinion, the best the NFL had ever seen."[15]

Those who played with and against him on the baseball diamond felt the same about Washington in their sport. "If it hadn't been for the color line, he would have made it to the majors before Robinson. He was better than Robinson," said a college opponent, Frank Peterson.[16] "It is very sad," said his UCLA baseball teammate Al Martel, "that Washington never had the same chance."[17]

Just as Jackie Robinson led a lifelong fight for equality and worked to provide opportunities for young people, so too did Kenny Washington. The methods of the two men differed. "I don't know whether Kenny with his quiet dignity or Jackie, the vibrant agitator, contributed more to social progress. But Washington never did less than bring us all closer together. His strength, tolerance, and patience were rare beacons," wrote John Hall in the *Times*.[18]

None other than Robinson himself put an exclamation mark upon Washington's legacy. In January 1957, while speaking on behalf of the NAACP's Fight for Freedom Fund, he said, "When you talk about the greatest players of all time, and you forget Kenny Washington, you are forgetting the greatest."[19]

NOTES

INTRODUCTION

1. John Newlands, "Oregon Grid Mentor Pays Tribute to Westwood Team," *UCLA Daily Bruin*, September 27, 1937, 3.
2. Braven Dyer, The Sports Parade, *Los Angeles Times,* October 21, 1936, 34.
3. Jack Singer, "Two Muir Tech Players Selected on All So Cal Prep Grid Team," *Los Angeles Times*, December 15, 1935, 2.
4. Braven Dyer, The Sports Parade, *Los Angeles Times*, September 27, 1937, A12.
5. Larry Mann, "UCLA Defeats Oregon 26–13; Uncovers Star," *Pomona (CA) Progress-Bulletin*, September 25, 1937, 8.
6. Ronald Wagoner, "UCLA's Eleven in 26–13 Win," *Pasadena Post*, September 25, 1937, 6.

CHAPTER 1

1. DeWitt Van Court, "Liable to Be Knockout on Tuesday Night," *Los Angeles Times*, October 21, 1912, 19.
2. "Baseball—Sports—Music—Theatricals," *Kansas City Star*, May 1, 1920, 12.
3. Almena Davis, "Tenacity of Purpose Outstanding Characteristic of Kenny 'General' Washington, His 'Best Girl' Says," *California Eagle*, December 14, 1939, 14.

CHAPTER 2

1. Braven Dyer, The Sports Parade, *Los Angeles Times*, May 31, 1959, 75.

2. Jim Tunney, in conversation with the author, April 27, 2020.

3. Lee Bastajian, "Tigers Trim Normans," *Los Angeles Daily News*, November 24, 1934, 10.

4. Jack Singer, "Tigers Capture Grid Battle," *Los Angeles Times*, November 24, 1934, 8.

5. Jack Singer, "Bowman Hailed as Best Lineman in Southland," *Los Angeles Times*, December 15, 1935, 20.

6. "Washington Leads Lincoln to 27–0 Win over Garfield in Prep Feature," *Los Angeles Times*, November 2, 1935, 9.

7. Jack Singer, "Washington Scores 4 Touchdowns as Lincoln Smothers Fairfax Team 31–6," *Los Angeles Times*, November 9, 1935.

8. Jack Singer, "Lincoln to Battle Fremont at Coliseum for City Prep Football Title," *Los Angeles Times*, November 22, 1935, A14.

9. Jack Singer, "All-City Dream Team Selected by Coaches," *Los Angeles Times*, December 1, 1935, 20.

CHAPTER 3

1. Braven Dyer, The Sports Parade, *Los Angeles Times*, May 3, 1937, 16.

2. Billy Rinehart, Northside Sportside, *Lincoln Heights Bulletin-News*, November 3, 1938, 4.

3. Claude Newman, "Reserves Show Up Weakly but Bruins in Win," *Hollywood Citizen-News*, September 25, 1937, 6.

CHAPTER 4

1. Frank Finch, "Bruin Grid Hopes at Half-Mast," *Los Angeles Times*, October 6, 1937, A13.

2. Harvey Rockwell, Sport Slants, *San Mateo Times*, October 11, 1937, 8.

3. Rockwell, Sport Slants, 8.

4. Bob Brachman, "'We Showed 'Em,' Roar Card Stars," *San Francisco Examiner*, October 10, 1937, 55.

5. Bill Tobitt, "Tribe Credits Tiny's New Necktie, Grayson's Raincoat with Victory," *Oakland Tribune*, October 10, 1937, A9.

6. Bruce Myers, Along the Bench, *Corvallis Gazette-Times*, October 19, 1937, 6.

7. Frank Finch, "Powerful Bears Tackle Bruins Today," *Los Angeles Times*, October 31, 1937, A11.

8. Henry Borba, Borba-rometer, *San Francisco Examiner*, November 2, 1937, 9.

9. "Texans Seek New Grid Date," Associated Press, October 14, 1938.

10. Wendell Smith, "Matty Bell Tells of Team Vote Which Erased Color Line," *Pittsburgh Courier*, October 29, 1938, 17.

11. "Bruins' Negro Foes 'Passed' by Mustangs," United Press, November 16, 1937.

12. Hank Hart, The Sports Parade, *Big Spring Daily Herald*, November 19, 1937, 8.

13. Chester L. Washington Jr., Sez Ches, *Pittsburgh Courier*, December 4, 1937, 16.

14. Editorial, *Dallas Campus*, November 24, 1937, 2.

15. Smith, "Matty Bell Tells of Team Vote Which Erased Color Line," 17.

16. B. J. Violett, "Teammates Recall Jackie Robinson's Legacy," *UCLA Today*, April 25, 1997.

17. Frank Finch, "Bruins Down Missouri," *Los Angeles Times*, November 28, 1937, A9.

CHAPTER 5

1. Braven Dyer, "Trojans Beat Bruins, 19–13," *Los Angeles Times*, December 5, 1937, 1.

2. Frank Finch, "Inside Story of Record Toss Revealed," *Los Angeles Times*, December 6, 1937, A9.

3. Bert LaBrucherie, "The Greatest Play I Ever Saw," *Cumberland Evening Times*, November 20, 1946, 18.

4. Frank Finch, "Spaulding Joshes Jones after Thriller," *Los Angeles Times*, December 5, 1937, 17.

5. Finch, "Spaulding Joshes Jones after Thriller," 17.

6. Grantland Rice, The Sportlight, *Spokesman-Review*, December 8, 1937, 13.

7. Milt Cohen, "Washington Hits Brace of Homers," *Daily Bruin*, February 18, 1938, 3.

8. John Hall, "The Story Teller," *Los Angeles Times*, November 7, 1972, 37.

9. Prescott Sullivan, Low Down, *San Francisco Examiner*, April 8, 1938, 22.

10. Jessica Pickens, "From Football to Ford: Woody Strode's Road to Hollywood," July 30, 2020, TCM.com.

CHAPTER 6

1. Braven Dyer, The Sports Parade, *Los Angeles Times*, November 3, 1937, A14.

2. J. Cullen Fentress, Gab Stuff, *California Eagle*, May 5, 1938, 13.

3. Bill Tobitt, "Two Bits Worth," *Oakland Tribune*, October 8, 1937, 34.

4. Chester L. Washington Jr., Sez Ches, *Pittsburgh Courier*, December 30, 1939, 16.

5. Prescott Sullivan, The Low Down, *San Francisco Examiner*, September 30, 1937, 5.

6. Bob Hogan, Sportlets, *Iowa City Press-Citizen*, September 20, 1938, 16.

7. Robert Edgren, "Coast Fans Howl for UCLAN Grid Star Kenny Washington," *Montana Standard*, December 24, 1939, 18.

8. Karin Cohen, in conversation with the author, May 17, 2020.

9. Paul Zimmerman, Sport Postscripts, *Los Angeles Times*, April 8, 1940, 19.

10. Bob Ray, "Stuhldreher Lauds Trio of Bruins," *Los Angeles Times*, November 13, 1938, 35.

11. Red McQueen, Hoomalimali, *Honolulu Advertiser*, December 22, 1938, 14.

12. Red McQueen, Hoomalimali, *Honolulu Advertiser*, January 4, 1939, 8.

13. Hank Casserly, Hank Says, *Madison Capital Times*, November 15, 1938, 15.

14. Al Wolf, Sportraits, *Los Angeles Times*, September 1, 1947, 15.

CHAPTER 7

1. Chester G. Hanson, "Determination Grid's Gift to Washington," *Los Angeles Times*, December 8, 1939, 22.

2. Frank Finch, "Jackie Robinson Enters UCLA; to Compete in Football, Track," *Los Angeles Times*, February 17, 1939, 33.

3. Eddie Brietz, Sports, *Daily Free Press*, August 22, 1940, 2.

4. "T.C.U. Outfit Good Losers," *Los Angeles Times*, September 30, 1939, 11.

5. B. J. Violett, "Teammates Recall Jackie Robinson's Legacy," *UCLA Today*, April 25, 1997.

6. Al Wolf, "Washington Leads Bruins to 20–6 Win over Grizzlies," *Los Angeles Times,* October 22, 1939, A9.

7. Curley Grieve, Sports Parade, *San Francisco Examiner*, November 30, 1939, 27.

8. Grieve, Sports Parade, November 30, 1939, 27.

9. Eddie West, West Winds, *Santa Ana Register*, December 28, 1939, 8.

CHAPTER 8

1. Charles Genuit, "Coach Jones Says UCLA Dangerous," *Los Angeles Daily News*, December 9, 1939, 12.

2. Helen F. Chappell, "Chatter and Some News," *Chicago Defender*, December 23, 1939, 6.

3. Ed Sullivan, Listen Kids, *St. Louis Post Dispatch*, December 13, 1939, 25.

CHAPTER 9

1. Carl J. Storck, "Pro Gridders Redouble Progressive Efforts in 1940," *Sheboygan Press*, January 6, 1940, 11.

2. Sam Balter, "Here's Sam Balter's Immortal Broadcast," *Pittsburgh Courier*, January 13, 1940, 16.

3. Roy Craft, "Lillard Eyed by Grid Czar," *Eugene Register Guard*, October 9, 1931, 7.

4. James Sheehy, "Midnight Flier Hits Open Switch," *Corvallis Gazette-Times*, October 16, 1931, 6.

5. Harold Parrott, "Joe Lillard Last of Negro Pro Grid Stars," *Brooklyn Daily Eagle*, November 12, 1935, 23.

6. Chester L. Washington Jr., Sez Ches, *Pittsburgh Courier*, August 31, 1940, 16.

7. Harold Parrott, "Louis Shuffle Grid Offense of Brown Bomber," *Brooklyn Daily Eagle*, November 15, 1935, 28.

8. Dave Farrell, "Asks MacPhail to Sign Negro Stars," *Pittsburgh Courier*, March 30, 1940, 17.

9. Robert Edgren, "Coast Fans Howl for UCLAN Grid Star Washington," *Montana Standard*, December 24, 1939, 18.

10. Bob Ray, The Sports X-Ray, *Los Angeles Times*, December 11, 1939, 23.

11. Dick Hyland, "Hyland Picks All-Coast Team," *Los Angeles Times*, December 17, 1939, A11.

12. Matt Weinstock, Town Talk, *Los Angeles Daily News*, December 9, 1939, 23.

13. Fred Russell, Sideline Sidelights, *Nashville Banner*, December 15, 1939, 34.

14. Groucho Marx, *"You Bet Your Life,"* season 9, episode 30, aired April 16, 1959, on NBC, posted March 15, 2014, YouTube video, 22:12, https://www.youtube.com/watch?v=T3IBxwm2LfA.

15. "Grid Board Ignores Kenny," *Los Angeles Times*, December 14, 1939, 11.

16. Ron Gemmell, Sports Sparks, *Salem (OR) Statesman Journal*, December 17, 1939, 8.

17. Art Cohn, Cohn-ing Tower, *Oakland Tribune*, December 17, 1939, 10-A.

18. "Labor Protests Washington Barring," *Los Angeles Sentinel*, December 28, 1939, 5.

19. Curley Grieve, Sports Parade, *San Francisco Examiner*, December 13, 1939, 22.

20. "Fans Protest as Washington off West Team," *Los Angeles Times*, December 20, 1939, 29.

21. Jerry Hawley, "Ovation Due Washington," *UCLA Daily Bruin*, December 8, 1939.

CHAPTER 10

1. "Mike Jacobs Seeks Kenny to Take Joe Louis' Place," *Pittsburgh Courier*, December 16, 1939, 16.

2. Almena Davis, "Tenacity of Purpose Outstanding Characteristic of Kenny 'General' Washington, His 'Best Girl' Says," *California Eagle*, December 14, 1939, 14.

3. "Kenny Washington to Try Fight Game," *Chicago Defender*, January 6, 1940, 24.

4. "Kenny Did It to Aid Mother," International News Service, December 22, 1939, 21.

5. J. Cullen Fentress, "Down in Front," *California Eagle*, January 4, 1940, 3B.

6. Harry Borba, "Ex-Bear to Play Right Half for Collegians Sunday," *San Francisco Examiner*, January 31, 1940, 24.

7. Leo C. Popkin interviewed by Douglas Bell for Academy Oral Histories, Margaret Herrick Library, Academy of Motion Picture Arts and Sciences, 2007.

8. Harry Levette, Behind the Scenes, *California Eagle*, November 21, 1940, 7.

9. Bob Ray, The Sports X-Ray, *Los Angeles Times*, November 19, 1940, A11.

10. "Kenny Washington, Former UCLA Football Star, Makes Harlem Film Debut, Thursday," *New York Age*, October 26, 1940, 4.

11. Earl J. Morris, Grand Town, *Pittsburgh Courier*, November 30, 1940, 20.

12. Lucas Jones, Slants on Sports, *Blackfoot Bingham County News*, September 28, 1940, 6.

13. Leo C. Popkin interviewed by Douglas Bell.

CHAPTER 11

1. "This All Star Is a Versatile Gent, Anahu!" *Chicago Tribune*, August 13, 1940, 19.

2. "Mates Praise Washington," *Chicago Tribune*, August 12, 1940, 22.

3. "Schiechl Shoots for Victory as a Nuptial Gift," *Chicago Tribune,* August 19, 1940, 21.

4. Loren Schultz, Sportlets, *Iowa City Press-Citizen*, September 23, 1940, 9.

5. "Protests Pour In after Radio Cuts Off Game," *Chicago Tribune*, August 31, 1940, 17.

6. Jimmy Powers, The Power House, *New York Daily News*, August 31, 1940, 192.

7. Chester L. Washington Jr., Sez Ches, *Pittsburgh Courier*, August 31, 1940, 16.

CHAPTER 12

1. Stanley Speer, "Bulldog Grids, Collegians to Vie Sunday," *Hollywood Citizen-News*, January 13, 1941, 12.
2. "Washington Leads Bears against Bulldogs Tomorrow," *Los Angeles Times*, January 11, 1941, 13.
3. Art Cohn, Cohn-ing Tower, *Oakland Tribune*, November 2, 1940, 14.
4. Paul Zimmerman, Sport Postscripts, *Los Angeles Times*, September 5, 1941, 23.
5. Dick Hyland, Behind the Line, *Los Angeles Times*, December 23, 1941, A10.
6. Dick Hyland, Behind the Line, *Los Angeles Times*, August 25, 1941, A11.
7. Paul Zimmerman, Sport Postscripts, *Los Angeles Times*, September 3, 1942, 17.

CHAPTER 13

1. Dick Hyland, Behind the Line, *Los Angeles Times*, December 23, 1941, A10.
2. Bob Smyser, "Hollywood in 17–10 Victory," *Los Angeles Times*, December 22, 1941, 31.
3. Lisle Shoemaker, "Bears Rally to Win, 17–10," *Los Angeles Daily News*, December 22, 1941, 28.
4. Kara Dixon Vuic, "Women May Soon Have to Register for the Draft," *Washington Post*, March 4, 2019.
5. "Kenny Washington Can't Play Football," *Chicago Defender*, November 20, 1943, 11.
6. "No Pro Ball for Kenny Washington," *Long Beach Independent*, November 10, 1943, 8.
7. Pete Koken, Whatz Doin' in Review, *Van Nuys News*, August 4, 1942, 6.

CHAPTER 14

1. Herman Hill, "Kenny Washington Had Many Thrills," *Pittsburgh Courier*, May 15, 1943, 19.
2. Hill, "Kenny Washington Had Many Thrills," 19.
3. Lowell Redelings, The Sports Speedometer, *Hollywood Citizen-News*, December 17, 1942, 16.
4. Herman Hill, "Will Give Negro Players Trial on Club," *Pittsburgh Courier*, February 6, 1943, 18.
5. Art Cohn, "Negroes Saved Boxing . . . Would Save Baseball," *Pittsburgh Courier*, April 24, 1943, 18.

6. Dick Hyland, Behind the Line, *Los Angeles Times*, December 23, 1941, A10.

CHAPTER 15

1. Al Wolf, Sportraits, *Los Angeles Times*, May 7, 1944, 4.

2. "Ken Washington Arrives for Clippers Opening," *San Francisco Examiner*, September 1, 1944, 17.

3. "Decision Made on Negro Star," United Press, September 1, 1944.

4. Prescott Sullivan, The Low Down, *San Francisco Examiner*, November 21, 1944, 17.

5. Sullivan, The Low Down, 17.

6. Prescott Sullivan, "Clippers, Ft. Warren Grid Clash Today," *San Francisco Examiner*, December 3, 1944, 17.

7. Wendell Smith, Smitty's Sports Spurts, *Pittsburgh Courier*, October 28, 1944, 12.

8. Dan Burley, Sports by Dan Burley, *New York Age*, December 10, 1949, 30.

9. "Ex-Bruin Opens against San Diego," *Hollywood Citizen-News*, September 25, 1945, 12.

10. "Mustang Pro Grids Face Wildcats Today," *Los Angeles Times*, September 24, 1944, 24.

11. Braven Dyer, The Sports Parade, *Los Angeles Times*, November 27, 1945, 10.

CHAPTER 16

1. Dink Carroll, Playing the Field, *Montreal Gazette*, October 25, 1945, 14.

2. Charles Maher, "The Long Run from 22nd Street to City Hall," *Los Angeles Times*, June 28, 1973, 17.

3. Carroll, Playing the Field, 14.

4. "Varied Comment of O.B., Writers on Negro's Case," *Sporting News*, November 1, 1945, 5.

5. "Bobo Newsom Has His Say," *Dayton (OH) Journal-Herald*, October 25, 1945, 12.

6. "The Monarchs to Appeal," *Kansas City Times*, October 24, 1945, 7.

7. "Rickey Counters Piracy Charge," *New York Daily News*, October 24, 1945, 59.

8. Wendell Smith, The Sports Beat, *Pittsburgh Courier*, December 1, 1945, 12.

9. Smith to Branch Rickey, December 19, 1945, Wendell Smith Papers, Manuscript Archive Collection, National Baseball Hall of Fame.

10. Jimmy Powers, The Powerhouse, *New York Daily News*, November 22, 1945, 52.

11. Roger Birtwell, "Air Duel Looms as Yanks Battle Champion Rams," *Boston Globe*, November 24, 1946, 24.

12. Birtwell, "Air Duel Looms as Yanks Battle Champion Rams," 24.

CHAPTER 17

1. Braven Dyer, The Sports Parade, *Los Angeles Times*, January 31, 1946, 10.

2. 1946 Halley Harding Speech, posted May 14, 2012, YouTube video, 4:35, https://www.youtube.com/watch?v=QTgzIDxKneQ.

3. Bob Kelley, Bob Kelley Says, *Long Beach Independent*, March 14, 1956, 8.

4. Paul Zimmerman, "Rams Ask 5 1946 Dates in Coliseum," *Los Angeles Times*, January 16, 1946, A8.

5. J. Cullen Fentress, "Grid Aces May Get Chance," *Pittsburgh Courier*, February 2, 1946, 12.

6. J. Cullen Fentress, "Ken Second to Play for Pro Gridders," *Pittsburgh Courier*, March 30, 1946, 16.

7. Wendell Smith, Training Camp Ticker Tape, *Pittsburgh Courier*, March 30, 1946, 17.

8. "Buster" Miller, Sports Parade, *New York Age*, March 30, 1946, 11.

9. Billy Rinehart, Northside Sportside, *Lincoln Heights Bulletin-News*, March 28, 1946, 9.

10. Claude Newman, Claude Newman Says, *Valley Times*, March 23, 1946, 6.

11. Dick Hyland, The Hyland Fling, *Los Angeles Times*, March 22, 1946, 7.

12. "Washington Okeh after Operation," *Los Angeles Daily News*, April 23, 1946, 19.

13. Maxwell Stiles, Styles in Sports, *Hollywood Citizen-News*, March 29, 1967, 6.

14. Claude Newman, Claude Newman Says, *Valley Times*, March 26, 1947, 10.

15. Pete Kokon, What's Cookin' with Kokon, *Valley Times*, August 10, 1946, 9.

16. Paul Zimmerman, "Hardy Opposes Waterfield in Ram Squad Tilt," *Los Angeles Times*, August 13, 1946, A6.

17. Merdies Hayes, "Woody Strode: Hollywood Mainstay," *Our Weekly* (Los Angeles), July 21, 2016.

18. Wendell Smith, "97,380 Fans See Negro Stars Play In 'Dream' Game," *Pittsburgh Courier*, August 31, 1946, 16.

CHAPTER 18

1. Pete Kokon, What's Cookin' with Kokon, *Valley Times*, October 22, 1946, 9.

2. Bob Hoenig, The Inside Outlook, *Hollywood Citizen-News*, October 22, 1946, 6.

3. Bob Hebert, "Rams Tame Lions on Waterfield's Passes," *Los Angeles Daily News*, October 21, 1946, 26.

4. Hoenig, The Inside Outlook, 6.

5. Marjorie Martin, "Grid Star Bob Waterfield Denies Rift with Jane," *Boston Daily Globe*, November 30, 1946, 1.

6. John B. Old, "Turned Down Yankee Pilot Job, Durocher Confides to the World," *Sporting News*, November 27, 1946, 7.

7. "Robinson Dinner Due Thursday," *Pasadena Star-News*, November 5, 1946, 13.

8. Wendell Smith, The Sports Beat, *Pittsburgh Courier*, October 19, 1946, 12.

9. Wendell Smith, The Sports Beat, *Pittsburgh Courier*, December 7, 1946, 16.

10. Wendell Smith, Sports Beat, *Pittsburgh Courier*, April 3, 1948, 14.

11. Frank Finch, "Washington to Report for Trial with Giants," *Los Angeles Times*, February 27, 1950, 58.

CHAPTER 19

1. Maxwell Stiles, "Rams in Better Shape, Open Practice at Loyola," *Long Beach Press-Telegram*, August 5, 1947, 10.

2. Maxwell Stiles, "Only a Reinjured Knee Will Keep Kenny Washington off Ram Team," *Long Beach Press-Telegram*, September 11, 1947, A11.

3. Bob Hoenig, The Inside Outlook, *Hollywood Citizen-News*, October 22, 1947, 22.

4. Paul Zimmerman, Sportscripts, *Los Angeles Times*, December 15, 1947, 27.

5. Bob Meyers, "Los Angeles Rams' Reeves in Grave Mood—Snyder's Almost in Grave Period," *Pasadena Star-News*, November 6, 1947, 24.

6. Meyers, "Los Angeles Rams' Reeves in Grave Mood," 24.

CHAPTER 20

1. Patricia Clary, "Rams Steal March on Other Pro Grid Squads," *Long Beach Press-Telegram*, July 17, 1948, 9.

2. "Thurmond Fires His Opening Gun," *Longview (TX) News-Journal*, August 1, 1948, 1.

3. Frank Finch, "Kingfish Says He's Through after This Year," *Los Angeles Times*, November 16, 1948, C3.

4. "Ken Washington Honored," *Los Angeles Mirror News*, December 7, 1948, 46.

5. Braven Dyer, Sports Parade, *Los Angeles Times*, December 10, 1948, 55.

6. Libby Clark, "West Coast Roundup," *Chicago Defender*, December 11, 1948, 9.

7. Paul Zimmerman, Sportscripts, *Los Angeles Times*, December 11, 1948, 33.

8. Ned Cronin, "Ned Cronin," *Los Angeles Daily News*, December 10, 1948, 50.

9. "Tay Brown Praises Talented Tartar Backs," *Los Angeles Times*, December 14, 1948, 49.

10. Paul Lowry, "Kenny Says Cheers Went to His Heart," *Los Angeles Times*, December 13, 1948, 59.

11. Elaine St. Johns, "Kenny Washington's Last Game First for Mom," *Los Angeles Mirror News*, December 13, 1948, 14.

12. St. Johns, "Kenny Washington's Last Game First for Mom," 14.

CHAPTER 21

1. A. S. "Doc" Young, "Maxwell Stiles Thinks Gridder Should Get It," *New York Age*, December 25, 1948, 19.

2. Bill Higgins, "Hollywood Flashback: In the 30s, Darryl F. Zanuck Had a Killer Instinct," *Hollywood Reporter*, June 23, 2016.

3. Edwin Schallert, "'Pinky' Fascinates as Race Issue Film," *Los Angeles Times*, October 22, 1949, 13.

4. Ezra Goodman, "Film Review," *Los Angeles Daily News*, October 22, 1949, 21.

5. Marjory Adams, "New Films," *Boston Globe*, October 8, 1949, 18.

6. Robert Ellis, "Hollywood at Dawn," *California Eagle*, October 20, 1949, 15.

7. Theatrical Editor, "Show Business," *California Eagle*, June 21, 1951, 6.

8. Bill Chase, "'Pinky' Best Anti-bias Film Yet," *New York Age*, Saturday October 1, 1949, 21.

9. Bob Thomas, "Film Story Challenges Robinson," *Pomona (CA) Progress-Bulletin*, February 9, 1950, 7.

CHAPTER 22

1. Arnott Duncan, Dunkin Dunc, *Arizona Republic*, March 1, 1950, 24.

2. A. S. "Doc" Young, "Kingfish Ken's Clouts Making Lippy Beam," *Sporting News*, March 15, 1950, 20.

3. Young, "Kingfish Ken's Clouts Making Lippy Beam," 20.

4. Jim Hackleman, The Hack Stand, *Honolulu Star-Bulletin*, November 27, 1972, 39.

5. Frank Finch, "Scouting the Pros," *Los Angeles Times*, March 19, 1950, A14.

6. Frank Finch, "Leo Says Kenny Too Green to Make Grade in Major Leagues," *Los Angeles Times*, March 24, 1950, 60.

7. "PCL Club May Sign Kenny Washington," *Long Beach Independent*, March 24, 1950, 24.

8. Finch, "Leo Says Kenny Too Green to Make Grade in Major Leagues," 60, 61.

9. Braven Dyer, "Scribes Howl for Investigation as Prexy Cops Harness Race," *Los Angeles Times*, April 4, 1950, CC.

10. "Kingfish Plans Trial Workout with Seraphs," *Los Angeles Times*, March 31, 1950, 55.

11. Al Wolf, Sportraits, *Los Angeles Times*, April 29, 1950, B2.

CHAPTER 23

1. Bernie Evans, "UCLA's Johnson Catching a Legend," *San Pedro (CA) News-Pilot*, October 18, 1973, 11.

2. "Kingfish Kenny Belting Ball, Not Throwing It," *Pasadena Independent*, January 30, 1956, 18.

3. Frank Finch, "Tank Warfare Looms in NFL," *Los Angeles Times*, July 5, 1949, 53.

4. Brad Pye Jr., "Prying Ye," *Los Angeles Sentinel*, November 20, 1969, B1.

5. Pye, "Prying Ye," B1.

6. Shav Glick, "Kenny Washington, Former Bruin Star, Dies," *Los Angeles Times*, June 25, 1971, C1.

7. Bob Meyers, "Kenny Washington Feted," Associated Press, October 4, 1970, 42.

8. John Hall, "We'll Miss Kenny," *Los Angeles Times*, June 28, 1971, 31.

9. Brad Pye Jr., "Kenny Washington—Mr. Versatile," *Los Angeles Sentinel*, July 1, 1971, B1.

10. "Kenny Washington Rites Planned Tuesday Morning," *Valley News*, June 27, 1971, 6.

11. "LA County Pays Tribute," *Long Beach Independent Press-Telegram*, June 27, 1971, 33.

12. Stanley O. Williford, "Washington's Friends Pay Last Respects," *Los Angeles Times*, June 30, 1971, 59.

EPILOGUE

1. Matt. 20:26–28 (New International Version).

2. William Shakespeare, *Twelfth Night, or What You Will*, stanza 155, line 3, act 2, scene 5 (New York: Macmillan, 1912), 52.

3. William C. Rhoden, "Sports of the Times; Greatness Is Now Harder to Define," *New York Times*, June 8, 2002, 10.

4. "Coliseum Features 'Court of Honor,'" *Pomona (CA) Progress-Bulletin*, November 23, 1973, C4.

5. Billy Rinehart, Northside Sportside, *Lincoln Heights Bulletin-News*, June 8, 1944, 3.

6. "Kenny Washington, All-Time UCLA Sports Hero, Dead at 52," *Monrovia (CA) Daily News-Post*, June 25, 1971, 12.

7. John Hall, "The Good Old Days," *Los Angeles Times*, October 29, 1968, 11.

8. Bernie Evans, "UCLA's Johnson Catching a Legend," *San Pedro (CA) News-Pilot*, October 18, 1973, 11.

9. Evans, "UCLA's Johnson Catching a Legend," 11.

10. John Hall, "UCLA Blazed Trail for Negro Athletes," *Miami Herald*, November 6, 1969, 42.

11. Libby Clark, "West Coast Roundup," *Chicago Defender*, December 11, 1948, 9.

12. NFL, "Kenny Washington Breaks the NFL's Color Barrier," NFL Films, posted February 22, 2016, YouTube video, 3:01, https://www.youtube.com/watch?v=7GstE32yLhU.

13. Lem Graves Jr., "Now, the Sky's the Limit," *Pittsburgh Courier*, May 3, 1947, 15.

14. "Washington's Farewell Ends LA Grid Career," *New York Daily News*, December 11, 1948, 17.

15. Shav Glick, "Kenny Washington, Former Bruin Star, Dies," *Los Angeles Times*, June 25, 1971, C1.

16. Steve Sneddon, From My Corner, *Reno Gazette-Journal*, June 26, 1971, 7.

17. John Hall, "The Story Teller," *Los Angeles Times*, November 7, 1972, 37.

18. John Hall, "We'll Miss Kenny," *Los Angeles Times*, June 28, 1971, 31.

19. Maxwell Stiles, Styles in Sports, *Los Angeles Mirror News*, March 7, 1959, 8.

BIBLIOGRAPHY

1946 Halley Harding Speech. Posted May 14, 2012. YouTube video, 4:35, https://www.youtube.com/watch?v=QTgzIDxKneQ.

Adams, Marjory. "New Films." *Boston Globe*, October 8, 1949, 18.

Associated Press. "Texans Seek New Grid Date." October 14, 1938.

Balter, Sam. "Here's Sam Balter's Immortal Broadcast." *Pittsburgh Courier*, January 13, 1940, 16.

Bastajian, Lee. "Tigers Trim Normans." *Los Angeles Daily News*, November 24, 1934, 10.

Birtwell, Roger. "Air Duel Looms as Yanks Battle Champion Rams." *Boston Globe*, November 24, 1946, 24.

Borba, Harry. Borba-rometer. *San Francisco Examiner*, November 2, 1937, 9.

———. "Ex-Bear to Play Right Half for Collegians Sunday." *San Francisco Examiner*, January 31, 1940, 24.

Brachman, Bob. "'We Showed 'Em,' Roar Card Stars." *San Francisco Examiner*, October 10, 1937, 55.

Brietz, Eddie. Sports. *Daily Free Press*, August 22, 1940, 2.

Burley, Dan. Sports by Dan Burley. *New York Age*, December 10, 1949, 30.

Carroll, Dink. Playing the Field. *Montreal Gazette*, October 25, 1945, 14.

Casserly, Hank. Hank Says. *Madison Capital Times*, November 15, 1938, 15.

Chappell, Helen F. "Chatter and Some News." *Chicago Defender*, December 23, 1939, 6.

Chase, Bill. "'Pinky' Best Anti-bias Film Yet." *New York Age*, Saturday October 1, 1949, 21.

Chicago Defender. "Kenny Washington Can't Play Football." November 20, 1943, 11.

———. "Kenny Washington to Try Fight Game." January 6, 1940, 24.

Chicago Tribune. "Mates Praise Washington." August 12, 1940, 22.

———. "Protests Pour In after Radio Cuts Off Game." August 31, 1940, 17.

———. "Schiechl Shoots for Victory as a Nuptial Gift." August 19, 1940, 21.

215

————. "This All Star Is a Versatile Gent, Anahu!" August 13, 1940, 19.

Clark, Libby. "West Coast Roundup." *Chicago Defender*, December 11, 1948, 9.

Clary, Patricia. "Rams Steal March on Other Pro Grid Squads." *Long Beach Press-Telegram*, July 17, 1948, 9.

Cohen, Milt. "Washington Hits Brace of Homers." *Daily Bruin*, February 18, 1938, 3.

Cohn, Art. Cohn-ing Tower. *Oakland Tribune*, December 17, 1939, 10-A.

————. Cohn-ing Tower. *Oakland Tribune*, November 2, 1940, 14.

————. "Negroes Saved Boxing . . . Would Save Baseball." *Pittsburgh Courier*, April 24, 1943, 18.

Craft, Roy. "Lillard Eyed by Grid Czar." *Eugene Register Guard*, October 9, 1931, 7.

Cronin, Ned. Ned Cronin. *Los Angeles Daily News*, December 10, 1948, 50.

Dallas Campus. Editorial. November 24, 1937, 2.

Davis, Almena. "Tenacity of Purpose Outstanding Characteristic of Kenny 'General' Washington, His 'Best Girl' Says." *California Eagle*, December 14, 1939, 14.

Dayton (OH) Journal-Herald. "Bobo Newsom Has His Say." October 25, 1945, 12.

Duncan, Arnott. Dunkin Dunc. *Arizona Republic*, March 1, 1950, 24.

Dyer, Braven. "Scribes Howl for Investigation as Prexy Cops Harness Race." *Los Angeles Times*, April 4, 1950, CC.

————. Sports Parade. *Los Angeles Times*, December 10, 1948, 55.

————. The Sports Parade. *Los Angeles Times*, October 21, 1936, 34.

————. The Sports Parade. *Los Angeles Times*, May 3, 1937, 16.

————. The Sports Parade. *Los Angeles Times*, September 27, 1937, A12.

————. The Sports Parade. *Los Angeles Times*, November 3, 1937, A14.

————. The Sports Parade. *Los Angeles Times*, November 27, 1945, 10.

————. The Sports Parade. *Los Angeles Times*, January 31, 1946, 10.

————. The Sports Parade. *Los Angeles Times*, May 31, 1959, 75.

————. "Trojans Beat Bruins, 19–13." *Los Angeles Times*, December 5, 1937, 1.

Edgren, Robert. "Coast Fans Howl for UCLAN Grid Star Kenny Washington." *Montana Standard*, December 24, 1939, 18.

Ellis, Robert. "Hollywood at Dawn." *California Eagle*, October 20, 1949, 15.

Evans, Bernie. "UCLA's Johnson Catching a Legend." *San Pedro (CA) News-Pilot*, October 18, 1973, 11.

Farrell, Dave. "Asks MacPhail to Sign Negro Stars." *Pittsburgh Courier*, March 30, 1940, 17.

Fentress, J. Cullen. "Down in Front." *California Eagle*, January 4, 1940, 3B.

————. Gab Stuff. *California Eagle*, May 5, 1938, 13.

————. "Grid Aces May Get Chance." *Pittsburgh Courier*, February 2, 1946, 12.

————. "Ken Second to Play for Pro Gridders." *Pittsburgh Courier*, March 30, 1946, 16.

Finch, Frank. "Bruin Grid Hopes at Half-Mast." *Los Angeles Times*, October 6, 1937, A13.

———. "Bruins Down Missouri." *Los Angeles Times*, November 28, 1937, A9.

———. "Inside Story of Record Toss Revealed." *Los Angeles Times*, December 6, 1937, A9.

———. "Jackie Robinson Enters UCLA; to Compete in Football, Track." *Los Angeles Times*, February 17, 1939, 33.

———. "Kingfish Says He's Through after This Year." *Los Angeles Times*, November 16, 1948, C3.

———. "Leo Says Kenny Too Green to Make Grade in Major Leagues." *Los Angeles Times*, March 24, 1950, 60, 61.

———. "Powerful Bears Tackle Bruins Today." *Los Angeles Times*, October 31, 1937, A11.

———. "Scouting the Pros." *Los Angeles Times*, March 19, 1950, A14.

———. "Spaulding Joshes Jones after Thriller." *Los Angeles Times*, December 5, 1937, 17.

———. "Tank Warfare Looms in NFL." *Los Angeles Times*, July 5, 1949, 53.

———. "Washington to Report for Trial with Giants." *Los Angeles Times*, February 27, 1950, 58.

Gemmell, Ron. Sports Sparks. *Salem (OR) Statesman Journal*, December 17, 1939, 8.

Genuit, Charles. "Coach Jones Says UCLA Dangerous." *Los Angeles Daily News*, December 9, 1939, 12.

Glick, Shav. "Kenny Washington, Former Bruin Star, Dies." *Los Angeles Times*, June 25, 1971, C1.

Goodman, Ezra. "Film Review." *Los Angeles Daily News*, October 22, 1949, 21.

Graves, Lem, Jr. "Now, the Sky's the Limit." *Pittsburgh Courier*, May 3, 1947, 15.

Grieve, Curley. Sports Parade. *San Francisco Examiner*, November 30, 1939, 27.

———. Sports Parade. *San Francisco Examiner*, December 13, 1939, 22.

Hackleman, Jim. The Hack Stand. *Honolulu Star-Bulletin*, November 27, 1972, 39.

Hall, John. "The Good Old Days." *Los Angeles Times*, October 29, 1968, 11.

———. "The Story Teller." *Los Angeles Times*, November 7, 1972, 37.

———. "UCLA Blazed Trail for Negro Athletes." *Miami Herald*, November 6, 1969, 42.

———. "We'll Miss Kenny." *Los Angeles Times*, June 28, 1971, 31.

Hanson, Chester G. "Determination Grid's Gift to Washington." *Los Angeles Times*, December 8, 1939, 22.

Hart, Hank. The Sports Parade. *Big Spring Daily Herald*, November 19, 1937, 8.

Hawley, Jerry. "Ovation Due Washington." *UCLA Daily Bruin*, December 8, 1939.

Hayes, Merdies. "Woody Strode: Hollywood Mainstay." *Our Weekly* (Los Angeles), July 21, 2016.

Hebert, Bob. "Rams Tame Lions on Waterfield's Passes." *Los Angeles Daily News*, October 21, 1946, 26.

Higgins, Bill. "Hollywood Flashback: In the 30s, Darryl F. Zanuck Had a Killer Instinct." *Hollywood Reporter*, June 23, 2016.

Hill, Herman. "Kenny Washington Had Many Thrills." *Pittsburgh Courier*, May 15, 1943, 19.

———. "Will Give Negro Players Trial on Club." *Pittsburgh Courier*. February 6, 1943, 18.

Hoenig, Bob. The Inside Outlook. *Hollywood Citizen-News*, October 22, 1946, 6.

———. The Inside Outlook. *Hollywood Citizen-News*, October 22, 1947, 22.

Hogan, Bob. Sportlets. *Iowa City Press-Citizen*, September 20, 1938, 16.

Hollywood Citizen-News. "Ex-Bruin Opens against San Diego." September 25, 1945, 12.

Hyland, Dick. Behind the Line. *Los Angeles Times*, August 25, 1941, A11.

———. Behind the Line. *Los Angeles Times*, December 23, 1941, A10.

———. "Hyland Picks All-Coast Team." *Los Angeles Times*, December 17, 1939, A11.

———. The Hyland Fling. *Los Angeles Times*, March 22, 1946, 7.

International News Service. "Kenny Did It to Aid Mother." December 22, 1939, 21.

Jones, Lucas. Slants on Sports. *Blackfoot Bingham County News*, September 28, 1940, 6.

Kansas City Star. "Baseball—Sports—Music—Theatricals." May 1, 1920, 12.

Kansas City Times. "The Monarchs to Appeal." October 24, 1945, 7.

Kelley, Bob. Bob Kelley Says. *Long Beach Independent*, March 14, 1956, 8.

Kokon, Pete. What's Cookin' with Kokon. *Valley Times*, August 10, 1946, 9.

———. What's Cookin' with Kokon. *Valley Times*, October 22, 1946, 9.

———. Whatz Doin' in Review. *Van Nuys News*, August 4, 1942, 6.

LaBrucherie, Bert. "The Greatest Play I Ever Saw." *Cumberland Evening Times*, November 20, 1946, 18.

Leo C. Popkin interviewed by Douglas Bell for Academy Oral Histories. Margaret Herrick Library. Academy of Motion Picture Arts and Sciences, 2007.

Levette, Harry. Behind the Scenes. *California Eagle*, November 21, 1940, 7.

Long Beach Independent. "No Pro Ball for Kenny Washington." November 10, 1943, 8.

———. "PCL Club May Sign Kenny Washington." March 24, 1950, 24.

Long Beach Independent Press-Telegram. "LA County Pays Tribute." June 27, 1971, 33.

Longview (TX) News-Journal. "Thurmond Fires His Opening Gun." August 1, 1948, 1.

Los Angeles Daily News. "Washington Okeh after Operation." April 23, 1946, 19.

Los Angeles Mirror News. "Ken Washington Honored." December 7, 1948, 46.

Los Angeles Sentinel. "Labor Protests Washington Barring." December 28, 1939, 5.

Los Angeles Times. "Fans Protest as Washington off West Team." December 20, 1939, 29.

———. "Grid Board Ignores Kenny." December 14, 1939, 11.

———. "Kingfish Plans Trial Workout with Seraphs." March 31, 1950, 55.

———. "Mustang Pro Grids Face Wildcats Today." September 24, 1944, 24.

———. "Tay Brown Praises Talented Tartar Backs." December 14, 1948, 49.

———. "T.C.U. Outfit Good Losers." September 30, 1939, 11.

———. "Washington Leads Bears against Bulldogs Tomorrow." January 11, 1941, 13.

———. "Washington Leads Lincoln to 27–0 Win over Garfield in Prep Feature." November 2, 1935, 9.

Lowry, Paul. "Kenny Says Cheers Went to His Heart." *Los Angeles Times*, December 13, 1948, 59.

Maher, Charles. "The Long Run from 22nd Street to City Hall." *Los Angeles Times*, June 28, 1973, 17.

Mann, Larry. "UCLA Defeats Oregon 26–13; Uncovers Star." *Pomona (CA) Progress-Bulletin*, September 25, 1937, 8.

Martin, Marjorie. "Grid Star Bob Waterfield Denies Rift with Jane." *Boston Daily Globe*, November 30, 1946, 1.

Marx, Groucho. "*You Bet Your Life.*" Season 9, episode 30, aired April 16, 1959, on NBC. Posted March 15, 2014. YouTube video, 22:12. https://www.youtube .com/watch?v=T3IBxwm2LfA.

McQueen, Red. Hoomalimali. *Honolulu Advertiser*, December 22, 1938, 14.

———. Hoomalimali, *Honolulu Advertiser*, January 4, 1939, 8.

Meyers, Bob. "Kenny Washington Feted." Associated Press, October 4, 1970, 42.

———. "Los Angeles Rams' Reeves in Grave Mood—Snyder's Almost in Grave Period." *Pasadena Star-News*, November 6, 1947, 24.

Miller, "Buster." Sports Parade. *New York Age*, March 30, 1946, 11.

Monrovia (CA) Daily News-Post. "Kenny Washington, All-Time UCLA Sports Hero, Dead at 52." June 25, 1971, 12.

Morris, Earl J. Grand Town. *Pittsburgh Courier*, November 30, 1940, 20.

Myers, Bruce. Along the Bench. *Corvallis Gazette-Times*, October 19, 1937, 6.

Newlands, John. "Oregon Grid Mentor Pays Tribute to Westwood Team." *UCLA Daily Bruin*, September 27, 1937, 3.

Newman, Claude. Claude Newman Says. *Valley Times*, March 23, 1946, 6.

———. Claude Newman Says. *Valley Times*, March 26, 1947, 10.

———. "Reserves Show Up Weakly but Bruins in Win." *Hollywood Citizen-News*, September 25, 1937, 6.

New York Age. "Kenny Washington, Former UCLA Football Star, Makes Harlem Film Debut, Thursday." October 26, 1940, 4.

New York Daily News. "Rickey Counters Piracy Charge." October 24, 1945, 59.

———. "Washington's Farewell Ends LA Grid Career." December 11, 1948, 17.

NFL. "Kenny Washington Breaks the NFL's Color Barrier." NFL Films. Posted February 22, 2016. YouTube video, 3:01. https://www.youtube.com/watch?v=7GstE32yLhU.

Old, John B. "Turned Down Yankee Pilot Job, Durocher Confides to the World." *Sporting News*, November 27, 1946, 7.

Parrott, Harold. "Joe Lillard Last of Negro Pro Grid Stars." *Brooklyn Daily Eagle*, November 12, 1935, 23.

———. "Louis Shuffle Grid Offense of Brown Bomber." *Brooklyn Daily Eagle*, November 15, 1935, 28.

Pasadena Independent. "Kingfish Kenny Belting Ball, Not Throwing It." January 30, 1956, 18.

Pasadena Star-News. "Robinson Dinner Due Thursday." November 5, 1946, 13.

Pickens, Jessica. "From Football to Ford: Woody Strode's Road to Hollywood." July 30, 2020. TCM.com.

Pittsburgh Courier. "Mike Jacobs Seeks Kenny to Take Joe Louis' Place." December 16, 1939, 16.

Pomona (CA) Progress-Bulletin. "Coliseum Features 'Court of Honor.'" November 23, 1973, C4.

Powers, Jimmy. The Power House. *New York Daily News*, August 31, 1940, 192.

———. The Powerhouse. *New York Daily News*, November 22, 1945, 52.

Pye, Brad, Jr. "Kenny Washington—Mr. Versatile." *Los Angeles Sentinel*, July 1, 1971, B1.

———. "Prying Ye." *Los Angeles Sentinel*, November 20, 1969, B1.

Ray, Bob. "Stuhldreher Lauds Trio of Bruins." *Los Angeles Times*, November 13, 1938, 35.

———. The Sports X-Ray. *Los Angeles Times*, December 11, 1939, 23.

———. The Sports X-Ray. *Los Angeles Times*, November 19, 1940, A11.

Redelings, Lowell. The Sports Speedometer. *Hollywood Citizen-News*, December 17, 1942, 16.

Rhoden, William C. "Sports of the Times; Greatness Is Now Harder to Define." *New York Times*, June 8, 2002, 10.

Rice, Grantland. The Sportlight. *Spokesman-Review*, December 8, 1937, 13.

Rinehart, Billy. Northside Sportside. *Lincoln Heights Bulletin-News*, November 3, 1938, 4.

———. Northside Sportside. *Lincoln Heights Bulletin-News*, June 8, 1944, 3.

———. Northside Sportside. *Lincoln Heights Bulletin-News*, March 28, 1946, 9.

Rockwell, Harvey. Sport Slants. *San Mateo Times*, October 11, 1937, 8.

Russell, Fred. Sideline Sidelights. *Nashville Banner*, December 15, 1939, 34.

San Francisco Examiner. "Ken Washington Arrives for Clippers Opening." September 1, 1944, 17.

Schallert, Edwin. "'Pinky' Fascinates as Race Issue Film." *Los Angeles Times*, October 22, 1949, 13.

Schultz, Loren. Sportlets. *Iowa City Press-Citizen*, September 23, 1940, 9.

Shakespeare, William. *Twelfth Night, or What You Will.* New York: Macmillan, 1912.

Sheehy, James. "Midnight Flier Hits Open Switch." *Corvallis Gazette-Times*, October 16, 1931, 6.

Shoemaker, Lisle. "Bears Rally to Win, 17–10." *Los Angeles Daily News*, December 22, 1941, 28.

Singer, Jack. "All-City Dream Team Selected by Coaches." *Los Angeles Times*, December 1, 1935, 20.

———. "Bowman Hailed as Best Lineman in Southland." *Los Angeles Times*, December 15, 1935, 20.

———. "Lincoln to Battle Fremont at Coliseum for City Prep Football Title." *Los Angeles Times*, November 22, 1935, A14.

———. "Tigers Capture Grid Battle." *Los Angeles Times*, November 24, 1934, 8.

———. "Two Muir Tech Players Selected on All So Cal Prep Grid Team." *Los Angeles Times*, December 15, 1935, 2.

———. "Washington Scores 4 Touchdowns as Lincoln Smothers Fairfax Team 31–6." *Los Angeles Times*, November 9, 1935.

Smith, Wendell. "97,380 Fans See Negro Stars Play in 'Dream' Game." *Pittsburgh Courier*, August 31, 1946, 16.

———. "Matty Bell Tells of Team Vote Which Erased Color Line." *Pittsburgh Courier*, October 29, 1938, 17.

———. Smith to Branch Rickey. December 19, 1945. Wendell Smith Papers. Manuscript Archive Collection, National Baseball Hall of Fame.

———. Smitty's Sports Spurts. *Pittsburgh Courier*, October 28, 1944, 12.

———. Sports Beat. *Pittsburgh Courier*, April 3, 1948, 14.

———. The Sports Beat. *Pittsburgh Courier*, December 1, 1945, 12.

———. The Sports Beat. *Pittsburgh Courier*, October 19, 1946, 12.

———. The Sports Beat. *Pittsburgh Courier*, December 7, 1946, 16.

———. Training Camp Ticker Tape. *Pittsburgh Courier*, March 30, 1946, 17.

Smyser, Bob. "Hollywood in 17–10 Victory." *Los Angeles Times*, December 22, 1941, 31.

Sneddon, Steve. From My Corner. *Reno Gazette-Journal*, June 26, 1971, 7.

Speer, Stanley. "Bulldog Grids, Collegians to Vie Sunday." *Hollywood Citizen-News*, January 13, 1941, 12.

Sporting News. "Varied Comment of O.B., Writers on Negro's Case." November 1, 1945, 5.

St. Johns, Elaine. "Kenny Washington's Last Game First for Mom." *Los Angeles Mirror News*, December 13, 1948, 14.

Stiles, Maxwell. "Only a Reinjured Knee Will Keep Kenny Washington off Ram Team." *Long Beach Press-Telegram*, September 11, 1947, A11.

———. "Rams in Better Shape, Open Practice at Loyola." *Long Beach Press-Telegram*. August 5, 1947, 10.

———. Styles in Sports. *Hollywood Citizen-News*, March 29, 1967, 6.

———. Styles in Sports. *Los Angeles Mirror News*, March 7, 1959, 8.

Storck, Carl J. "Pro Gridders Redouble Progressive Efforts in 1940." *Sheboygan Press*, January 6, 1940, 11.

Sullivan, Ed. Listen Kids. *St. Louis Post Dispatch*, December 13, 1939, 25.

Sullivan, Prescott. "Clippers, Ft. Warren Grid Clash Today." *San Francisco Examiner*, December 3, 1944, 17.

———. Low Down. *San Francisco Examiner*, April 8, 1938, 22.

———. The Low Down. *San Francisco Examiner*, September 30, 1937, 5.

———. The Low Down. *San Francisco Examiner*, November 21, 1944, 17.

Theatrical Editor. "Show Business." *California Eagle*, June 21, 1951, 6.

Thomas, Bob. "Film Story Challenges Robinson." *Pomona (CA) Progress-Bulletin*, February 9, 1950, 7.

Tobitt, Bill. "Tribe Credits Tiny's New Necktie, Grayson's Raincoat with Victory." *Oakland Tribune*, October 10, 1937, A9.

———. "Two Bits Worth." *Oakland Tribune*, October 8, 1937, 34.

United Press. "Bruins' Negro Foes 'Passed' by Mustangs." November 16, 1937.

———. "Decision Made on Negro Star." September 1, 1944.

Valley News. "Kenny Washington Rites Planned Tuesday Morning." June 27, 1971, 6.

Van Court, DeWitt. "Liable to Be Knockout on Tuesday Night." *Los Angeles Times*, October 21, 1912, 19.

Violett, B. J. "Teammates Recall Jackie Robinson's Legacy." *UCLA Today*, April 25, 1997.

Vuic, Kara Dixon. "Women May Soon Have to Register for the Draft." *Washington Post*, March 4, 2019.

Wagoner, Ronald. "UCLA's Eleven in 26–13 Win." *Pasadena Post*, September 25, 1937, 6.

Washington, Chester L., Jr. Sez Ches. *Pittsburgh Courier*, December 4, 1937, 16.

———. Sez Ches. *Pittsburgh Courier*, December 30, 1939, 16.

———. Sez Ches. *Pittsburgh Courier*, August 31, 1940, 16.

Weinstock, Matt. Town Talk. *Los Angeles Daily News*, December 9, 1939, 23.

West, Eddie. West Winds. *Santa Ana Register*, December 28, 1939, 8.

Williford, Stanley O. "Washington's Friends Pay Last Respects." *Los Angeles Times*, June 30, 1971, 59.

Wolf, Al. "Horrell Fails to Find 'Swelled Heads' in Bruin Ranks." *Los Angeles Times*, October 2, 1939, 31.

———. Sportraits. *Los Angeles Times*, May 7, 1944, 4.

———. Sportraits. *Los Angeles Times*, September 1, 1947, 15.

———. Sportraits, *Los Angeles Times*, April 29, 1950, B2.

———. "Washington Leads Bruins to 20–6 Win over Grizzlies." *Los Angeles Times*, October 22, 1939, A9.

Young, A. S. "Doc." "Kingfish Ken's Clouts Making Lippy Beam." *Sporting News*, March 15, 1950, 20.

————. "Maxwell Stiles Thinks Gridder Should Get It." *New York Age*, December 25, 1948, 19.

Zimmerman, Paul. "Hardy Opposes Waterfield in Ram Squad Tilt." *Los Angeles Times*, August 13, 1946, A6.

————. "Rams Ask 5 1946 Dates in Coliseum." *Los Angeles Times*, January 16, 1946, A8.

————. Sport Postscripts. *Los Angeles Times*, April 8, 1940, 19.

————. Sport Postscripts. *Los Angeles Times*, September 5, 1941, 23.

————. Sport Postscripts. *Los Angeles Times*, September 3, 1942, 17.

————. Sportscripts. *Los Angeles Times*, December 15, 1947, 27.

————. Sportscripts. *Los Angeles Times*, December 11, 1948, 33.

INDEX

ABOUT THE AUTHOR

Dan Taylor is the author of five books. His prior works include *Lights, Camera, Fastball: How the Hollywood Stars Changed Baseball* (2021); *Fates Take-Out Slide* (2017), in collaboration with George Genovese; *A Scout's Report: My Seventy Years in Baseball* (2015); and *Rise of the Bulldogs* (2009). Taylor is a former award–winning television sportscaster and the television broadcaster for the Fresno Grizzlies. He is a member of the Society for American Baseball Research and contributes to their biography project. Taylor is also a member of the Pacific Coast League Historical Society. He resides in Fresno, California.